The Volume Factor

ENDORSEMENTS

"*Volume*, the often ignored metric, is one of the most powerful drivers of market moves. This book is an incredible resource of not only the role of *Volume* but also how it can be used to unlock some amazing trading signals. Buff's volume based indicators are some of the most inspired indicators I've seen in my nearly 30 years of Technical Analysis work. No matter what your level of proficiency with Technical Analysis is, these are indicators that should be in your daily tool-kit. There are so many high points in this book like Buff's explanation of price momentum in terms of Newtonian physics and the critical section on Risk Management. Make sure you don't skip the introduction on this book either, Buff's candor as he describes his experience and observations in the market is refreshing and will help anyone who is open to self-reflection. This is an incredible book that will give any Fund Manager, Advisor or Trader critical insights into what drives the market, the confidence to hold a position, and the hidden clues of when it's time to get out."

—**Mathew Verdouw,** CMT, CFTe Founder & CEO Optuma

"Think you understand volume in the market? Guess again learn the truth from Buff's groundbreaking research"

— **Larry Willliams,** Legendary trader

"Analysts debate the importance of volume in modern markets. Some say changes in market structure make it less meaningful. Others insist principles from the 1800s still apply exactly as they did back then. Buff uses data to settle the question definitively and shows both sides are wrong. He introduces new indicators offering unique insights into market action. He explains how to calculate the indicators and how to use them in trading. This is groundbreaking work and Buff has changed the way I will look at markets in the future. VPCI and VMI are now standard indicators on my charts. After reading this book, you'll certainly find tools to add volume to your work too."

— **Michael Carr,** CMT

"Buff's comprehensive exploration of volume delves into a diverse array of studies, spanning factor models and sector analysis, exemplifying a wealth of research that is both exhaustive and unassailable. These studies resonate with resonance, earning resounding endorsements from both practitioners and academics alike. A case in point is the compelling demonstration of their applicability in the context of retirement planning with regular withdrawals, serving as a sterling example of their real-world effectiveness."

— **Dr. Matthew Lutey,** Indiana University NW

"With clarity and depth, Buff explores how incorporating *Volume* as an idiosyncratic investment factor can enhance outcomes for professional investors and ultimately, their clients."

— **Joseph Alkaraki,** VP Investment Management Industry

"Those with a mathematical bent will be sure to benefit from this exhaustive and well-researched explanation of volume and why it should be part of every technician's toolbox."

— **Martin Pring**

"*The Volume Factor* is the financial edge every investor wants. Buff Dormeier shows how anyone can "follow the money." His award-winning tools dive into money flow in a unique way. Buff adds, "volume analysis doesn't judge whether price is reasonable or not, rather whether the trend is likely to continue." Asset managers will want this book."

— **Jerry Blythe,** emeritus member CMTA

"Buff's new book *Volume Factor* is a treasure trove of analysis. Buff has brought risknanalysis and overlays into his methods, adjusting price by volume and money flow. He applies these methods to capital flows to increase returns while reducing risk. We found his first book, Investing with *Volume* Analysis of "great technical importance that demands immediate attention." Volume Factor extends these ideas with new discoveries and is a resource every portfolio manager should have on his desk. Buff continues to make important contributions, expanding the growing field of technical analysis. We thank Buff for his great work."

— **Karen Granville on behalf of Joe Granville** (1923-2013)

"Buff, you have contributed so much to technical analysis it was like Joe found a tune and you took it and put it into orchestration"

— **Karen Granville**

THE VOLUME FACTOR

The Missing Piece:
Goals-Based Investment Strategies
To Achieve Successful Investment Outcomes

BUFF PELZ DORMEIER, CMT®

NEW YORK
LONDON • NASHVILLE • MELBOURNE • VANCOUVER

The Volume Factor

Tactical Goal Based Investment Strategies for Financial Advisors, Endowments and Institutional Investors

Published in New York, New York, by Morgan James Publishing. Morgan James is a trademark of Morgan James, LLC. www.MorganJamesPublishing.com

Proudly distributed by Publishers Group West®

Holy Bible: English Standard Version. Crossway Bibles, 2001.

ISBN 9781636983226 paperback
ISBN 9781636983233 ebook
Library of Congress Control Number: 2023945692

Interior Design by:
Christopher Kirk
www.GFSstudio.com

Thank you, Father, for adopting me as your child, at the priceless inconceivable cost secured through the lifeblood of your beloved Son. Dear Lord Jesus,
I extend my gratitude for descending from your heavenly throne to inhabit this world you created in splendor which has been marred in our corruption.

Thank you for trading the company of your Father and the adoration of angels for the scorn and ridicule of mankind. To you, the flawless, righteous, and unblemished Creator, I am thankful for shouldering my sin and my punishment, bearing the full just wrath of our Father that I may be eternally adorned in your righteousness. To you who is eternal, the author of all life, I am grateful for your selfless death, granting me the gift of eternal life beside you.

Your ways are above my ways. Your thoughts are above my thoughts. You dwell in eternity creating time, matter and energy. As well as the dimensions known, as well as those unknown, the vastness of space, the intelligence of design, and the miracle of life. I am redeemed by your Son, sealed by your Spirit and held eternally secure by the firm strong grasp of the Father's hand.

You are omnipotent, peerless in your might. You are the almighty, there is none like you. Your nature is good, unblemished, just, unwavering, and genuine. You are good, pure, righteous, faithful and true. You are kind, gentle, peaceful, forgiving, and compassionate. And where your unfailing love meets your perfect justice, you provide your amazing grace.

You left heaven to be born a man, live a sinless life, die a sacrificial death to be resurrected back to life, and triumphantly ascend back to heaven. You promise to return and reign restoring all things anew. Until that glorious day and forever more, hold up your rod providing me your strength to obey and honor you with purity.

I thank you for your provision and ask your favor rest upon this reader,
that your face would shine upon them, be gracious to them, and provide them peace.

TABLE OF CONTENTS

INTRODUCTION 1

CHAPTER 1: Investment Factors 10
CHAPTER 2: Setting The Stage Volume As An Investment Factor 23
CHAPTER 3: The Volume Factor In Trends 27
CHAPTER 4: Volume and Momentum – The Volume Factor 63
CHAPTER 5: Risk Management – Math Always Wins 96
CHAPTER 6: Bull Run, Bear Hide – Volume Factor Strategies For Growth And The Endowment Method Of Withdrawal 135
CHAPTER 7: Sector Investing 153
CHAPTER 8: The Dividend Tree and the Income Method of Drawal 170
CHAPTER 9: Volume Factor Direct Indexing...............................186
CHAPTER 10: Yield Matters 192

CONCLUSION 200
ABOUT THE AUTHOR...205
ACKNOWLEDGMENTS..207
GLOSSARY 209
BIBLIOGRAPHY...217

Important Information Regarding Hypothetical, Back-Tested Performance

Much of the model data presented throughout this book is hypothetical in nature. The results shown are not based on any advisory client assets. The performance results do not represent the results of actual trading of investible assets or securities. The hypothetical results do not reflect payment of any sales charges or fees an investor may pay to purchase the securities underlying the models or fees associated with funds or investment strategies that are intended to track the performance of the models. The imposition of these fees and charges would cause performance to be lower than the performance shown.

The hypothetical results presented in this book are presented solely for analysis purposes and are subject to inherent limitations, including the following: they are designed with the benefit of hindsight, based on historical data, do not reflect actual trading, and do not reflect the impact that certain economic and market factors might have had on the decision or rule-making process. No hypothetical, back-tested or simulated performance can completely account for the impact of financial risk in actual performance.

The hypothetical results are provided for analysis purposes only and should not be taken as an indication of actual results of any investment strategy. There are frequently material differences between hypothetical, back-tested or simulated performance results and actual results subsequently achieved by any investment strategy. Back-tested performance is hypothetical and is calculated by retroactively applying a back-tested model designed with the benefit of hindsight. Back-tested data represents the application of a specific methodology and selection of model constituents in hindsight. The back-tested performance differs from actual performance because the allocation rules may be adjusted at any time, for any reason and can continue to be changed until desired or better performance results are achieved.

Past performance of a model is not a guarantee of future results. Actual performance of the any of models discussed in this book may vary significantly from the hypothetical results shown.

INTRODUCTION

"I am a searcher...
I always was... and I still am...
searching for the missing piece."
—Louise Bourgeois

After years in the financial industry, I have finally figured it out. I spent the majority of my career seeking to master the markets. From the beginning of my quest, I understood that there is no holy grail. I also understood that there is always someone smarter and wiser, empowered with superior resources. The best one can aspire is an edge. For a while now, I have been blessed with a sharp edge. After decades of practice, however, I have come to realize that having an edge, while critically important, is only one piece of a much larger puzzle. To help people reach their financial goals, one's edge must be strategically and tactically employed.

But I am getting ahead of myself. Let's first take a step back. What is the larger puzzle? For most investors, the puzzle is not the building of wealth. Rather, the dilemma is figuring out how to make their money work for them. The problem resides somewhere between one's investment strategy and one's financial plan. It is here, in the mean or space between an individual's investment strategy and their financial goals, where investors and planners frequently miss the mark. This is the missing puzzle piece. This is the puzzle piece I've finally figured out.

In my previous book, *Investing with Volume Analysis*, I discussed volume analysis and my investment edge, volume. This new book, *The Volume Factor*, explains how to employ that edge to realize one's financial goals. However, if you are looking for market indicators and strategies, you will not be disappointed, as I also share more of my proprietary indicators and explain exactly how to employ them.

Goals-based investing is the nexus between determining financial goals and achieving successful financial outcomes. Goals-based investing is the strategy and the ensuing processes that allow you, an astute investor, to accomplish your life goals. The capacity to achieve life goals is where true treasure lies.

MY STORY

So, how did I get here? Allow me to share a bit of my background. I attended a state school, Indiana State, as a Division 1 athlete. While there, I learned that talent must be combined with hard work to compete. I also learned that putting in extra work pays strong dividends. More importantly, unwavering effort – grit – almost always yields exponential results. This is the law of incremental returns, a law that applies to life as well as to investing. These principles of hard work and effort later framed my career.

After a short stint in the not-for-profit world, I quickly pivoted to the industry I grew up in, the brokerage business, where I fell in love with the markets. I then worked for Charles Schwab while studying to be a market analyst. Quickly, I advanced to Schwab 500, the department initially designed to work with the top 500 clients of the firm. While there, I began to apply my analytical studies within the profession through Socratic client conversations.

A problem arose. Often, some of our top clients would wait five deep for an opening to speak to me while other team members sat idle. I met with leadership and convinced them that web-based investing would become a threat to all of our positions. To defend against these trends, we needed to provide "value through advice." As a result, we (I, Jay Farmer, and Chuck Sampson), formed Schwab's Technical Analysis Team, providing hand-selected advisors with the skills necessary to offer advice in their conversations with clients. So, when you see the Schwab "value of advice" commercials, you now know how it all started.

From there, I put my research and analysis theories into practice as the portfolio manager for a family-office investment firm in Indianapolis. Following this, I joined my father's investment practice. I understood that the transaction brokerage model was on the path to extinction, and in response, we strategically pivoted to fiduciary discretionary portfolio management. Subsequently, I came to believe that the next phase would be financial planning. We moved to a new firm that had developed state-of-the-art goals-based planning resources. Today, we are at Kingsview Partners, where I am helping to scale our portfolio management business while introducing goals-based and targeted outcome investing concepts to financial advisors. I believe this model of goals-based investing will become the new field that fuses financial planning with investment strategy.

GOALS-BASED INVESTING

What is goals-based investing? In working with the affluent, I have found that most investors live between two extremes in understanding their spending. The first error many people make is spending too much or, more specifically, spending too much at the wrong time. This error leads to a reduced lifestyle for their remaining days. The second fallacy is the opposite of the first but leads to the same outcome. This error is the fear of running out of money.

Living a life with financial insecurity leads to the reality of a reduced lifestyle. In either case, life is lived, but those dreams that can be accomplished only through wealth are not fully realized, a true tragedy.

What if there was a way to know just how much you could confidently spend or give away, with confidence that you will remain financially secure? This is the goal of financial planning. Financial planners utilize asset allocation models and modern portfolio theory to predict how long one's money will last. The problem with traditional investment allocation models and modern portfolio theory is that they deal with historical probabilities and uncertainties. The financial planner is left to either acquire or design an investment model for their client that "fits" the plan. This investment model should consider the investor's financial objectives and risk tolerance. Such a model is designed to meet a long-term risk/return goal but not focused on meeting a defined targeted investment objective.

BEHAVIORAL FINANCE

However, according to Ken Haman, a variable of planning exists that remains unaccounted for more often than not. Contrary to what many believe, investing may be just as much about managing emotions as it is about evaluating investments. The investment process should also consider our emotional compulsions to achieve favorable outcomes and our fear of unfavorable results. Investors worry, "Am I going to be okay?" and "How do I protect myself from harm?" Accounting for emotional concerns is the practice of behavioral finance.

What is behavioral finance? According to Investopedia, behavioral finance asserts that rather than being rational and calculating, people often make financial decisions based on emotions and cognitive biases. Here is one example. A financial advisor creates an appropriate asset allocation model for a client based on the client's objectives and risk tolerance. Yet, during bull markets, the client is upset that they are not earning as much as the top-performing benchmarks. Then, during market pullbacks, they complain because they are losing money.

Over the course of time, humanity has sought security by gathering into groups, developing tools and weapons, cultivating fields, breeding livestock, building villages, and surrounding those villages with walls. Achievements and gains in wealth are followed by the desire to increase security and minimize risk. Eventually, civilization accumulated wealth in the form of currency as opposed to physical possessions.

Today, investments are considered "securities" because money offers a feeling of security and certainty regarding the future. As people eventually required less protection from wild animals and invaders, they began to protect themselves by accumulating wealth. Now, instead of worrying about becoming tonight's dinner for a wolf or our warring neighbor's next conquest, we fear the decline of our net worth. The insight behind critical behavioral finance is that investors still perceive information and then react based on their personal experiences and interpretations.

Behavioral finance is as real as human history. Market behavior is driven by two powerful emotions, which have driven humanity from the beginning. Genesis 3:6 says: "When the woman saw that the tree was good for food and that it was a delight to the eyes, and that the tree was desirable to make *one* wise, she took from its fruit and ate; and she also gave to her husband with her, and he ate."

The first dominating emotion of humans is lust, the desire for more and better. An affluent friend of mind, T.P., favored the following motto: "I want it all." It may sound greedy, but it is unequivocally honest. We all want it all. We all want to win. It is human nature. Buying securities gives us a crack at obtaining this goal.

Genesis 3:10 says, "I heard the sound of you in the garden, and I was afraid because I was naked; so I hid myself." One of the most powerful of all human emotions is fear. When gripped by fear, a person is incapable of reasoning. Someone in a state of fear loses their capacity to reason; emotional instinct takes over. Intrinsic value is absolutely meaningless to a person riveted by fear. Cash is where such investors typically hide.

These two emotions play out daily in the stock market in the form of demand, the desire for profit and supply, and the fear of loss. As an investor, it is helpful to know which personality is the controlling market force. Is it the bears (supply) or the bulls (demand)? Price is the end result of buyers and sellers determining who is in control at any given moment. Through volume, one can gauge the price movement's legitimacy and stamina.

Investors' reactions to changing values can be perfectly rational at times and wildly irrational at other times. This is because the brain is capable of using automatic mechanisms or "shortcuts," as opposed to facts and data, to perceive and react to information. Research in behavioral finance has identified patterns that explain how the brain naturally processes information. One pattern stems from reactions during moments of anxiety or urgency. Investors feel vulnerable when bombarded with more information than they are able to process. To cope, our minds create mental shortcuts, built-in heuristics, to ease the challenge of deciding.

Heuristics are our preset patterns of decision-making. Unfortunately, while they work well enough in many situations, we need to improve our heuristics when making investment decisions. Herein lies the typical client-advisor dance. When the market soars higher, the client wonders why his portfolios are not measuring up to the top-performing indexes touted on the financial networks. The client asks his advisor why they are not receiving the returns reported in the broadcasts. The advisor reminds their client of their unique objectives and custom benchmark, designed around their specific risks and goals. However, over the course of the bull market, the client gets their way as the advisor wears down, while the client's investments become increasingly aggressive during up markets.

During down markets, the advisor now believes they have good news to report. That is, the client is finally beating those formerly high-flying benchmarks. However, the client could not care less. They are presently gripped in the fear that comes from losing money or perhaps better stated, losing security. The client no longer cares about their financial plan's benchmark; zero is their new goal. If their pain persists too long or becomes too acute, these emotional investors flee to cash.

Driven by these behavioral finance realities, goals-based investing maintains all the tools of the advisor. These tools include a financial plan based upon the client's goals and risk tolerance and a form-fitting asset allocation model utilizing the diversification benefits of modern portfolio theory. But where strategic modern portfolio theory stops, tactical post-modern portfolio management begins.

RISK MANAGEMENT

Postmodern, active tactical management is nothing new. What is different about our approach is that it employs strategic, tactical strategies targeting the desired goals-based outcome. In the distribution phase, goals-based outcomes take three forms: yield, volatility, or a combination of the two. Yield outcomes are derived from a distribution strategy targeting a specific yield. An investor with a targeted yield lives off the income of the portfolio. So long as the yield is achieved, the client's income goals are met. The key to this method is maintaining the portfolio yield at a growth rate above inflation.

Another goals-based investment distribution method is driven by growth and volatility. Volatility-based outcomes are connected to the endowment method of withdrawal. The goal of the endowment withdrawal method is to provide capital growth with a flexible allowance to meet life's expenditures. Under the endowment method of withdrawal, the income target is based upon the account's value at a predetermined period, such as an annual anniversary. The greater the returns, the more capital is withdrawn. However, the weaker the returns, the less capital is withdrawn.

The difficulty of the endowment method is creating a sufficiently stable yield by which to plan. The greater the portfolio's volatility, the greater the difficulty in maintaining future income. For example, if a portfolio were to drop 20%, with a 5% distribution level, then the portfolio would need to return 33.33% the following year to meet the same distribution level. This is because the 20% capital drop plus the 5% withdrawal rate equates to a 25% drop in value. A portfolio that is down 25% needs an approximate 33 1/3% return on the remaining capital to get back to even (100 -25 = 75, 75 * 1.33 = 100). Thus, low volatility is required for the endowment methodology to be successful. A tactical risk management overlay is essential to the success of a goals-based investment process.

VOLUME FACTOR RISK OVERLAYS

Tactical asset management must be more consistent at best. Some trend-following strategies have done an excellent job of decreasing risk while improving returns. However, trend-following systems need improvement. Trend-following techniques typically do not return to the market until well after the significant bottoming returns have been made. Unfortunately, the strongest phase of a bull market is typically its birth. By following capital flow trends instead of price trends and combining these trends with volume capitulation indications, the Volume Factor risk overlay system aims to follow market trends while reemploying capital during rare capitulation events.

You may have heard the phrase, "You cannot time the market." I will not weigh in on whether or not one can time the market. However, I have developed strong confidence that it is undoubtedly possible to gauge the "health" of the market. This is roughly analogous to a doctor gauging a patient's health. Doctors use medical tools to assess the general health of their patients. You understand this drill because your own health is assessed every time you undergo a physical examination. Medical professionals check your heart, lungs, throat, pulse, height, weight, and blood pressure, and they may order blood work or other diagnostics. From this data, your doctor can gauge the state of your health.

Similarly, in today's sports science, metrics are used to assess athletes' performance and injury potential. Likewise, market technicians use analytical tools to gauge the health of both bull and bear markets. Specific tools I commonly use in my analysis are capital-weighted volume, capital-weighted dollar volume, the advance-decline line, new highs and lows, and the percentage of stocks above trend. These are just a few, but much like a physical examination, they provide me with the data needed to gauge the market's internal health. Understanding the health condition of markets is helpful in determining how a market may perform in the future, as well as its susceptibility to injury.

The ability to effectively assess the health of the market is the differentiator empowering our tactical goals-based strategies. Goals-based investing is the fusion of modern and post-modern tactical management with investment planning. All of these tools have been around for a long time, so why has this not been done before? The answer is that it has, but with very inconsistent results. Poor, inconsistent tactical investment results occur because they lack critical innovation. And that critical innovative edge, the missing piece, is the title of this work, *The Volume Factor*.

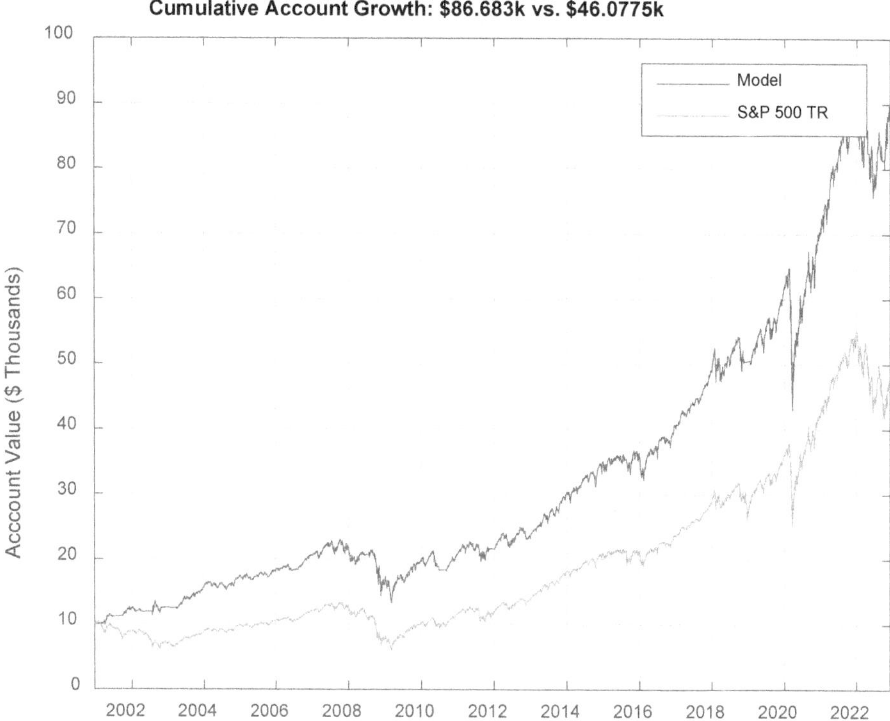

The Volume Factor represents a distinctive approach to tactical asset management. The securities industry is rich in highly educated, book-smart professionals. Portfolio managers all know the same theories and use the same tools, resources, research, data sets, and providers. They manage their assets according to what they have learned in school and their accreditation societies. As a result, it should not surprise anyone that their investment philosophies generally tend to be similar in nature. Yes, they have wide variations in style, but within their own stylistic framework, generally, investment managers' views of the investing climate are homogeneous. As a result, their portfolio products are similar variations of the same thing. Additionally, their performance typically tracks a similar index. Sometimes they are a bit ahead, and at other times they are a bit behind. This similarity creates job stability and leads to ordinary performance.

This is not the goal or approach with the Volume Factor. At birth, I was given the name "Buff." In my 53 years, I have never known another authentic Buff. Perhaps that is why I detest the ordinary. I seek an extraordinary life. Nothing else will do. My heart's desire is to deliver meaningful results to my relationships. My daily prayer is to be a blessing overflowing into the lives I touch.

VOLUME FACTOR INVESTMENT MODELS

My Volume Factor investment models seek to be much more than the standard off-the-shelf investment product easily classified into widely known investment categories. A standout cannot rely solely on the same accepted knowledge their peers already share. To be exceptional, one must break new ground in terms of discovery and be able to effectively apply an enlightened perspective. Investing should be about process over product.

Once again, by following capital trends instead of price trends and combining these trends with volume capitulation indications, the Volume Factor risk overlay system seeks to follow market trends while reemploying capital during rare capitulation events. Reduced volatility allows for more consistent withdrawals while simultaneously meeting the behavioral finance needs of investors, allowing investors to remain in the markets when they are rising while allocated in safe and defensive positions as they decline.

Additionally, the Volume Factor can be employed to analyze individual securities, allowing our models to be continually reallocated with only those specific investments demonstrating volume factor qualities. Infusing the Volume Factor edge into goals-based investing creates the necessary framework to produce successful outcomes. Successful outcomes are what the Volume Factor is all about.

To introduce a distinctive model approach like the Volume Factor to the mainstream, I needed to convince those with access to partner with me. That proved to be a challenging task. Why? Because most believed in the same traditional concepts producing ordinary results. Authentic and unique outside-the-box thinking is considered dangerous. Technical analysis, although practical, is too often considered fringe. My work with volume analysis is unique and highly differentiated. Is the proof in the pudding, or are these objectives sensationalistic?

My Volume Factor models are built on new concepts. Not only are the indicators proprietary, but the tools used for their construction are rare, as is the data. The processes employed strive for results some may consider unrealistic or even ludicrous. In *The Volume Factor*, the reader is introduced to investment models constructed in data blocks built by contrasting the elasticity of uncommon data sets. These building blocks are then reassembled into formulas, and these formulas are then combined to make algorithms. Following this, the algorithms are forged to create a system designed to attempt to realize specific investment outcomes.

The Volume Factor systems are designed to outperform over full market cycles. They are far from foolproof. Over short-term periods, there are many catalysts for price change. My volume-based data and analytics may provide valuable information leading to informed investment decisions. However, our supply-demand side perspective is not always a puissant impetus for price movement.

The goal of *The Volume Factor* is to introduce the reader to goals-based investment models, providing investors with what they really want and often need but are constantly told they cannot achieve. That is, to participate in the investments most in vogue when the markets are up and to be "safely" positioned when the markets are down. A cynic by nature, I, too, would be very skeptical of the ambitions laid out in this work. Yet, the data has convinced me otherwise.

However, please don't think my goal is to convince you. I am not persuading; I am giving back. You can choose to receive or reject this information, be it understanding or foolishness; only time and your own personal experience will tell. The culmination of this work was not built upon an island but, rather, was carefully constructed by expanding upon previously discovered information formerly concealed, ignored, or neglected. I hope to advance and elevate the fantastic work of others to new heights with *The Volume Factor*. It is both a responsibility and a labor of love, dedicated to those who invested in me, which I now share with you.

CHAPTER 1:

INVESTMENT FACTORS

"Every picture's painted differently, every one has got a vision in their mind. That fills the heart with answers, and the missing piece that we hope to find.

—Terri Clark

Some of the data presented in this chapter is hypothetical and back-tested data. This data is not based on any advisory client assets. Past performance of a model is not a guarantee of future results. Actual performance may vary significantly from the hypothetical results shown. Please see the section titled 'Important Information Regarding Hypothetical, Back-Tested Performance' for a full description of this data and the limitations associated with it.

Presently, baby boomers are plowing money into the stock markets, preparing for their upcoming retirement. According to Forbes Financial Council, over the course of the next decade, on average, 10,000 baby boomers will retire each day. Meanwhile, the highest earnings demographic, the millennial population, notorious for doing things 10 years late, is just beginning to gear up their investment savings plans. How are these new fund flows being allocated?

According to CNBC, passive investing now accounts for 45% of all United States funds, up from 25% just a decade ago. Over the past few decades, capital-weighted indexes have become America's de facto investment option. It is not that passive investment strategies, primarily undertaken through capital weighting, are a poor choice. On the contrary, capital weighting is a type of cross-sectional momentum investing with excellent results.

In a capital-weighted index, as index members gain or lose relative momentum, they rise or fall in their weightings. Given the vast allocations of these new net inflows being invested in this mindless strategy, holdings are becoming ever more concentrated. At the time of this writing (May 2023), the top five holdings of the S&P 500 accounted for approximately 20% of the index's weightings. This means that just five stocks control 20% of the movements of the index composed of 500 members.

Consequently, baby boomers who are primarily invested in the S&P 500 have subjected themselves to concentration risk and, ever more so, the sequence of returns risk of reverse dollar cost averaging. The sequence of returns risk is the risk of receiving low or negative returns early on or when withdrawals are taken from an investment portfolio. This risk is significantly elevated when investors sell down their investment assets to supplement their lifestyle in retirement. Investors selling the index unwittingly cause the index products to liquate holdings, creating a spiraling decline.

According to Forbes, millennial investors are the most risk-averse demographic, despite the fact that they are the youngest demographic. Thus, they will likely be fickle investors in a less favorable investment climate. Far and away, these two demographics, baby boomers and millennials, represent the most significant percentage of the American investment population.

Combining these risks via the sequence of returns for baby boomers, coupled with millennials' risk aversion, multiplies the probability and the volatility associated with an S&P 500 unwinding event. Unwinding is when an index product, whether an ETF or a fund, must sell positions in its underlying holdings to satisfy redemption sales. In capital-weighted indexes, the position sales match those of their size weightings. Thus, the larger the position weighting, the more that stock is required to be sold off. Over the past decade, as more money poured into the S&P 500, the largest weightings grew ever larger. However, an unwinding event would be especially devastating to those employing this passive index strategy and to those holding large concentrations of the heavily weighted issues in the S&P 500.

FACTOR INVESTING

As opposed to mindlessly following the movements of the herd, *factor investing* provides an alternative investment strategy to passive investing. **Factor investing involves** choosing or weighting investments based on their characteristics or attributes. Think about factor investing much like the screening of a group of job candidates. For example, a hiring manager may desire candidates with specific experience or educational levels. Other options might be more subjective, such as strong leadership skills, high motivation, and the ability to follow directions. Similarly, scouts look for traits, aka "factors," in the players they recruit. As Chris Ballard, General Manager of the Indianapolis Colts, explains, "Traits are the most important thing that we look for. It's the character, the mental toughness, the competitive spirit, the intelligence. That's what separates good players from great players."

Likewise, equities traits may be fundamental or technical in nature. The fundamental attributes of a company include earnings, profitability, cash flow, and revenue. Likewise, stocks have technical traits, such as price momentum and volatility, all of which stem from shareholder behavior. Still, other attributes, such as size or dividends, may not be as easily characterized as singularly fundamental or technical in nature. According to BlackRock, only five broad factor categories presently exist: value, size, quality, momentum, and low volatility.

The primary thesis of this work is that **volume** should be included among these broad factors. **Volume is the linchpin** that leads to successful goals-based investing outcomes.

SEEK TO OUTPERFORM: SINGLE FACTORS & MULTIFACTOR

Combining factors can reduce volatility of returns

Single factor strategies have low historical correlation, so combining them within Multifactor ETFs can deliver greater consistency of returns.

U.S. factors calendar year fund returns (%)

2014	2015	2016	2017	2018	2019	2020	2021	2022	Annual return 2014 - YTD
Min Vol 16.34	Momentum 9.12	Value 15.68	Momentum 37.60	Min Vol 1.36	Quality 34.14	Momentum 29.69	Value 28.98	Min Vol -9.35	Momentum 11.75
Size 15.78	Quality 5.56	Size 13.32	Quality 22.26	Momentum -1.77	Size 29.06	Quality 16.96	Quality 26.90	Value -14.14	Min Vol 10.30
Momentum 14.48	Min Vol 5.50	Min Vol 10.50	Value 21.97	Quality -5.77	Min Vol 27.77	Size 16.30	Size 25.03	Size -15.84	Quality 9.95
Value 12.29	Size 0.37	Quality 9.18	Min Vol 18.97	Size -6.51	Momentum 27.57	Min Vol 5.60	Min Vol 20.80	Momentum -18.23	Size 9.76
Quality 11.62	Value -3.54	Momentum 4.89	Size 18.88	Value -11.18	Value 27.47	Value -0.32	Momentum 13.45	Quality -20.39	Value 7.46

Source: Morningstar as of 12/31/2022. Min Vol represented by the iShares MSCI USA Min Vol Factor ETF. Size represented by the iShares MSCI USA Size Factor ETF, Momentum represented by the iShares MSCI USA Momentum Factor ETF, Value represented by the iShares MSCI USA Value Factor ETF, Quality represented by the iShares MSCI USA Quality Factor ETF

Performance data represents past performance and does not guarantee future results. Investment return and principal value will fluctuate with market conditions and may be lower or higher when you sell your shares. Current performance may differ from the performance shown.

The strategic bundling of factors is called "multifactor investing." Similarly, smart beta is another investment strategy that ascribes weights to portfolio characteristics. Often, "smart beta" and "multifactor" are used interchangeably. Although both strategies aim to achieve better risk-adjusted returns than traditional market-cap-weighted index funds, smart beta does not necessarily need to be factor-based. Additionally, smart beta can serve as a "passive" rules-based strategy, deviating from the market-cap-weighted index. Smart beta criteria can be chosen based on academic research, market trends, factors, and other investor preferences.

A multifactor portfolio may be passive, active, or even tactical in nature. Instead of weighting securities in the portfolio based solely on their market capitalization, multifactor strategies use a variety of factors – such as value, momentum, low volatility, quality, and size – to construct a portfolio emphasizing specific characteristics believed to drive higher returns. Typically, multifactor portfolios employ more sources of excess returns (alpha) and are more diversified than a single-factor, smart beta strategy. Multifactor strategies seek to identify and invest in stocks that exhibit positive characteristics across multiple factors. Overall, both smart beta and multifactor strategies are designed to provide investors with an alternative to traditional market-cap-weighted index funds while seeking to generate better risk-adjusted returns.

These innovative smart beta/multifactor strategies can be packaged into quantitatively driven indexes, creating intelligent alternatives to capital-weighted indexes. Packaging these strategies into an ETF provides investors with a low-cost, transparent, and liquid investment while also incorporating the attributes of active management. If you believe this to be an enticing active management alternative, know that the investment management industry agrees, as evidenced by the historic 20% growth rate in new strategic smart beta/multifactor products.

Yet, investors should also be aware of the potential drawback of these strategies. First, many factors have identical names but carry different definitions and formulas. This creates a confusing environment for advisors and consumers. Second, these strategies are relatively new. Thus, many smart beta, factor, and multifactor ETFs do not have long-term track records but, rather, rely heavily on underlying backtested index results.

OPTIMIZATION AND BACKTESTING

The *Volume Factor* is no different in this regard. I believe in backtesting. It is heavily utilized throughout the industry and in this book. However, backtested results may be misleading or may even be a product of random chance. In some situations, (not in *The Volume Factor*), backtesting may be optimized (sometimes even with Artificial Intelligence) to advance the desired results.

Optimization is the practice of continually re-backtesting an indication or a combination of indications to determine the optimal settings. I believe optimization is a bad idea. Habitually, optimizers tend to optimize and keep on optimizing until they discover a successful combination. The result is a backtest characterized by a process of evolution, not mindful creation.

With optimization, tens of thousands of combinations are data-mined until the most successful combination is produced. However, indicators should be thoughtfully created under a specific set of mindful conditions to uncover specific sets of information (not randomized). A law of nature called entropy tells us that order degenerates toward disorder. Therefore, random processes cannot yield useful, intelligent information. With optimization, or curve-fitting, one simply identifies the randomized combinations that worked best in the past. But why should they work in the future? Suppose you invest money using an optimized investment system. You then enter a long-term losing streak not experienced in the backtesting. Do you keep losing, or do you reoptimize?

I don't have enough faith in optimization to make an informed investment decision. As opposed to an illogical methodology, I suggest a simplified approach. Instead of optimizing parameters, settings should be based on the investment horizon. What do I mean by that? For example, to contrast data sets over the course of a week versus a month, the proper indicator settings would be five business days (one week) and 20 business days (four weeks). Maintaining consistent settings corresponding to the calendar keeps it simple and realistic. My belief is that if a backtest does not "work" over the course of a specified time frame, yet supposedly does work over another specified time frame, then the backtest does not work at all.

So, assuming the backtests are fair and legitimate, I have found evidence of outperformance garnered through factor investing to be abundant through many sources. Typically, these accepted factors have been shown to add alpha and improve risk-adjusted return rates above indexing. **Figure 2** shows BlackRock's five factors plus their multifactor strategy versus the S&P 500 index backtested to 2006.

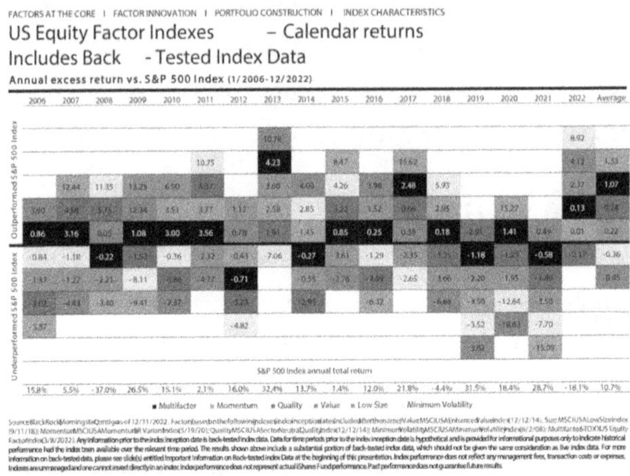

Figure 3 illustrates the same factors applied to the international markets versus the MSCI EFA index. Although these traditional factors may yield incremental improvements, *The Volume Factor* introduces a new factor exhibiting superior alpha generation. In fact, this book is devoted to that factor: volume. When properly understood within the context of price trends, **volume reveals the forces of supply and demand**. When correctly applied, the *Volume Factor could be the most prominent factor behind price discovery to date.*

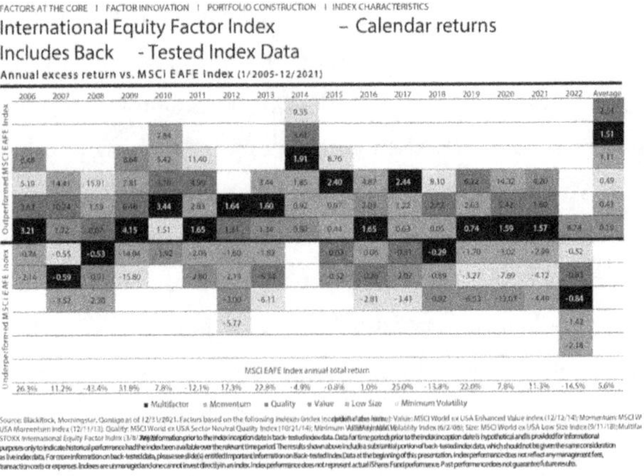

Of the five accepted factors proposed by BlackRock, two, value and quality, are fundamental factors, and two, volatility and momentum, are technical factors. However, many characteristics can be encompassed within these broad factor categories. Moreover, each of these characteristics has many variations within their calculations. Such variety can lead to a factor "flavors" list, similar to listings of ice cream flavors, brands, and recipes. The factor characteristic must prove itself across time, economies, and geography to be isolated as an actual factor. The factor must also utilize a systematic approach of rational explanation as to why a characteristic adds value. We will start with the factor that is neither technical nor fundamental in nature: the size factor.

THE SIZE FACTOR

The first factor we will review is the most controversial, size. No doubt there is much evidence that small companies often perform differently than large companies. The small capitalization size factor premium was first hypothesized in 1981 by Rolf Banz in the *Journal of Financial Economics*. His research, titled "The Relationship Between Return and Market Value of Common Stocks," concluded that "small NYSE firms have had significantly larger risk-adjusted returns than large-cap NYSE stocks over a forty-year period." Many other sources have confirmed that small stocks, while more volatile, have outperformed their larger counterparts.

In recent years, however, large stocks have outperformed small stocks. Much of the evidence is cyclical in nature. Small stocks tend to outperform large stocks during economic turning points. The theory is that small companies are more nimble and able to adjust during swift economic shifts. Small company growth is expected to outperform in the later bubbling stages of an economic upturn, when the economy is expanding, and interest rates are high and rising. The economic phase that typically follows the end of the expansion is the beginning of an economic downturn when interest rates are high and falling and the economy is stalling out. This type of economic environment is expected to be favorable to small-cap value stocks.

Offering an alternative opinion to size as a factor, Ron Alquist, Ronen Israel, and Tobias Moskowitz of AQR Capital Management conclude that size factor returns are "less stable, less persistent, and less robust than these other factors." In their study, titled "Fact, Fiction, and the Size Effect," published in the *Journal of Portfolio Management* in 2018, these authors theorized there is an absence of risk-adjusted return premiums in small versus large stocks. If there is a return premium in small caps, it is primarily due to a liquidity risk premium associated with illiquid small stocks. Additionally, as AQR's research explains, "using 90+ years of U.S. data, there is no evidence of a pure size effect. Moreover, it may not have existed in the first place if not for data errors and insufficient adjustments for risk and liquidity."

The majority of the original studies demonstrating slight cap outperformance ascribed to size are explained by survivorship bias. Survivorship bias occurs when index data used to calculate historical performance fail to account for delisted stocks that are removed from the database. These delisting events tend to be adverse events, such as bankruptcies. **After adjusting for the bullish survivorship bias, the vast majority of outperformance by a small cap over a large cap is negated**, while the risk remains higher.

Historically, small caps were expected to outperform due to their explosive growth potential. More recently, though, this growth has been subdued due to the rise of private equity at the expense of early public issuance. In the 1980s and 1990s, the average age of a company at IPO from inception was eight years, and the average capitalization was $50 million. By 2020, the average company IPO age was more than 12 years, and the capitalization was over $250 million. This leaves the typical IPOs of today at just barely small-cap status. Today's IPOs are also less profitable on average. Additionally, growth sectors such as technology now only represent less than 14% of the Russell 2000, while nearly 35% of private equity is technology. Thus, much of the explosive growth potential of new and rising small companies has been replaced by private equity, which is now more patient in raising new equity from the public markets.

THE VOLATILITY FACTOR

The first technical factor we cover is volatility. Specifically, low-volatility stocks tend to outperform. The first low-volatility index created was the S&P 500 low-volatility index in April 2011. At first glance, the factor of low volatility may appear too good to be true. Could lower risk (via low volatility) mean higher returns? Low-volatility strategies work. Why? It's the math. Although low volatility has lower upside capture, lower downside captures more than makes up for it.

Perhaps the first observation of this phenomenon was made by Robert Haugen and A.J. Heins in a study published in 1972 titled "On the Evidence Supporting the Existence of Risk Premiums in the Capital Market." The study, which analyzed the performance of U.S. stocks from 1926 to 1969, concludes, "Over the long run, stock portfolios with less variance in monthly returns have experienced greater average returns than their 'riskier' counterparts." This low-volatility factor approach generally outperforms during high volatility/rapidly declining market climates.

Exhibit 1 summarizes a selection of low-volatility indices based on various benchmarks over the last 15 years, displaying the improved risk/return ratios of each low-volatility index compared to its corresponding parent benchmark. The data illustrate low volatility's potential to offer higher risk-adjusted returns than the market benchmark from which they were derived.

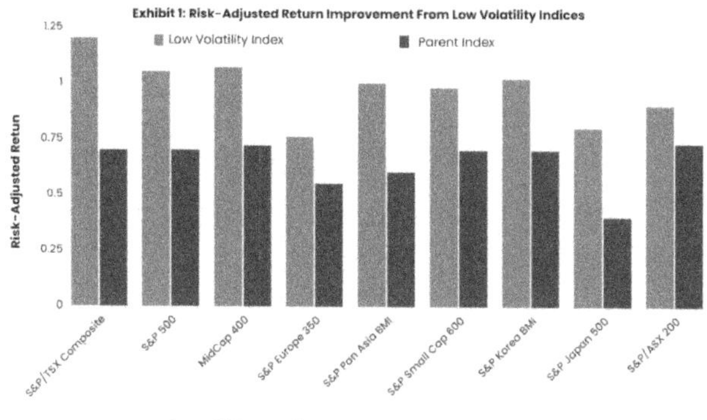

Exhibit 1: Risk-Adjusted Return Improvement from Low Volatility Indices. Source: S&P Dow Jones Indices LLC. Data from April 2003 to April 2018. Index performance is based on annualized monthly total return in local currency, except for the S&P Pan Asia BMI, which uses USD. The chart is provided for illustrative purposes and reflects hypothetical historical performance associated with backtested performance.

Like all factor strategies, there are various approaches to building a low-volatility portfolio. Most, however, define low volatility as low standard deviation. Again, like many of the technical factors, volatility is relative in contrast to the index or other index components.

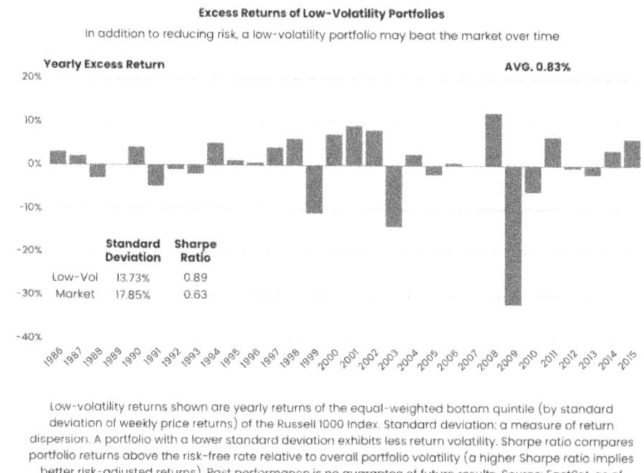

Low-volatility returns shown are yearly returns of the equal-weighted bottom quintile (by standard deviation of weekly price returns) of the Russell 1000 Index. Standard deviation: a measure of return dispersion. A portfolio with a lower standard deviation exhibits less return volatility. Sharpe ratio compares portfolio returns above the risk-free rate relative to overall portfolio volatility (a higher sharpe ratio implies better risk-adjusted returns). Past performance is no guarantee of future results. Source: FactSet, as of Mar. 31, 2016.

Exhibit 2, from Fidelity's Darby and Frank Nielson and Bobby Barnes' "An Overview of Factor Investing," shows that Russell 1000 stocks with low price volatility narrowly outperformed over time, with less risk – leading to higher risk-adjusted returns. In addition, lower-risk stocks tend to hold up better during down markets, when investor uncertainty is elevated. As a result, low-volatility strategies generate lower drawdowns and benefit from the compounding effects of excess returns during bear markets.

THE VALUE FACTOR

The value factor is based on a belief that a given security is inexpensive relative to some measure of fundamental value. This discount, or value, should lead to future outperformance compared to pricier issues. Value investors believe stocks are ultimately a product of their future earnings. An explanation of why a stock may appear cheap is the associated risk in meeting its future earnings potential.

The work of Benjamin Graham and David Dodd, in their book *Security Analysis*, popularized value investing. Performing a value-oriented security analysis could not have come at a better time, as the SEC was formed contemporaneously. New security laws provided visibility in corporate balance sheets and communications, opening the practice of value investing to the public as opposed to the privileged few with special access or connections.

Popular methodologies of value factor investing are price-to-book, price-to-sales, and earnings yield.

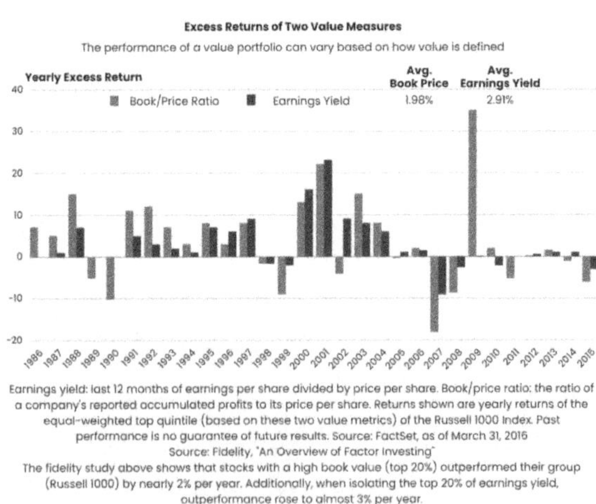

Earnings yield: Last 12 months of earnings per share divided by price per share. Book/price ratio: The ratio of a company's reported accumulated profits to its price per share. Returns shown are yearly

returns of the equal-weighted top quintile (based on these two-value metrics) of the Russell 1000 Index. Past performance is no guarantee of future results. Source: FactSet, as of Mar. 31, 2016.

Source: Fidelity, "An Overview of Factor Investing"

The Fidelity study above shows that stocks with a high book value (top 20%) outperformed their group (Russell 1000) by nearly 2% per year. Additionally, when isolating the top 20% of earnings yield, outperformance rose to almost 3% per year.

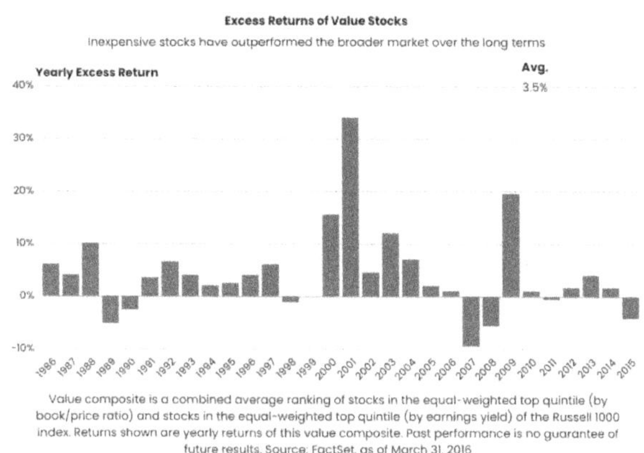

Value composite is a combined average ranking of stocks in the equal-weighted top quintile (by book/price ratio) and stocks in the equal-weighted top quintile (by earnings yield) of the Russell 1000 Index. The returns shown are yearly returns of this value composite. Past performance is no guarantee of future results. Source: FactSet, as of Mar. 31, 2016

Source: Fidelity, "An Overview of Factor Investing"

Although value stocks may appear cheap, often they are inexpensive for good reasons. As a result, the value factor may dramatically underperform at times. In other words, cheap stocks can become even cheaper. Value is one of the factors that may underperform for months and even years. Consequently, value is typically found to be the most volatile or risky of the factors. Value's higher volatility often leads to smaller risk-adjusted returns than the other factors.

THE QUALITY FACTOR

The quality factor is a key concept in portfolio management. It refers to the tendency of high-quality companies to outperform lower-quality companies over the long haul. Quality is generally defined as a company's financial strength, profitability, stability, and growth prospects.

In portfolio management, the quality factor is often used to construct well-diversified and balanced portfolios. By selecting companies with solid financials, consistent earnings growth, and high returns on capital, portfolio managers can reduce the risk of holding lower-quality companies that may be more susceptible to market volatility and economic downturns. Such quality portfolios focus on identifying companies with strong competitive positions, consistent earnings growth, and attractive valuations.

One of the key benefits of the quality factor is its ability to provide downside protection during market downturns. By holding high-quality companies, investors can both reduce the impact of market volatility on their portfolios and generate higher risk-adjusted, long-term returns.

Although the value factor often sees greater reductions during market drawdowns, quality stocks typically hold up better during significant declines. Low volatility can buffer price in large declines but can also severely lag during market run-ups, whereas quality generally performs soundly in strong market upswings. These attributes make quality a beneficial factor in multifactor models.

However, it's important to note that investing in high-quality companies assumes risks and uncertainties, just like any other strategy. In particular, the quality factor may underperform during periods of market exuberance, when investors are more focused on growth and momentum.

The quality factor has been extensively studied in portfolio management, and numerous academic papers and empirical studies have examined its impact on investment performance.

One such paper is another study by AQR Capital Management titled "Value and Momentum Everywhere," by Clifford Asness, Tobias Moskowitz, and Lasse Pedersen. This research was published in the *Journal of Finance* in 2013, and it examined the performance of various investment factors, including value, momentum, and quality, across different asset classes and geographies. The study found that the quality factor was a significant driver of outperformance in both developed and emerging equity markets. A quality-based investment strategy generated higher risk-adjusted returns than a traditional market-cap-weighted approach.

Another study, "Quality Minus Junk" by Clifford Asness, Andrea Frazzini, and Lasse Pedersen, published in 2018 in the *Journal of Portfolio Management*, examined the performance of a quality-based investment strategy in the U.S. equity market over a 40-year period. The researchers found that a long/short portfolio of high-quality companies outperformed a long/short portfolio of low-quality companies by an average of 2.13% per year, with higher Sharpe ratios and lower volatility. The study also found that the quality factor was a distinct and robust driver of stock returns, independent of other factors such as value and momentum.

A similar study by Fidelity Investments examined the performance of a quality factor-based investment strategy in the U.S. equity market over a 25-year period. The study found that a portfolio of high-quality companies outperformed the broader market by an average of 2.5% per year, with lower volatility and higher risk-adjusted returns.

These studies provide compelling evidence in support of the efficacy of the quality factor in portfolio management. By selecting high-quality companies with solid financials, stable earnings, and attractive valuations, investors may generate higher risk-adjusted returns and reduce the impact of market volatility on their portfolios.

THE MOMENTUM FACTOR

The momentum factor is a key concept in portfolio management. It refers to the tendency of assets that have performed well in the recent past to continue to perform well in the future. Momentum investing is based on the idea that trends in asset prices are likely to persist over time. The momentum factor contends that investors can generate higher returns by buying assets trending upward and selling those trending downward.

Numerous academic and research papers have studied the momentum factor and its impact on investment performance. One such paper, published in the *Journal of Finance* in June 1992, is titled "The Cross-Section of Expected Stock Returns." Authored by Eugene Fama and Kenneth French, the study examined the performance of a momentum-based investment strategy in the U.S. equity market over a 30-year period. The study found that a portfolio of high-momentum stocks outperformed the broader market by a significant margin, with annualized returns 3-4% higher than the S&P 500 index.

Another momentum study, written by Kalok Chan, Allaudeen Hameed, and Wilson Tong and published in the *Journal of Financial Economics*, is titled "Momentum Strategies in International Stock Markets." The study, published in June 2000, examined the performance of a momentum-based investment strategy across 11 different international equity markets over a 20-year period. These researchers found that the momentum factor was a significant driver of outperformance in all of the markets reviewed. A momentum-based investment strategy generated higher risk-adjusted returns than a traditional market-cap-weighted approach.

A similar study by AQR Capital Management is titled "Fact, Fiction and Momentum Investing." Published in the *Journal of Portfolio Management* in 2014, it examined the performance of the momentum factor across different asset classes, including equities, fixed income, currencies, and commodities. The study found that the momentum factor was a significant driver of outperformance in all asset classes examined, and that a momentum-based investment strategy generated higher risk-adjusted returns than a traditional buy-and-hold approach.

These studies provide compelling evidence in support of the efficacy of the momentum factor in portfolio management. By selecting assets with recent strong performance and avoiding those with recent weak performance, investors can generate higher risk-adjusted returns and reduce the impact of market volatility on their portfolios.

Momentum could also be a key driver in multifactor investing. *One drawback of factors is that they fall in and out of favor.* Thus, an investor employing a factor strategy may require much patience to see the factor play out. However, momentum could be employed to choose the factors currently demonstrating promise. “Momentum in Factor Portfolios,” published in the *Journal of Portfolio Management* in 2018 by Huseyin Gulen and Yuhang Xing, examined the effectiveness of using momentum to gauge the timing of factors. The authors found that momentum-based factor portfolios outperformed traditional buy-and-hold factor portfolios, suggesting that momentum can serve as a valuable tool in enhancing multifactor investment strategies.

Another study, titled “Momentum Investing in Factor Portfolios,” published by Tobias Moskowitz and Yao Hua Ooi in the *Journal of Alternative Investments* in 2017, investigated the performance of momentum-based factor investing strategies in different market environments. The authors found that momentum can be a valuable addition to multifactor investing, particularly during market stress, when traditional factor strategies may underperform.

These studies suggest that infusing momentum into factor-based investment strategies may help investors improve their risk-adjusted returns and provide a more robust approach to multifactor investing.

In the next chapter, we will present the title of this work, *The Volume Factor.*

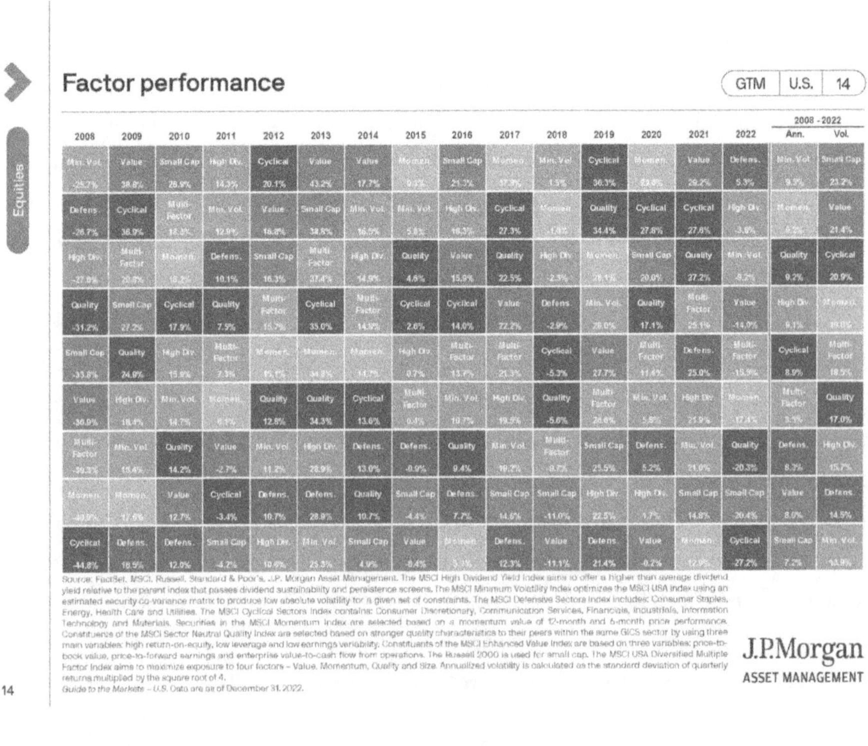

Equities

Factor performance

GTM | U.S. | 14

2008	2009	2010	2011	2012	2013	2014	2015	2016	2017	2018	2019	2020	2021	2022	2008 - 2022 Ann.	2008 - 2022 Vol.
Min. Vol. -25.7%	Value 38.8%	Small Cap 26.9%	High Div. 14.3%	Cyclical 20.1%	Value 43.2%	Value 17.7%	Momen. 9.3%	Small Cap 21.3%	Momen. 37.8%	Min. Vol. 1.5%	Cyclical 36.3%	Momen. 29.6%	Value 29.2%	Defens. 5.3%	Min. Vol. 9.3%	Small Cap 23.2%
Defens. -26.7%	Cyclical 36.9%	Multi-Factor 18.3%	Min. Vol. 12.9%	Value 16.8%	Small Cap 38.8%	Min. Vol. 16.5%	Min. Vol. 5.6%	High Div. 16.3%	Cyclical 27.3%	Momen. -1.8%	Quality 34.4%	Cyclical 27.6%	Cyclical 27.6%	High Div. -3.6%	Momen. 8.2%	Value 21.4%
High Div. -27.8%	Multi-Factor 20.8%	Momen. 16.2%	Defens. 10.1%	Small Cap 16.3%	Multi-Factor 37.4%	High Div. 14.9%	Quality 4.6%	Value 15.9%	Quality 22.5%	High Div. -2.3%	Momen. 26.1%	Small Cap 20.0%	Quality 27.2%	Min. Vol. -9.2%	Quality 9.2%	Cyclical 20.9%
Quality -31.2%	Small Cap 27.2%	Cyclical 17.9%	Quality 7.5%	Multi-Factor 15.7%	Cyclical 35.0%	Multi-Factor 14.8%	Cyclical 2.6%	Cyclical 14.0%	Value 22.2%	Defens. -2.9%	Min. Vol. 28.0%	Quality 17.1%	Multi-Factor 25.1%	Value -14.0%	High Div. 9.1%	Momen. 19.0%
Small Cap -33.8%	Quality 24.9%	High Div. 15.9%	Multi-Factor 7.3%	Momen. 15.1%	Momen. 34.8%	Momen. 14.7%	High Div. 0.7%	Multi-Factor 13.7%	Multi-Factor 21.3%	Cyclical -5.3%	Value 27.7%	Multi-Factor 11.4%	Defens. 25.0%	Multi-Factor -15.9%	Cyclical 8.9%	Multi-Factor 18.5%
Value -36.9%	High Div. 18.4%	Min. Vol. 14.7%	Momen. 6.1%	Quality 12.8%	Quality 34.3%	Cyclical 13.6%	Multi-Factor 0.4%	Min. Vol. 10.7%	High Div. 19.5%	Quality -5.6%	Multi-Factor 28.6%	Min. Vol. 5.8%	High Div. 21.9%	Momen. -17.4%	Multi-Factor 8.5%	Quality 17.0%
Multi-Factor -39.3%	Min. Vol. 18.4%	Quality 14.2%	Value -2.7%	Min. Vol. 11.2%	High Div. 28.9%	Defens. 13.0%	Defens. -0.9%	Quality 9.4%	Min. Vol. 19.2%	Multi-Factor -8.7%	Small Cap 25.5%	Defens. 5.2%	Min. Vol. 21.0%	Quality -20.3%	Defens. 8.3%	High Div. 15.7%
Momen. -40.9%	Momen. 17.6%	Value 12.7%	Cyclical -3.4%	Defens. 10.7%	Defens. 28.9%	Quality 10.7%	Small Cap -4.4%	Defens. 7.7%	Small Cap 14.6%	Small Cap -11.0%	High Div. 22.5%	High Div. 1.7%	Small Cap 14.8%	Small Cap -20.4%	Value 8.0%	Defens. 14.5%
Cyclical -44.8%	Defens. 18.5%	Defens. 12.0%	Small Cap -4.2%	High Div. 10.6%	Min. Vol. 25.3%	Small Cap 4.9%	Value -8.4%	Momen. 5.3%	Defens. 12.3%	Value -11.1%	Defens. 21.4%	Value -0.2%	Momen. 12.9%	Cyclical -27.2%	Small Cap 7.2%	Min. Vol. 13.9%

Source: FactSet, MSCI, Russell, Standard & Poor's, J.P. Morgan Asset Management. The MSCI High Dividend Yield Index aims to offer a higher than average dividend yield relative to the parent index that passes dividend sustainability and persistence screens. The MSCI Minimum Volatility Index optimizes the MSCI USA index using an estimated security co-variance matrix to produce low absolute volatility for a given set of constraints. The MSCI Defensive Sectors Index includes: Consumer Staples, Energy, Health Care and Utilities. The MSCI Cyclical Sectors Index contains: Consumer Discretionary, Communication Services, Financials, Industrials, Information Technology and Materials. Securities in the MSCI Momentum Index are selected based on a momentum value of 12-month and 6-month price performance. Constituents of the MSCI Sector Neutral Quality Index are selected based on stronger quality characteristics to their peers within the same GICS sector by using three main variables: high return-on-equity, low leverage and low earnings variability. Constituents of the MSCI Enhanced Value Index are based on three variables: price-to-book value, price-to-forward earnings and enterprise value-to-cash flow from operations. The Russell 2000 is used for small cap. The MSCI USA Diversified Multiple Factor Index aims to maximize exposure to four factors – Value, Momentum, Quality and Size. Annualized volatility is calculated as the standard deviation of quarterly returns multiplied by the square root of 4.

Guide to the Markets – U.S. Data are as of December 31, 2022.

14

J.P.Morgan
ASSET MANAGEMENT

CHAPTER 2:

SETTING THE STAGE VOLUME AS AN INVESTMENT FACTOR

"A Jedi's strength flows from the force."

—Yoda.

Before we begin presenting the evidence, it's important to first note that investment factors require a rational theory. The rationale behind the factor must be reasonable and logical to be considered a market factor. This chapter lays out the case in support of volume analysis as a logical and reasonable market factor. We will begin assembling our foundational rationale encompassing volume theory with the very basic fundamentals and then work our way toward a deeper understanding of why volume analysis is effective.

Although market volume is a crucial piece of investment information, the majority of the public is ignorant of volume. Financial analysts do not often consider volume, whereas technical analysts underutilize it. Yet volume provides essential information in two critical ways: one by indicating a price change before it happens and two by helping the technician interpret the meaning of a price change as it happens.

Vince Lombardi and John Wooden both are famous for focusing on the fundamentals by maintaining a simplified approach. In that spirit, let us begin with the basic fundamentals of technical analysis. I am reminded of Vince Lombardi's quote, "Gentlemen this is a football." In the realm of technical analysis, it just doesn't get any more basic than price. So, what is price?

When I, as an investor, purchase a security, what is my opinion of that security? I'm bullish. I believe the price will rise; why else would I buy it? But to take ownership, my buy order must be matched. What do you suppose is the seller's opinion of that same security? While there could be a multitude of reasons to sell, most likely, the seller is bearish. They believe the price will decline; otherwise, they would not sell it.

Therefore, price is an agreement to disagree between two parties with opposite opinions of future price direction. That agreement to disagree is called price in the exchange markets.

In this way, price represents the conviction, emotions, and will volition of investors. Price is truth. It does not matter what the talking heads on TV say, and the same holds true for the analyst price targets, the outlook concerning intrinsic value, anything, and everything else. A stock is worth its traded price, period. Opinions do not cover margin calls.

Billions are spent every year researching security and market valuations. Price discovery truly is a beautiful economic mechanism. In this way, price is the market's DNA because it represents all the collective knowledge of the markets. Now, on to our topic, volume. If price is the market's DNA, then volume is the market's RNA. Like RNA decodes and interprets DNA, volume interprets and decodes price.

Volume is synonymous with force. A quick lookup of "force" in the dictionary provides the following definition: "Force is a power made operative against support or resistance."

Technical analysis 101: What is support? Support is an area where buyers reside. What is resistance? Resistance is an area where sellers reside.

Technical Analysis 102: What is an uptrend? An uptrend is a rising support line. And what is a downtrend? A downtrend is a falling resistance line.

Now let us advance to Technical Analysis 400: Volume is the force required to sustain price trends.

Switching over to the physics dictionary, force is defined as a vector quantity producing acceleration. This confirms a major tenant of technical analysis going back to the days of Charles Dow over a century ago: Volume leads price. This means that significant changes in volume trends often precede major price movements.

In summary, consider Yoda. What did he say before engaging in an important mission? "May the force be with you." Volume, my friends, is the force of the exchange markets. If you take one thing from this chapter, remember that volume is the force, and you, as an investor, want to make sure you are on the right side of it. *"Sometimes, the missing puzzle piece is right in front of you; you just have to see it."*

So why did the market go up today, and why did it go down yesterday? It went up today because there were more buyers than sellers, and it went down yesterday because there were more sellers than buyers. That's the technical analysis, right? That's what we hear on the financial networks.

"Ils ne comprennent pas." That's French for "They do not understand." In an exchange market, the number of shares purchased always equals the number of shares sold, which equals the total volume exchanged.

Here is a simple formula to help you remember: B=S=T, which stands for buy volume = sell volume = total volume. Now let's put this knowledge into practice. Let's say I receive a volume analysis trade signal from my Volume Analysis MetaStock add-on. I want to buy the stock the moment I receive the signal – no time to waste. I put in an order to buy 1,000 shares of ABC stock at the market. Unbeknownst to me, an institution is selling 100,000 shares, because ABC stock has just reached its intrinsic value target. The institution puts in a limit order to sell 100,000 of its shares. My 1,000 shares are matched against 1,000 of the institution's shares. The question is, who is in control? Is it me, the buyer with a market order? Or is it the seller, which has 100 times as many shares of stock but is employing a limit order?

We do not know the answer for certain – that is, until the order is executed. If that trade goes through on an uptick, it indicates my demand is greater than their supply. Conversely, if the trade goes through on a downtick, then there is more supply than demand. These interactions occur tens of thousands of times every second, five days a week, in the equity exchanges. If these accumulations of ticks over time are moving higher, then we know demand is in control, visualized by an uptrend. This is a security that is being accumulated over the course of time. In contrast, if these accumulations of trade ticks are moving downward over the course of time, then we know that supply is in control. This is visualized through a downtrend in a security that is being distributed over time.

What if there was a way to look deep inside these supply and demand interactions to determine if the volume supports the price action? That is the goal of volume analysis. Volume is the performance driver in every strategy I have developed. In my professional expert opinion, volume is the unknown investment factor. In fact, volume research has repeatedly been applied and tested by technicians, fundamental analysts, and academicians. It is one of the few indicators or data sets on which they mostly agree. *The Volume Factor* strives to provide an edge so that you, too, can follow the flows of capital.

Here are four reasons I infuse volume data into both my security selection process and my risk management overlay. Those who follow price trends and price momentum alone may be investing toward the peak of an advance. They also are often inclined to be shaken out by price whipsaws. However, combining volume with price helps to alleviate the common trend and momentum issues of buying at the peak and those dreaded whipsaws.

Like any good sermon, below, I provide four rational points, all beginning with the same letter: "R." These are the four R's of volume:

R-1: Responsiveness – Volume provides quicker information, and volume leads price. It is widely known and acknowledged that changes in volume generally occur before significant price movements.

R-2: Reliability – Volume confirms price. If price is the market's testimony, then volume is its polygraph. Volume validates and substantiates price. The more investors participate at a given price level, the more that price point is validated. In this way, volume may not only more rapidly propel an investor into a trend movement, faster but may also simultaneously increase the probability that the price's trend momentum will continue into the future.

R-3: Risk – By differentiating legitimate trends from failing trends and identifying trend weakness early on, investors correctly utilizing volume data should be better positioned to reduce the risks to their portfolios.

R-4: Returns – Returns are deemed the most important of the four R's. If volume can identify a trend earlier while creating a higher probability of being positioned correctly, then volume should also tilt the odds in our favor, potentially positioning the volume investor with an opportunity to realize better returns.

In summary, technicians, fundamental analysts, and academicians have studied volume and have often arrived at similar conclusions, making volume one of the few pieces of data on which they mostly agree. Yet, volume is underappreciated and underutilized in market analysis. Price is the agreement to disagree between buyers and sellers, while volume constitutes the force required to sustain price trends. Significant changes in volume trends often precede major price movements, rendering volume a leading indicator of price. Additionally, analyzing volume in conjunction with price reveals supply and demand dissymmetries, which are useful in determining how volume may support or contradict the price trend. In this way, volume both leads and confirms price. As we progress, we will combine and contrast volume with price to unravel the volume factor – the "force" behind both individual security selection and index analysis.

CHAPTER 3:

THE VOLUME FACTOR IN TRENDS

"Sometimes, the answer is hidden within the missing puzzle piece."

Some of the data presented in this chapter is hypothetical and back-tested data. This data is not based on any advisory client assets. Past performance of a model is not a guarantee of future results. Actual performance may vary significantly from the hypothetical results shown. Please see the section titled 'Important Information Regarding Hypothetical, Back-Tested Performance' for a full description of this data and the limitations associated with it.

In the last chapter, we reviewed the four R's of volume: Responsiveness, Reliability, Risk, and Return. In this chapter, and throughout this book, we will lay out the case that these old volume adages are important market factors. However, the underlying analysis must be fully understood for these adages to be correctly applied. Let's begin by building a conceptual understanding of how volume analysis works through the following analogy/visualization. *"The Volume Factor is the bridge connecting technical analysis to financial planning."*

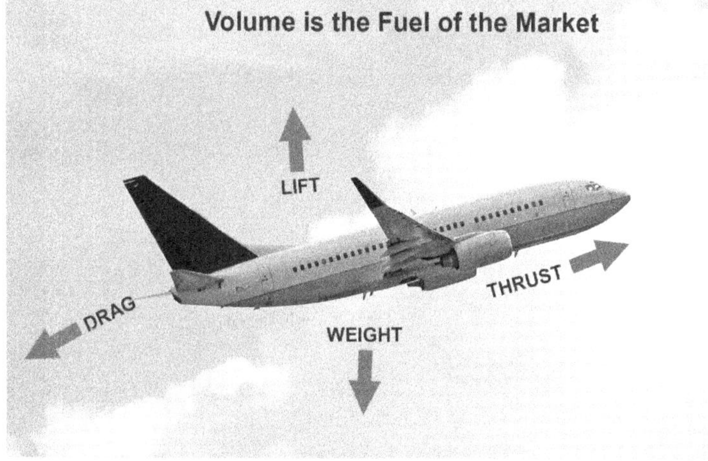

Think about volume analysis like this: Visualize yourself as the pilot of an airplane. You desire the plane to climb higher. To make the plane ascend, you must change the trajectory upward. That requires more fuel for thrust or the aircraft will likely stall. **Volume, or capital, is the fuel of the market**. It takes more and more people willing to participate at ever-increasing prices to keep the proverbial plane ascending. If the market is moving ever higher with fewer and fewer capital flows, then the market or security lacks sufficient fuel or thrust to continue and will likely stall. Now let's apply this theory to our four R's.

VOLUME LEADS PRICE

Responsiveness – Volume can provide essential information by indicating an impending price change before it happens. Volume may be highly telling, particularly when the volume reaches extreme levels, whether high or low. During such times, volume offers far superior information than price alone may provide. As authors Simon Gervails, Ron Kaniel, and Dan Minglegrin of "The High-Volume Return Premium," a white paper from the University of Pennsylvania's Rodney L. White Center for Financial Research, explain, "We find that individual stocks whose trading activity is unusually large (small) over periods of a day or week, as measured by trading volume during those periods, tend to experience large (small) subsequent returns." These researchers further state, "A stock that experiences unusually large trading activity over a particular day or a week is expected to appreciate subsequently." Illustrated in Figure 1 are the test results of Wharton's 33-year study comparing stocks that experienced relatively high-volume surges compared to stocks with normal and low volumes.

The High-Volume Return Premium

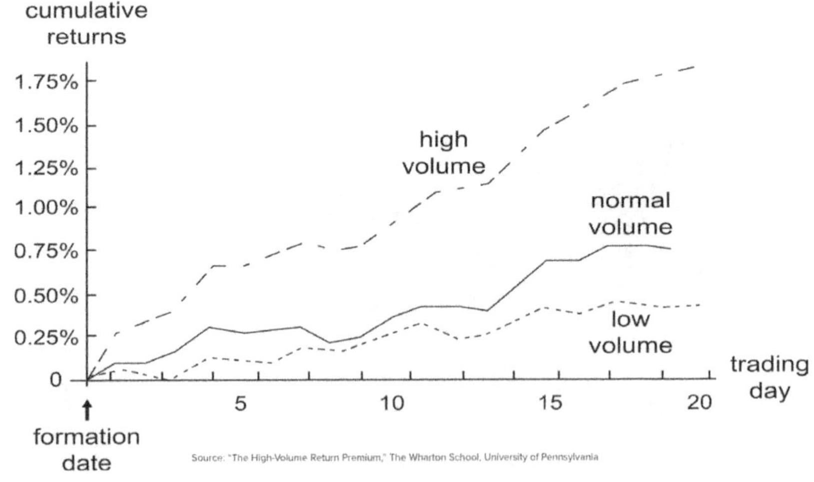

Source: "The High-Volume Return Premium," The Wharton School, University of Pennsylvania

Ron Kaniel, Dong Li, and Laura Starks of the University of Texas confirmed these conclusions. Their research paper, "The High-Volume Return Premium and the Investor Recognition Hypothesis: International Evidence and Determinants," concludes, **"We study the existence and magnitude of the high-volume return premium across equity markets in 41 different countries and find that the premium is a strikingly pervasive global phenomenon.** Moreover, we find evidence that the premium is a significant presence in almost all developed markets and in a number of emerging markets as well."

VOLUME INTERPRETS PRICE

Reliability – The second critical way volume provides information is by helping the technician to interpret price. *Volume enables the analyst to interpret the meaning of price through the lens of the corresponding volume.* As authors Lawrence Blume, David Easley, and Maureen O'Hara (1994) reported in "Market Statistics and Technical Analysis: The Role of Volume," published in the *Journal of Finance*: "We show that volume provides information on information quality that cannot be produced by the price statistic. We show how volume, information precision, and price movements relate, and demonstrate how sequences of volume and prices can be informative. We also show that traders who use information contained in market statistics [volume] do better than traders who do not. Technical analysis thus arises as a natural component of the agents' learning process."

However, price alone represents the vast majority of the work within technical analysis. As such, the Volume Factor elevates volume's significance as an essential element of investment analysis. Yet, doing so without also discussing price is insufficient. Volume can only be appropriately understood alongside price, and price cannot be adequately assessed without volume. Independently, both price and volume convey incomplete market information. However, when examined together, they provide indications of supply and demand that neither could provide independently. As Ying (1966), in his groundbreaking work on price-volume correlations, explained, "Price and volume of sales in the stock market are joint products of a single market mechanism; any model that attempts to isolate prices from volumes or vice versa will inevitably yield incomplete if not erroneous results." Next, we will explore two similar and related volume indicators: tick-based and volume-weighted indicators.

TICK-BASED AND VOLUME-WEIGHTED INDICATORS

An exchange market works much like an auction, where price is formed by two investors, each with a different opinion about the security's future price direction, agreeing to exchange a financial instrument. If the agreement occurs during an uptick, the buyer applies more demand than the seller's exerted supply. Likewise, if the agreement occurs during a downtick, the seller's actions wield greater force than the buyers. *Tick volume decisively quantifies the relationship between price and volume.*

Former president and founder of Worden Brothers, Don Worden, developed the concept of money flow in the late 1950s under the name "tick volume." Today, tick volume is primarily publicized by Laszlo Birinyi as "money flow." When investors use the term "tick," they refer to an individual trade. An uptick, or +tick, is a trade that occurs at a price higher than the last trade. A downtick, or -tick, is a trade that occurs at a lower price than the previous trade. **Tick volume refers to the volume of shares traded per tick.**

Tick volume analysis evaluates price and volume changes on a tick-by-tick basis. Uptick volume is the volume that occurs during upticks. Likewise, downtick volume is the volume occurring during downticks. It gets muddy in the common instance of trades that occur at the previous price, an unchanged tick. In such a scenario, the commonly accepted view is to treat the unchanged tick volume as if it were a part of the previous tick. Thus, if the previous tick was up, the unchanged tick's volume would also be considered an uptick volume, and vice versa.

Price-weighted tick volume uses tick data to "weight" each trade's volume by its corresponding price. The upticks are subtracted from the downticks, and this information is accumulated over time. In essence, tick volume/money flow is volume-weighted by the corresponding price accumulated on a tick-by-tick basis:

Tick Volume/Money Flow = Cumulative Sum (Tick Price * Uptick's Volume) minus Cumulative Sum (Tick Price * Downtick's Volume)

This calculation precisely measures the supply relative to the demand on a per-trade basis and accumulates the difference over time. It reveals whether money flows into or out of a stock based on upticks as buys and downticks as sales.

As an example, we will use two ticks to calculate money flow. The first tick goes through on an uptick of 100 shares at $100. Immediately, the next tick goes through on a downtick at $99.99 on 10,000 shares. The money flow is $989,000: calculated as (($100 *100 shares) - ($99.99 * 10,000)), meaning that $989,000 more in stock was sold than purchased. This illustration shows how money flow can widely veer from the price direction by giving more substantial weight to large-volume transactions. This information is used much in the same way as our other volume indicators. When money flow rises, it suggests that demand is building, indicating the price is poised to continue rising. When money flow falls, it means that supply is building, indicating the price could fall.

However, as the exchange markets become increasingly automated, the decimalization of security prices has strongly reduced the reliability of this method of intraday analysis. Trades completed by scalpers and market makers are most often filled from existing inventories, rendering the accumulation of upticks and downticks much more obscure. Additionally, institutions typically "work" their block trades throughout the trading session to avoid public transparency. Often this practice includes selling into upticks at the offer and buying into downticks at the bid.

The subsequent development in ticked-based analysis is Volume-Weighted Average Price (VWAP). This method was first introduced to the trading community in the March 1988 *Journal of Finance* article titled *"The Total Cost of Transactions on the NYSE"* by Stephen Berkowitz, Dennis Logue, and Eugene Noser. VWAP is the average price at which investors participated over a given period, which is typically one trading day. This is calculated by multiplying and dividing the total by the number of shares traded, aligning each price tick by the corresponding volume and then summing the results of all of these trades.

VWAP = Sum of Trade's Price * Trade's Volume/Sum of Trading Volume

VWAP is more commonly used as a statistic rather than an indicator. The industry standard is to determine a security's accumulation or distribution throughout the trading session. VWAP is the benchmark utilized to compare the average price actually paid to the average price all investors paid for the stock throughout the trading day. *Following VWAP assists institutions in reducing the impact of their large trading operations.*

The next innovation in volume analysis was moving from solely ticked based on a "reflection of time" – whether VWAP or accumulation (tick volume) – to a much more flexible approach. I am referring to my own Volume-Weighted Moving Averages, or VWMAs. Like tick volume and VWAP, VWMAs calculate average fund flows into and out of securities. However, *unlike tick volume, it is not an accumulation indicator.* And, unlike VWAP, VWMAs are not reset at the beginning of a new trading period. Moreover, VWMAs can use either ticks or time in their calculations, but more commonly, they use time.

This example is in days, but VWMAs could be set to any time frame (minutes, weeks, months), ticks, or trading block sizes. The VWMA is calculated by weighting each frame's (time, tick, or block) closing price with the frame's (time, tick, or block) volume compared to the total volume during the range:

Volume-Weighted Average = Sum {Closing Price (I) * [Volume (I)/ (Total Range)]}, where I = given day's action.

Let's now use the four R's of volume with VWMAs to prove volume's significance as an investment factor. We will accomplish this by infusing volume data into a simple trading strategy.

For your review, the 4 R's of volume are listed below:

R #1 is **Responsiveness**

Volume provides quicker information, and "volume leads price," the latter of which has been a mantra since the days of Charles Dow. As a result, changes in volume generally occur before significant price movements.

R #2 is **Reliability**

Volume confirms price. If price is the market's testimony, then *volume is its polygraph*. Volume validates and substantiates price. The more investors participate at a given price the more that price point is validated. In this way, volume may more rapidly propel an investor into a trend movement and increase the probability that the price's trend momentum will continue.

R #3 is **Risk**

By differentiating legitimate trends from failing trends and identifying trend weaknesses early on, investors should be better positioned to reduce the risks to their portfolios.

R #4 is **Returns**

If we can identify a trend earlier and have a higher probability of being positioned correctly, then we are tilting the odds in favor and positioning ourselves with the opportunity to realize better returns.

VWMAS' -VS- SMAS' Responsiveness

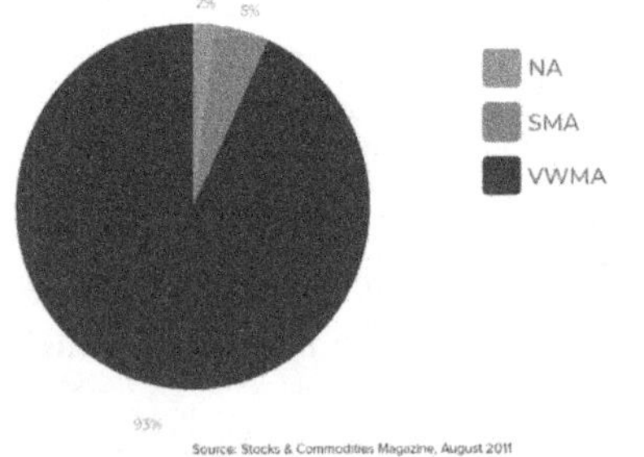

This study compares simple moving averages (SMAs) to VWMAs. It was conducted on 60 stocks chosen by size, volatility, and volume attributes over 5,000 trading days. A method is needed to objectively tally the results, as well as a credible sample. A reliable test must use the scientific method and be both unbiased and comprehensive. To accomplish this, the test was broken into several comprehensive parts.

First, securities were selected across three areas of capitalization: small, as measured by the S&P Small Cap Index; medium, as measured by the S&P 400 Index; and large, as measured by the S&P 100 Index. Equally important are the trading characteristics of each security. Thus, securities were further broken down into the characteristics of volume and volatility. When these traits are combined, a total of 12 groups are formed: small-cap high volume, low small-cap volume, high small-cap volatility, small-cap low volatility, mid-cap high volume, mid-cap low volume, mid-cap high volatility, mid-cap low volatility, large-cap high volume, large-cap low volume, large-cap high volatility, and large-cap low volatility.

Regarding responsiveness, 93% of all the issues showed faster signals with VWMAs than with SMAs. On the other hand, only 5% of the SMAs showed better responsiveness, and 2% of the time, the difference was insignificant.

VWMAs' -VS- SMAs' Reliability

Obtaining faster signals is relatively easy. All one needs to do is shorten the data set to receive quicker alerts. That's true in technical analysis, fundamental analysis, economics, and virtually any realm of science or social science. However, the cost of a faster signal has always been at the expense of reliability and accuracy.

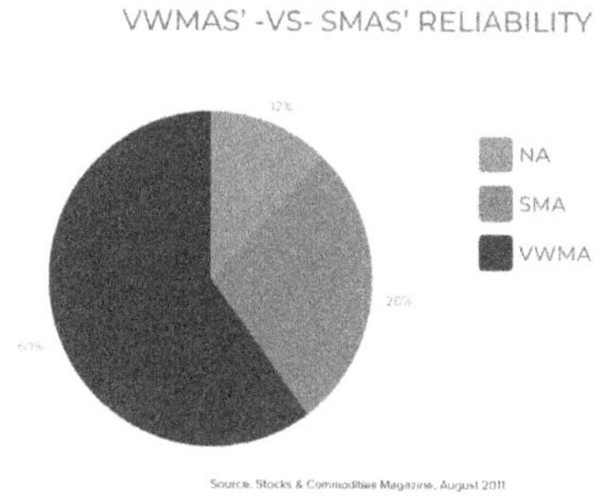

Source: Stocks & Commodities Magazine, August 2011

Yet, with volume analysis, we can receive faster signals while simultaneously improving the reliability of those signals. This slide shows that 60% of the issues showed enhanced accuracy with the volume infused VWMA. In contrast, only 28% showed improvement with volume excluded, and 12% of the time, there was no significant difference in accuracy. From these two studies, we can surmise that volume not only leads price, but also confirms price.

VWMAs' -VS- SMAs' Risk

The next R is Risk. Of the 60 securities tested, 44, or 70%, experienced lower drawdowns utilizing the volume-infused moving averages (VWMAs), compared to only 16, or 30% of those without volume (SMAs). Thus, applying volume infor-

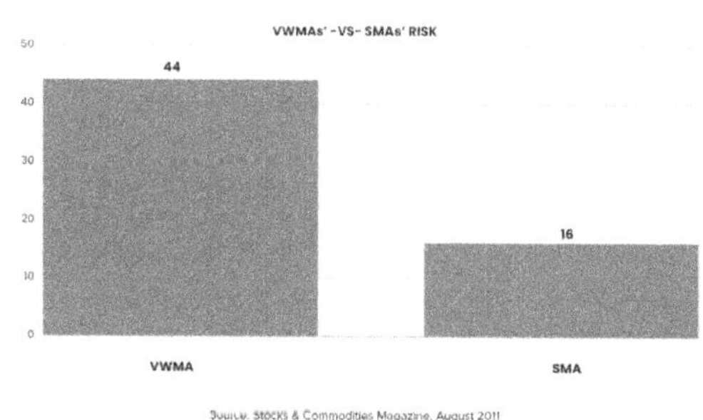

Source: Stocks & Commodities Magazine, August 2011

mation to our moving average crossover trading system significantly reduced the investment risk assumed.

VWMAs' -VS- SMAs' RETURNS

Finally, combining the three categories, small, mid, and large, with the four factors, low volume, high volume, high volatility, and low volatility, creates 12 subgroups. Eleven of the twelve subgroups demonstrated profit improvement with the volume infused VWMAs.

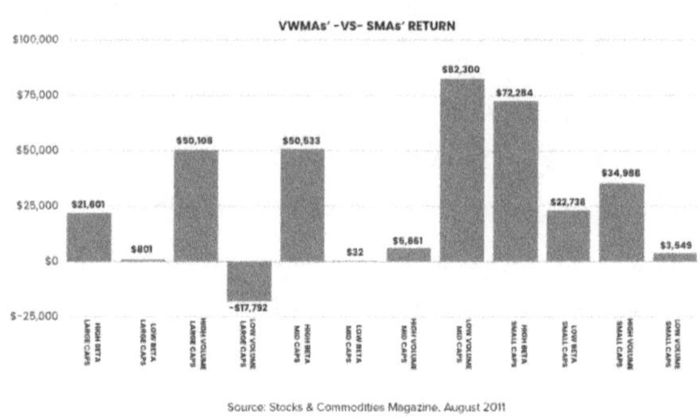

Source: Stocks & Commodities Magazine, August 2011

Because volume leads price, it makes sense to introduce volume into momentum indicators, allowing momentum indicators to respond even faster. In addition, because volume confirms a trend, volume weighting can enhance trend indicators infused with volume information, allowing the indicators to be more reliable. Likewise, because volume leads price, one can combine momentum with volume information to create indicators that provide quicker and more reliable signals. This leads us to the next volume-weighted analysis innovation, the Trend Thrust Indicator, or TTI.

TREND THRUST INDICATOR

The Trend Thrust Indicator is best explained by first introducing another one of my volume price trend indicator innovations, the Volume-Weighted MACD, which is an adaptation of the Moving Average Convergence Divergence (MACD) created by Gerald Appel. The MACD is used by traders and investors to identify trends and potential entry and exit points in financial markets. It consists of two exponential moving averages (EMAs), a faster one and a slower one, and a histogram that represents the difference between the two. Investors use **MACD to gauge the strength of the momentum.** When the histogram is above the zero line, it indicates that the momentum is bullish, and when it is below the zero line, it indicates that the momentum is bearish. The wider the histogram, the stronger the momentum.

To create the VW MACD, we simply swap out the EMAs used to calculate the MACD differential using VWMAs. The benefits of swapping the EMAs with VWMAs in the

MACD are similar to our research with VWMAs and SMA crossovers. However, with the Trend Thrust Indicator, we take these volume advantages up several notches.

The Trend Thrust Indicator is an enhanced version of the VW MACD, but the TTI also applies advanced adaptive logic derived from volume ratios applied within the calculation. In 1935, Harold M. Gartley stated the following: *"As the stock market student progresses in his learning, he finds that relative figures are almost always more useful than raw data (actual figures). The more advanced observers thus study not only actual volume of trading in stock, for a given period, but also the ratio or percent which that volume represents of the total volume."* With this concept in mind, the TTI utilizes adaptive volume ratios to exaggerate volume's impact on the volume-weighted moving average. This means TTI places greater emphasis on those price trends with higher volume and less focus on time periods with lighter volume.

Comparing MACD, VW MACD, And TTI

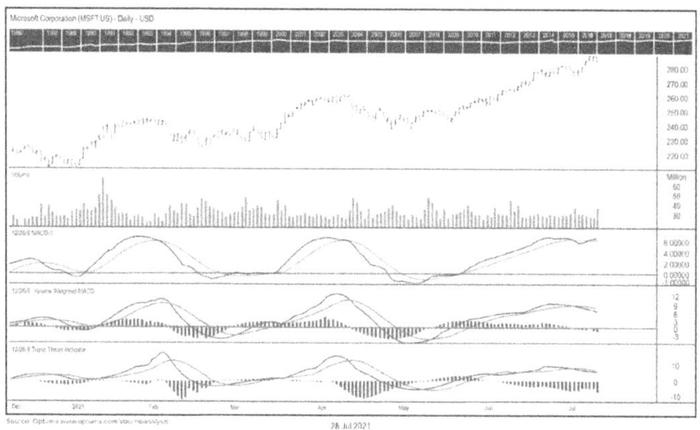

Source: Optuma www.optuma.com/volumeanalysis

The three indicators are depicted together in Figure 6 on MSFT using Optuma software. Optuma has most of my proprietary volume indicators available to its users (free trials are available at www.optuma.com/volumeanalysis). The first pane under price and volume is Gerald Appel on MSFT using Optuma software. Finally, the bottom is the TTI. The TTI looks similar to the MACD indicators but tends to lead and have fewer signals.

60 Securities Chosen By Strongest Size And Factor Qualities

Now back to the drill used to validate VWMAs. The TTI/MACD test was broken down into the same comprehensive parts. Again, securities were selected across three areas of capitalization: small as measured by the S&P Small Cap Index, medium as measured by the S&P 400 Index, and large as measured by the S&P 100 Index.

The three securities were then further broken down into the characteristics of volume and volatility. When these traits are combined, a total of 12 groups is formed: small-cap high volume, low small-cap volume, high small-cap volatility, small-cap low volatility, mid-cap high volume, mid-cap low volume, mid-cap high volatility, mid-cap low volatility, large-cap high volume, large-cap low volume, large-cap high volatility, and large-cap low volatility. Next, we evaluate the original MACD signals against the TTI using the classic crossover signals of Gerald Appel's original MACD settings.

60 Securities by three sizes of capitalization and four styles selected by the most prominent characteristics

Large Cap Low Volatility	*Large Cap High Volatility*	*Large Cap High Volume*	*Large Cap Low Volume*
PG	EP	CSCO	ATI
HNZ	AES	MSFT	BCC
CLI	DAL	INTC	BDK
MMM	ATI	ORCL	ROK
ETR	NSM	GE	CPB
Mid Cap Low Volatility	***Mid Cap High Volatility***	***Mid Cap High Volume***	***Mid Cap Low Volume***
EQT	ACF	ATML	WPO
BOH	BRW	MCHP	BDG
CLI	RSAS	IDPH	TECUA
HE	WIND		
	GILD	KELYA	
NFG	TQNT	ACF	CRS
Small Cap Low Volatility	***Small Cap High Volatility***	***Small Cap High Volume***	***Small Cap Low Volume***
CLP	REGN	PSUN	NPK
CHG	FLOW	ADPT	HGGR
ESS	NOR	KLIC	OXM
GBP	OCA	PCLE	SKY
SHU	CRY	CERN	LAWS

Three sizes of capitalization and four styles. A long position was taken when the spread crossed above the average spread. A short position was entered when the spread crossed under the average spread. A $10,000 position was taken with each cross. Commissions were not included.

TTI -VS- MACD, Percentage Profitable

Knowing stocks typically trend approximately one-third of the time, the MACD crossover signals of Gerald Appel correspond well with stocks' trending patterns. However, when infused with volume, the TTI reliability improves from 34.6% to over 51.6%. Even though price is not trending, volume flows still validate price movements. The TTI exploits this data, turning out more reliable signals. Of the 60 securities tested, all 60 demonstrated higher profitability with the TTI compared to the MACD.

60 securities by three sizes of capitalization and four styles selected by the most prominent characteristics

Large Cap Low Volatility	**Large Cap High Volatility**	**Large Cap High Volume**	**Large Cap Low Volume**
PG	EP	CSCO	ATI
HNZ	AES	MSFT	BCC
CL	DAL	INTC	BDK
MMM	ATI	ORCL	ROK
ETR	NSM	GE	CPB
Mid Cap Low Volatility	**Mid Cap High Volatility**	**Mid Cap High Volume**	**Mid Cap Low Volume**
EQT	ACF	ATML	WPO
BOH	BRW	MCHP	BDG
CLI	RSAS	IDPH	TECUA
HE	WIND	GILD	KELYA
NFG	TQNT	ACF	CRS
Small Cap Low Volatility	**Small Cap High Volatility**	**Small Cap High Volume**	**Small Cap Low Volume**
CLP	REGN	PSUN	NPK
CHG	FLOW	ADPT	HGGR
ESS	NOR	KLIC	OXM
GBP	OCA	PCLE	SKY
SHU	CRY	CERN	LAWS

TTI (BLUE) -VS- MACD (RED), Profitability Percent In The Seven Factors

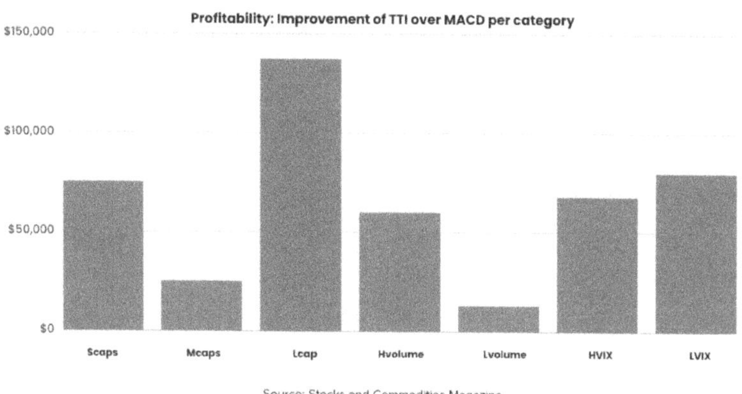

Overall, large caps using the volume enhanced TTI produced $137,138 more than the MACD. Thus, the TTI produced more profitable results among all three categories of capitalization.

Percent Profitable, Seven Factors

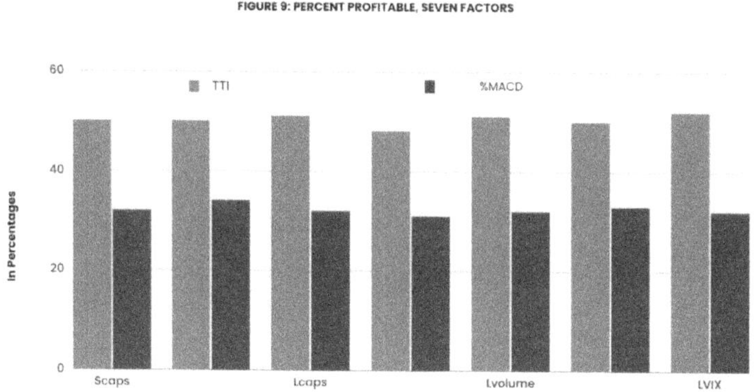

Figure 9 shows the reliability of seven factor groups by the percent profitability. Every factor group incorporating TTI improves upon the MACD trending patterns. However, when infused with volume, the TTI are more reliable.

Figure 9 shows the reliability of the seven factor groups by the percent profitable. Every factor group incorporating TTI improves upon the MACD trending patterns. However, when infused with volume, the TTI are more reliable.

With regard to profitability, as one might expcct, greater reliability begets greater profitability across all seven size and factor groups.

THE VOLUME PRICE CONFIRMATION INDICATOR

The differentiator in our approach to volume analysis is not only the data, but also its interpretation. Volume analysis is most effective in the context of market trends. Yet, most volume tools neglect trend data. However, what if there were a way to look deep inside price and volume trends to determine whether current prices are supported by volume? This is the objective of the Volume Price Confirmation Indicator (VPCI), a methodology that measures the symmetrical relationship between price and volume trends.

Many technical indicators have been developed to decode the price/volume relationship. However, the key to grasping volume information is not the volume data itself or its direct relationship with price movements. Rather, it is **best understood in terms of volume's relationship with the price trend**. The VPCI was uniquely developed to unveil critical information from this volume/price relationship.

There are many volume indicators, and most work well. However, they can work much better. Most other volume indicators are constructed through individualized pieces of data, as opposed to trend data. In contrast, the Volume Price Confirmation Indicator is unique in revealing the asymmetry between price trends and their corresponding volume flows via trend data.

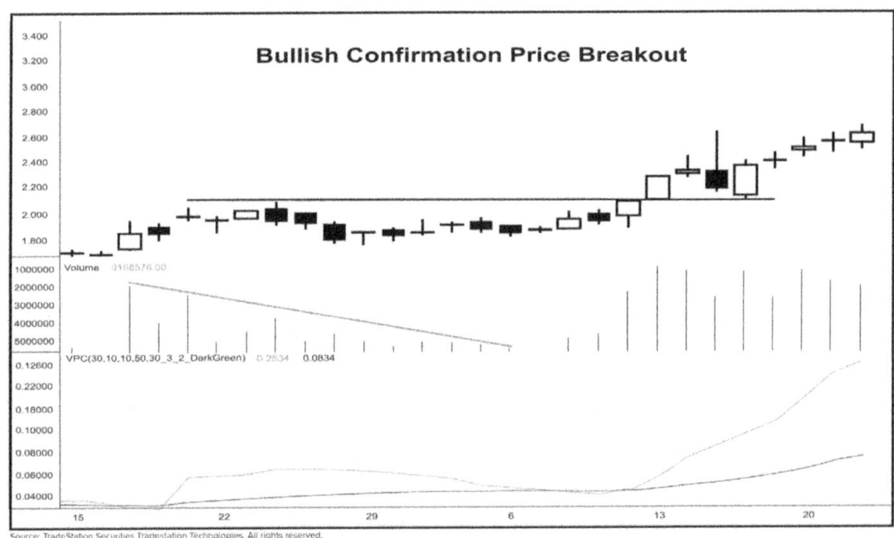

Source: TradeStation Securities Tradestation Technologies. All rights reserved.

Figure 11 shows a chart with price at top, volume in the middle, and the VPCI at bottom. The VPCI is capturing the asymmetry between price and volume trends. It moves up when the volume is confirmed and down when the volume is contradicting price. Here, you can see in Figure 11 that the price pattern is sideways, while volume begins a downward trend. Then, VPCI crosses over above its moving average at VPCI point 1. Shortly afterwards, the price breaks out at price point 1, with VPCI rising rapidly as the price follows.

The VPCI exposes the relationship between the prevailing price trend and its corresponding volume as either confirming (rising/above zero) or contradicting (falling/below zero) the price trend. This information gives possible indications of impending price movements.

The VPCI calculates the asymmetry between price trends and volume-weighted price trends. This is primarily derived by examining the difference between a volume-weighted moving average (VWMA) and the corresponding simple moving average (SMA). These differences expose information about the inherent relationship between price and money flow. For example, although SMAs demonstrate a stock's changing price levels, they do not reflect the amount of investor participation. With VWMAs, however, price emphasis is adjusted proportionally to each day's volume and then compared to the average volume over the range under study.

Here's an example of calculating a two-day moving average using both the SMA and VWMA for a security trading at $10 a share with 100,000 shares changing hands on the first day, and at $12 a share with 300,000 shares changing hands on the second day. The SMA calculation is day one's price plus day two's price divided by the number of days, or (10+12)/2, which equals 11. The VWMA calculation would be day one's price of $10 multiplied by day one's volume, which is expressed as a fraction of the total range (100,000/400,000 = 1/4), plus day two's price of $12 multiplied by day two's volume of the full range expressed as a fraction (300,000/400,000 = 3/4), which equals 11.5. The difference of .5 represents volume's confirmation of price. Had the SMA /VWMA numbers been flipped, the .5 change in the calculation would represent volume's contradiction of the price trend.

VPCI Basic Building Block VWMA – SMA

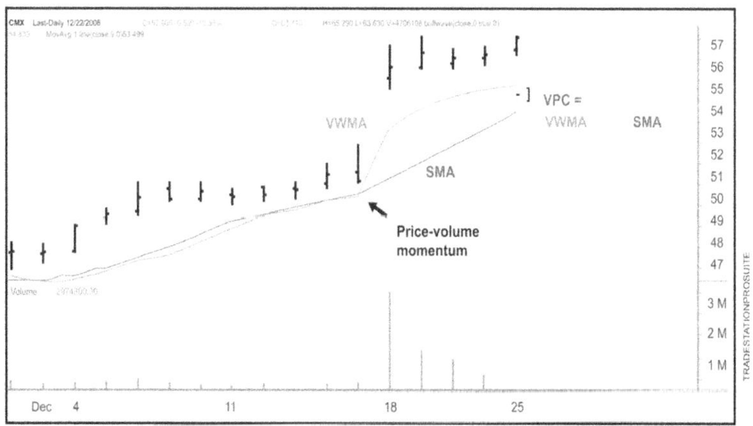

Source: TradeStation Securities Tradestation Technologies.

The Volume Price Confirmation Indicator reveals asymmetry in the intrinsic relationship between price trends and their corresponding volume flows.

Deriving VPCI's Components

The VWMA measures investor commitments expressed through price, weighted by each day's corresponding volume, compared to the total volume over time. Thus, volume-weighted averages weigh prices in exact proportion to the volume traded during each time period. Therefore, we can begin investigating the VPCI, keeping in mind how VWMAs work. The VPCI involves three calculations.

First, Volume Price Confirmation (VPC) is calculated by subtracting a long-term SMA from the same time frame's VWMA. Essentially, this calculation is the unseen nexus between price and price proportionally weighted to volume. This difference, when positive, is the VPC+ (volume-price confirmation), and when negative, the VPC- (volume-price contradiction). This computation represents the intrinsic relationship between price and volume symmetrically distributed over time.

The result is revealing. For example, a 50-day SMA might be $48.50, whereas a 50-day VWMA is $50. The difference of 1.5 represents price-volume confirmation (VWMA – SMA) (see Figure x). If the calculation were negative, it would represent a price-volume contradiction. This calculation alone provides purely unadorned information about the otherwise unseen relationship between price and volume.

The next step is to calculate the volume price ratio (VPR). VPR accentuates the VPC+/- relative to the short-term price-volume relationship. The VPR is calculated by dividing the short-term VWMA by the short-term SMA.

For example, assume the short-term time frame is 10 days, the 10-day VWMA is $68.75, and the 10-day SMA is $55. The VPR would equal 68.75/55, or 1.25. This factor will be multiplied by the VPC (+/-) calculated in the first step. Volume-price ratios greater than 1 increase the weight of the VPC+/-. Volume-price ratios less than 1 decrease the weight of the VPC+/-.

The third and final step is calculating the volume multiplier (VM). The VM's objective is to overweight the VPCI when volume increases and underweight the VPCI when volume decreases. This is done by dividing the short-term average volume by the long-term average volume. As an illustration, assume SMA's short-term average volume for 10 days is 1.5 million shares a day, and the long-term average volume for 50 days is 750,000 shares per day. The VM equals 2 (1,500,000/750,000). This calculation is then multiplied by the VPC after it has been multiplied by the VPR.

Now we have all of the information necessary to calculate the VPCI. First, the VPC+ confirmation of +1.5 is multiplied by the VPR of 1.25, giving 1.875. Then, 1.875 is multiplied by the VM of 2, revealing a VPCI of 3.75. This number is indicative of an issue under strong volume-price confirmation. This information will be best utilized in the context of the current price trend and relative to current VPCI levels.

CONFIRMING SIGNALS

Several VPCI signals may be employed in conjunction with price trends and price indicators. These include a VPCI greater than zero, which shows the relationship between price trends and volume, and is confirming or contradicting the price trend. Also important, a rising or falling VPCI provides trend direction, revealing the trend of volume confirmation or contradiction.

A smoothed volume-weighted average of VPCI, called "VPCI smoothed," demonstrates how much the VPCI has changed from previous VPCI levels and is used to indicate momentum. Bollinger Bands may also be applied to the VPCI, exposing VPCI extremes (more about this in subsequent chapters). Fundamentally, the VPCI reveals the proportional imbalances between price trends and volume-adjusted price trends. You can see the four divisions of the price/volume relationship in Table 2.

FOUR QUADRANTS OF THE PRICE/VOLUME RELATIONSHIP

Price Expansion & Volume Expansion	Price Contraction & Volume Contraction
Trend Up & Volume Rising **Strong Demand** **Greed w/ Energy = Ingigorated Greed** Phase 1 Phase 2 Price 10 12 Volume 100 300 VWMA = .25*10+.75*12 VCP = 11.5(VWMA) -11(SMA) Price Trend+2(Rising) -VS- VCP = +.5(Rising) **Bullish** **Uptrend Confirmation**	**Trend Down & Volume Falling** **Weak Supply** **Fear w/ Entropy = Apathy** Phase 1 Phase 2 Price 12 10 Volume 300 100 VWMA = .75*12+.25*10 VCP = 11.5(VWMA) -11(SMA) Price Trend-2(Falling) -VS- VCP = +.5(Rising) **Bullish** **Downtrend Contradiction**
Trend Up & Volume Falling Weak Demand Greed w/ Entropy = Complacency Phase 1 Phase 2 Price 10 12 Volume 300 100 VWMA = .75*10+.25*12 VCP = 10.5(VWMA) -11(SMA) Price Trend+2(Rising) -VS- VCP = -.5(Falling) Bearish Uptrend Contradiction	Trend Down & Volume Rising Strong Supply Fear w/ Energy = Fear Phase 1 Phase 2 Price 12 10 Volume 100 300 VWMA = .25*10+.75*12 VCP = 10.5(VWMA) -11(SMA) Price Trend-2(Falling) -VS- VCP = -.5(Fising) Bearish Downtrend Confirmation
Price Expansion & Volume Contraction	Price Contraction & Volume Expansion

Interpreting VPCI Within Price Trends

Greed

Referencing Table 2, we begin in the upper left-hand quadrant. An uptrend with increasing volume is a market characterized by greed, supported by the fuel (volume) needed to grow. This is the most bullish condition to maintain a healthy uptrend.

Complacency

In the lower-left quadrant, an uptrend without volume forms a complacent market. Combining the variables of an upward price trend with low volume equates to greed deprived of the fuel (volume) needed to sustain itself. Investors without the influx of other investors (volume) will eventually lose interest, and the uptrend should subsequently break down. Thus, the uptrend is contradicted by the lack of supporting volume.

Fear

We are moving now to the lower right side of the table. A falling price trend reveals a market driven by fear. Adding energy to fear can be likened to adding fuel to the fire and is generally bearish until the VPCI reverses. In this way, rising volume confirms the downtrend.

Apathy

Staying on the right side in the upper right quadrant, a falling price trend without volume reveals apathy, or, in other words, fear absent of energy. In such cases, weak-minded investors, overcome by fear, become irrationally fearful until the selling climax reaches a state of maximum homogeneity. Although these price declines are violent, the volume is relatively weaker. In other words, fewer and fewer shareholders are willing to sell at ever-decreasing prices. At this point, ownership held by vulnerable investors has been purged, producing a type of heat death (capitulation). In this way, relatively lower volume indicates a likely trend reversal.

When using VPCI, it's important to note that volume leads or precedes price action. Unlike most indicators, the VPCI often gives indications before price breaks, and trend reversals occur. A cheat sheet of the price-volume trend rules is illustrated in Table 3.

Table 3	VPCI Price Implications		
Price	***VPCI***	***Price Relationship***	***Implications***
Rising	Rising	Confirmation	Bullish
Rising	Declining	Contradiction	Bearish
Declining	Rising	Contradiction	Bullish
Declining	Declining	Confirmation	Bearish

We use Figure 14 of Toyota Motors ™ to illustrate the use of the VPCI indicator. At point 1, TM is breaking out of a downtrend, and the VPCI confirms this breakout immediately as it rises, crossing over VPCI smoothed and then the zero line. This is an example of VPCI's bullish confirmation of the price trend.

Later, the VPCI begins to fall during the uptrend, suggesting complacency. By point 2, VPCI crosses under VPCI smoothed, warning of a possible pause within the new uptrend. This is a classic example of a VPCI bearish contradiction. Before reaching point 3, VPCI creates a pattern forming a V bottom. This bullish sign indicates that the sell-off has washed out many sellers. Still later, at point 3, VPCI confirms the earlier bullish V pattern with a bullish crossover, leading to a strong bull rally.

VPCI IN ACTION

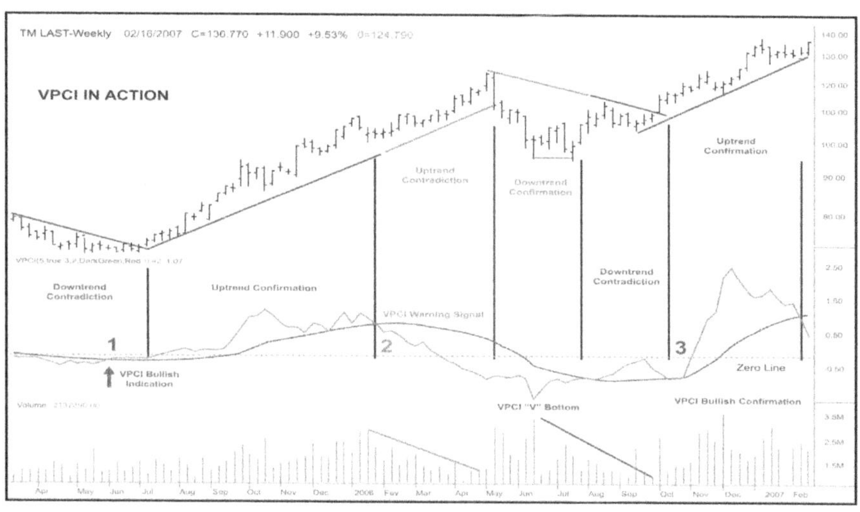

Source: TradeStation Securities Tradestation Technologies. All rights reserved.

THE STUDY

Through our volume knowledge and prior testing, it might seem a foregone conclusion that the VPCI is an effective indicator to confirm price trends. However, an accurate and measurable test must be completed to prove any hypothesis conclusive. Therefore, the VPCI indicator was tested via a trading system using two moving average systems.

The first study backtested the 5- and 20-day crossover system. A long position is taken when the short-term moving average crosses above the long-term moving average. A short position is enacted when the short-term moving average crosses under the long-term moving average. These actions tend to represent short-term changes in momentum and trend. The second (comparative) study also tested the 5- and 20-day crossover, but only kept the trades when the VPCI also previously crossed over a smoothed VPCI. This indicates a rising VPCI, or price confirmation. The VPCI setting will be the same as the moving averages: 20 days for the long-term component and 5 days for the short-term component.

This study has several limitations, but these settings were deliberately chosen to keep the analysis simple, pure, and unbiased. The first limitation is that the 5-day and 20-day moving average settings are too short to indicate a strong trend. This diminishes the effectiveness of the VPCI as a price trend confirmation and contradiction indicator. However, these settings are quick, creating more trades, thus allowing for a larger sample size. Also, setting the VPCI at 5 and 20 days when the price data are only 20 days old (length of long-term moving average) is too brief. Using these time settings, the VPCI might give signals ahead of the price trend or momentum indications according to the moving averages. However, the settings were kept the same to avoid potential interpretations that they were optimized. To overcome this clear deficiency, a 10-day look-back delay was applied to the VPCI, and a 5-day look-back delay on the VPCI smoothed. This delay allows the VPCI confirmation signal to be more in tune with the lagging moving average crossover. Ideally, one would use trend lines or other trend indications with the VPCI corresponding to the time frame invested or traded.

It is time to test our hypothesis once again. By now, you know the drill. Here are the 60 stocks chosen by size and most significant factor. To maintain the system's objectivity, both long- and short-system-generated trades were considered in our tests. A $10,000 position was taken with each crossover. Commissions were not included. The test period used was August 15, 1996, through June 22, 2004, for a total of 2,000 trading days measured by reliability and profitability.

60 Securities Chosen By Strongest Size And Factor

The test portfolio consisted of 60 stocks from different capitalization, volume and volatility groups.

Large-Cap Low Volatility	*Large-Cap High Volatility*	*Large-Cap High Volume*	*Large-Cap Low Volume*
PG	EP	CSCO	ATI
SO	AES	MFST	HET
BUD	DAK	INTC	BDK
WFC	ATI	ORCL	GD
PEP	NSM	GE	CPB
Mid-Cap Low Volatility	***Mid-Cap High Volatility***	***Mid-Cap High Volume***	***Mid-Cap Low Volume***
MDU	ESI	ATML	WPO
ATG	LTXX	SNDK	BDG
WPS	NGN	COMS	TECUA
HE	WIND	MLMN	KELYA
NFG	SEPR	CY	CRS
Small-Cap Low Volatility	***Small-Cap High Volatility***	***Small-Cap High Volume***	***Small-Cap Low Volume***
UNS	BRKT	CYBX	NPK
UBSI	ZIXI	MOGN	GMP
CIMA	MZ	KLIC	SXI
CTCO	LENS	HLIT	SKY
ATO	CRY	YELL	LAWS

To ensure unbiased results, five securities were backtested in each of these 12 subgroups, for a total of 60 securities, to ensure a significant sample size. Ensuring unbiased credibility, the five securities representing each group were not randomly selected but, rather, were chosen by identifying leaders with the various characteristics being measured. Thus, for high volume, the five highest-volume securities were chosen; likewise, for low volume, the five lowest-volume securities were chosen. The five highest-volatility and the five lowest-volatility securities from each of the three capitalization groups, as identified by Bloomberg on June 22, 2004 (see appendix for stock list), were used in this study. Any duplicated securities (high-volume and high-beta stocks were occasionally duplicated) were only used once. Securities that lacked sufficient history were removed and replaced with the next best suitable issue. Sixty securities were selected, forming 12 groups, four types, and three categories, to test the hypothesis.

Profitability Improvement

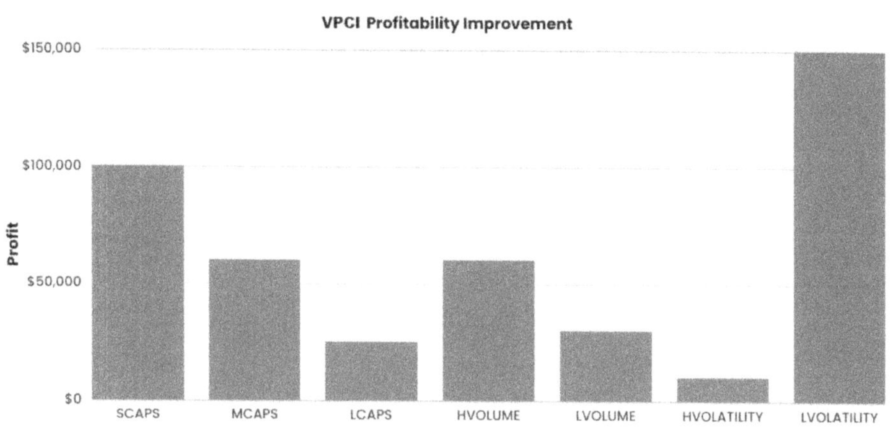

Source: www.activetradermag.com • March 2005 • ACTIVE TRADER

Applying the VPCI to the moving-average crossover system boosted overall profitability $211,997. Of the 60 stocks tested, 39 (65%) had better results using the VPCI.

To review, profitability was tested using only a 5- and 20-day moving average crossover and then retested using only those trades also displaying VPCI confirmation signals. Once again, the results were quite impressive. Broadly, the VPCI improved profitability in the three size classes, small, mid, and large caps, as well as all four style classifications, high and low volume, and high and low volatility (see Figure 15). In addition, 9 of the 12 subgroups showed improvement. The exceptions were mid-cap high-volatility issues and small and large low-volume issues. Of the 60 issues tested, 39 (65%) demonstrated improved results using VPCI confirmation signals. Overall, profitability in these issues was boosted by $211,997 with VPCI.

Reliability

In this study, reliability was measured by examining the percentage of trades that were profitable. By employing VPCI in the 5-day/20-day crossover system, overall profitability improved an average of 3.21% per issue. Improvement was realized by adding VPCI in all three size groups and all four style groups. Of the 12 subgroups, 10 showed improvement after adding the VPCI.

VPCI Percent Profitable

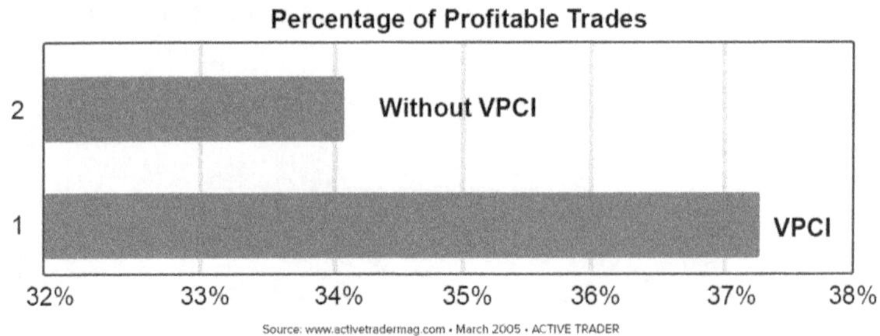

By incorporating the VPCI, the percentage of winning trades increased an average of 3.21% (10 of 12 stock subgroups had higher winning percentages). Large-cap and small-cap low-volatility stocks were the two exceptions.

Improved profitability resulted when adding the VPCI. The large and small-cap low-volatility category issues were the only exceptions. Overall, more than 43 of 60 issues (71%) showed improvement when including VPCI.

Risk-Adjusted Returns

Another way to look at profitability is through the Sharpe ratio. The Sharpe ratio takes the total return subtracted from the risk-free rate of return (U.S. Treasury note) and divides the result by the portfolio's monthly standard deviation. Thus, the **Sharpe ratio gives us a risk-adjusted rate of return**. *VPCI bettered the results once again* across all three size categories and all four style groups. VPCI realized improvement in 9 of the 12 subgroups. Mid-cap high volatility, large-cap low volatility, and large-cap low volume were the exceptions. Overall, the Sharpe ratio showed significant improvement with the addition of VPCI.

Profit Factor

Another way to look at risk-adjusted returns is through the profit factor. The profit factor considers how much money can be gained for every dollar lost within the same strategy. The profit factor measures risk by comparing the upside to the downside. The profit factor is calculated by dividing gross profits by gross losses. For instance, one issue might generate $40,000 in losses and $50,000 in gross profits, whereas a second issue might generate $10,000 in losses and $20,000 in gross profits. Both issues generate a $10,000 net profit. However, an investor can expect to make $1.25 for every dollar lost in the first system but $2 for every dollar lost in the second system. The figures of $1.25 and $2 represent the profit factor. VPCI significantly improved in this area (see Figure 17). Again, VPCI showed improvements in large, mid, and small-cap stock categories and in all four factor groups: low and high volume and low and high volatility. Among the 12 subgroups, only large-cap low-volatility issues did not show improvement with VPCI. Overall, the profit factor was improved by 19 %, meaning one can expect to earn 19% more profit for every dollar put at risk when employing VPCI in the trading system.

VPCI Profit Factor Improvement

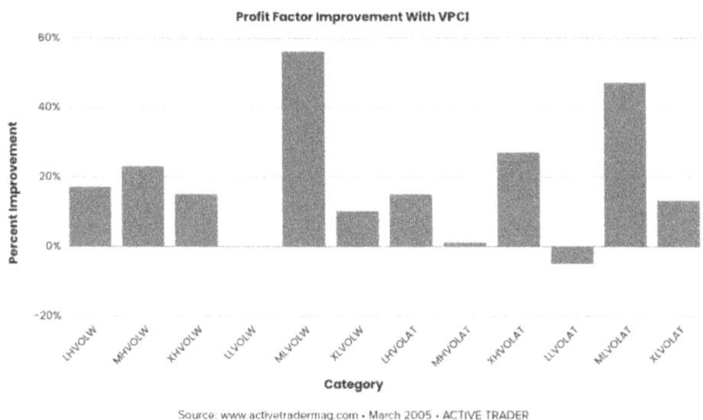

Overall, profit factor (gross profits divided by gross losses) improved by 19% with the VPCI. Of the 12 subgroups, only large-cap low-volatility (LLVOLAT) stocks did not show improvement with the VPCI.

Other Applications: Comparing the VPCI to Other Price-Volume Indicators

The critical insight in volume analysis is discovering volume's relationship to the price trend. The VPCI is unique in this way, as it is the only volume indicator exposing the asymmetry of price and volume trends through trend data as opposed to siloed price and volume data.

There are many price-volume indicators one can choose from to compare the use of VPCI. However, the most acclaimed is the original On-Balance-Volume. Recognizing volume as the force behind price, Joe Granville created OBV by assigning up days as positive volume (measured by an up close) and subtracting volume on down days. OBV is then price-directed volume with the accumulation of +/- volume flows based on price direction.

Granville's original objective with OBV was to uncover hidden coils in an otherwise non-eventful, non-trending market. With his OBV indicator, Granville became a renowned market strategist. He also popularized OBV and the wisdom of using volume in securities analysis.

VPCI differs from OBV in that VPCI calculates the proportional imbalances between price trends and volume-weighted price trends. This exposes the influence that volume has on a price trend. Although both OBV and VPCI contain volume-derived data, they convey different information. In comparison, VPCI is not an accumulation of history like OBV but is, rather, a snapshot of the influence of volume on price trends.

This enables VPCI to provide faster signals than an accumulation indicator, similar to the behavior of an oscillator. In contrast to OBV, VPCI's objective is not to uncover hidden coils in trendless markets, but to evaluate the health and sustainability of existing trends.

To illustrate the effectiveness and proper use of VPCI, a test was conducted comparing VPCI to OBV. The most general VPCI buy signal is the VPCI crossing above the VPCI smoothed line in an up-trending market. This indicates that VPCI is rising relative to previous VPCI levels. The traditional OBV does not have a lagging trigger like VPCI smoothed. OBV was adjusted by adding an eight-period simple moving average of OBV. The net effect gives OBV a corresponding trigger similar to VPCI smoothed. OBV crossovers of OBV smoothed provide indications that OBV is rising relative to previous OBV levels. Remember, VPCI is designed to be used in a trending market with a trending indicator. Thus, two additional tools are required to complete this test. First, an indicator is necessary to verify whether or not the market is trending. A 7-day Average Directional Index (ADX) indicator fulfills this criterion. Next, a trend indicator revealing the trend's direction is required. The MACD with the traditional (12, 26, 9) settings was used as the criterion for this test.

Finally, a test subject is needed that illustrates how these indicators work across a broad market. Perhaps there is no better or more popular vehicle for this experiment than the SPDR S&P 500 exchange-traded fund, SPY. The test period was from inception in February 1993 until the end of 2006. The results were not optimized in any way, shape, or form. In this system, long positions are taken only when the above conditions are met, accompanied by OBV crossovers in the first test and VPCI crossovers in the second test. In addition, long positions are exited with cross-under of OBV smoothed in the first test or with VPCI cross-under in the second study (see Figure 18). Although this test was created rather simplistically and traditionally for both observational and credibility purposes, the results are quite stunning (see Figures 18 and 19).

VPCI MACF OBV ADX

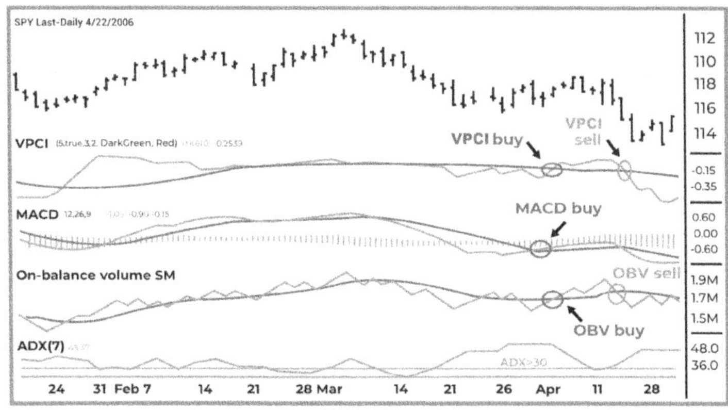

(Created with TradeStation. Tradestation Technologies, INC. All rights resever)

S&P 500 ETF On-Balance Volume Equity Curve

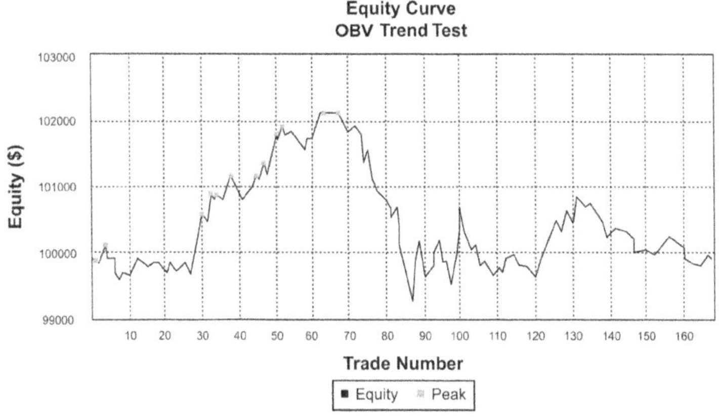

Created with TradeStation. Tradestation Technologies, Inc. © All rights reserved.

SPY, VPCI Equity Curve

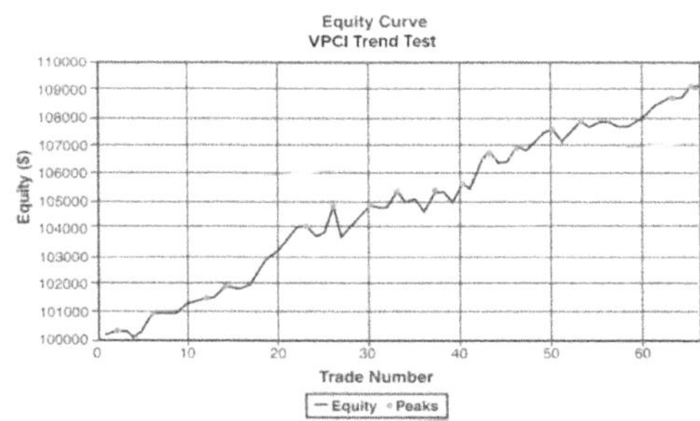

Created with TradeStation. TradeStation Technologies, Inc. © All rights reserved.

Excluding dividends and interest, OBV's annualized rate of return in the system was –1.57%, whereas VPCI's annualized return was 8.11%, an outperformance of over 9.5% annualized. In addition, VPCI improved reliability, giving profitable signals over 65% of the time compared to OBV, at only 42.86%.

Another consideration in evaluating performance is risk. VPCI had less than half the risk as measured by volatility, and it had 7.42 standard deviations compared to OBV, with 17.4 standard deviations from the mean. It is not surprising, then, that VPCI had much better risk-adjusted return rates. VPCI's Sharpe ratio from inception was .70, and it had a profit factor of 2.47 compared to OBV, with a –0.09 Sharpe ratio and a profit factor of less than 1 (see Table 5).

Admittedly, this testing environment is uneven. VPCI uses information from volume-weighted prices to gauge the health of existing trends. In contrast, OBV accumulates volume flows as directed by price changes to uncover hidden coils. Thus, the conditions set up in this system, a trending market with apparent price direction, is one condition in which VPCI is designed to succeed. Although OBV was not necessarily set up for failure, this study illustrates how less savvy practitioners often fail to use the indicators' information correctly or coordinate the indicators properly.

COMPARING STRATEGIES' RETURNS

Table 5: Comparing Strategies' Returns

SPY ADX + MACD System 1993 - 2006

Strategy*	Annual Return	Time Invested	Std Dev	5yr Shape	% Profitable	Profit Factor
Buy Hold	9.94%	100%	17.75%	0.10	N/A	N/A
MACD	-3.88%	24.79%	13.03%	0.27	41.79%	0.97
VPCI	8.11%	35.63%	7.42%	0.74	65.15%	2.47
OBV	-1.57%	27.02%	17.40%	0.05	42.86%	1

***Dividends not included**

*Dividends not included

What if an investor had only used the MACD to buy and sell signals within this same system without using the VPCI information? This investor would have lost out on a nearly 12% annualized return – that difference coming from VPCI's positive 8.11% versus MACD's negative 3.88% – while significantly increasing risk. What if this investor had only employed a buy-and-hold approach? Although this investor would have realized a slightly higher return, they would have endured much more significant risks.

The VPCI strategy returned nearly 90% of the buy-and-hold strategy with about 60% less risk as measured by standard deviation. Looking at risk-adjusted returns another way, the **five-year Sharpe ratio** for the S&P 500 SPY ETF was only 0 .1 compared to the VPCI system of 0.74. Additionally, the VPCI investor was invested only 35% of the time, allowing the investor to invest in other investments or sit on cash. During the 65% of the time not invested, an investor would have only needed a 1.84% money market yield to exceed the buy-and-hold strategy. Moreover, an investor would have experienced much smoother performance without nearly as steep capital drawdowns. The VPCI's worst drawdown was only a measly –2.71% compared to the underlying investments' worst year of -22.81%, over a 20% numerical difference in the rate of return.

ANNUAL RETURNS OF EACH STRATEGY

Strategy*	1993	1994	1995	1996	1997	1998	1999
Buy-Hold	3.61	-2.21	34.95	20.1	31.44	27.04	19.11
MACD	0.31	5.42	0.88	12.63	14.72	-12.93	-30.6
VPCI	2.93	6.42	6.12	19.83	19.09	8.9	3.17
OBV	-1.03	-1.24	0	18.81	7.3	12.4	-12.43
Strategy*	**2000**	**2001**	**2002**	**2003**	**2004**	**2005**	**2006**
Buy-Hold	-10.68	-12.87	-22.81	26.12	8.62	3.01	13.74
MACD	9.26	11.12	0.9	1.34	1.8	1.69	-11.32
VPCI	-2.71	21.28	-0.65	10.4	4.27	4.8	9.29
OBV	-26.55	-28.34	12.45	-12.79	33.32	-15.58	-8.33

Annual Returns. Here you see the annual returns of the various strategies from 1993 to 2006. Note that the worst annualized VPCI return was only -2.71%

*Annual rates of return without dividends

Listed above are the year-over-year returns. Notice that there are only two losing years, 2000 and 2002. But remember, this was early 2000, when cash earned a high interest rate. If the cash was invested in T-bills while not deployed in SPY, this system would not have suffered a losing year.

So, if the VPCI does this for a losing system, imagine what it could do in a winning strategy. That scenario is what we will look at next while bringing the VPCI, ADX, and MACD system up to date.

VPCI + ADX + MACD S&P 500 Components 01/01/1993 - 07/13/2021

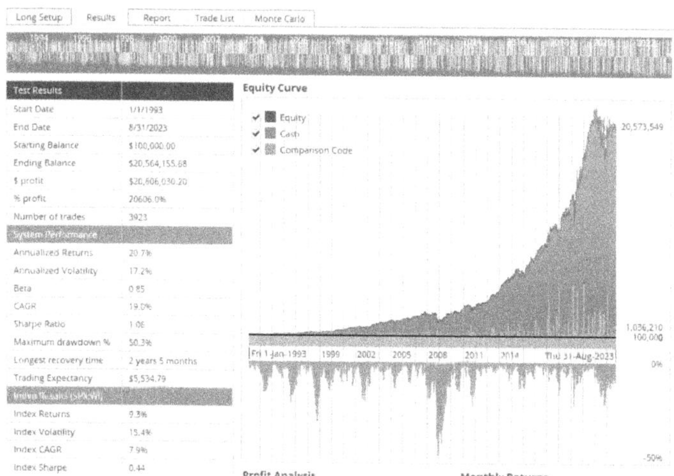

Source: Optuma www.optuma.com/volumeanalysis

What is the winning system? Before going there, let us first examine why the ADX and MACD system did not work on the SPY. This system is designed to identify strong trends.

Broad markets comprise many different stocks, in differentiated industries, and consist of multiple styles and factors. By design, broad markets are diverse and thus do not exhibit strong trends that individual stocks typically exhibit.

Taking this into account, our winning system is the exact same system, but this time, as opposed to investing in the SPY ETF instrument, we will invest in the components of the S&P 500 meeting the system criteria. That is a considerable difference. In our example, we take 5% positions in S&P 500 components meeting the criteria of ADX > 30, MACD crossover, and VPCI confirmation. We will then sell when the VPCI contradicts. Again, the exact same system, just with the S&P 500 components as opposed to the ETF itself. This study is up to date as of July 13, 2021.

First notice above in Figure 21 that the SPX over this time period appreciated 9.6%, annualized. Our $100,000 investment in 1993 grew to $1 million by buying and holding the SPX. That is the red line in the mountain graph. The yellow bars show our systemCI confirmation. We will then sell when the VPCI blue mountain chart shows the VPCI ADX MACD system's growth of nearly $4.4 million, with annual returns of 17.5% compared to the SPX returns of 9.6%. Again, this is the same system, this round using the components of the S&P 500 versus the SPDR S&P 500 Index ETF. This backtest was conducted on the Optuma platform, which we employ throughout this book.

VPCI + ADX + MACD -VS- VPCI + ADX +TTI

MACD VS TTI

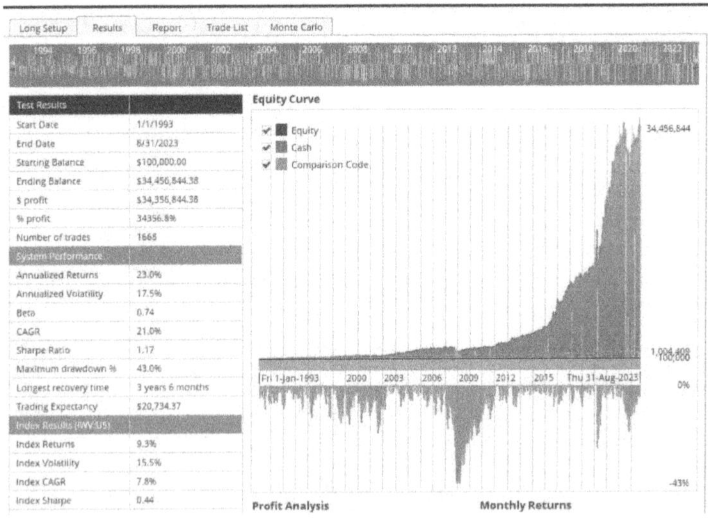

Source: Optuma www.optuma.com/volumeanalysis

The question often asked of me is, why not swap the MACD with the TTI in the DOW Award system? That is what this chart (Figure 22) shows, with the MACD on the left and the TTI on the right.

Notice that the return improves from approximately $4.4 million with MACD to just under $6.9 million with TTI. However, the annualized return is not much better, 17.5% versus 17.8%. The close total return can be explained by the VPCI being the trigger on the sales side of both systems. However, a couple of differences are noted below, as VPCI and TTI are more aligned with their logic.

First, there are fewer trades and fewer sales, keeping the model much more invested. However, despite the greater investment, the volatility drops from 24% to 18% with TTI, while the maximum drawdown drops from 75% to just 35%. The recovery time falls from 7.5 years to just three years. Thus, TTI returns improve the system, and the risk-adjusted returns are much more significant when utilizing TTI. This is evident in the Sharpe ratio of 0.62 under the original MACD/VPCI systems to the Sharpe ratio of 0.85 under the adjusted TTI/VPCI system.

VPCI + ADX +TTI NASDAQ 100 01/01/1993 - 07/13/2021

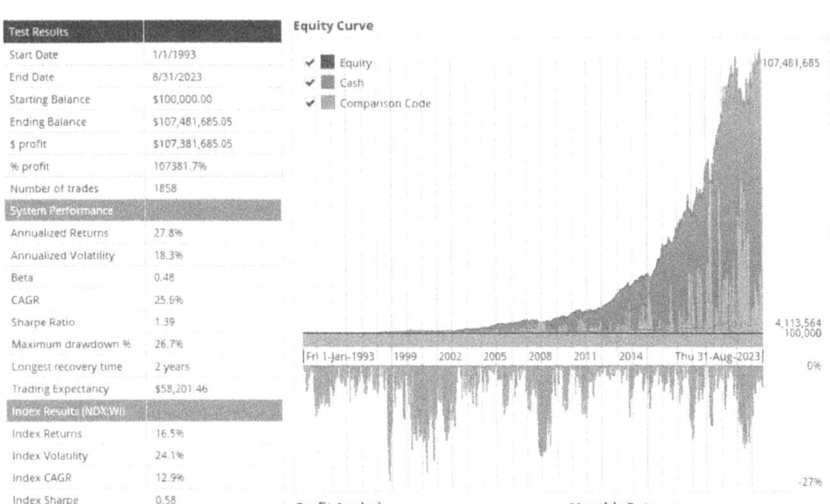

Test Results	
Start Date	1/1/1993
End Date	8/31/2023
Starting Balance	$100,000.00
Ending Balance	$107,481,685.05
$ profit	$107,381,685.05
% profit	107381.7%
Number of trades	1858
System Performance	
Annualized Returns	27.8%
Annualized Volatility	18.3%
Beta	0.48
CAGR	25.6%
Sharpe Ratio	1.39
Maximum drawdown %	26.7%
Longest recovery time	2 years
Trading Expectancy	$58,201.46
Index Results (NDX:WI)	
Index Returns	16.5%
Index Volatility	24.1%
Index CAGR	12.9%
Index Sharpe	0.58

Source: Optuma www.optuma.com/volumeanalysis

Finally, let us do this same test again, only using the NDX components instead of the SPX components. The NASDAQ 100 has significantly outperformed the SPX over the last couple of decades. But what makes this study even more interesting is that these NASDAQ 100 issues exhibit greater volatility and trending patterns. These qualities are preferable in a trend-following system.

Here, $100,000 invested in the NASDAQ 100 Index grows to $4.1 million, while the TTI VPCI system grows to a whopping $23.4 million. That equates to an average annualized return of 17.2% for the NDX versus 23.2% for the TTI VPCI combination. Meanwhile, the volatility drops from the NASDAQ 100's 24% down to 19.5% under the TTI/VPCI Trend System. Most importantly, from a practical behavioral finance perspective, the recovery time in our volume-infused system falls to less than a year as opposed to well over a decade with the NDX Index.

EMPLOYING THE VPCI

Price can be considered as the emotion, conviction, and volition of investors. Logically, you can then define a price trend as the emotion, conviction, and volition of investors expressed over time. A buyer's underlying emotion or motivation is greed. Greed is the desire to obtain a profit. Greed, or an uptrend, needs fuel to build and sustain itself. In a healthy market, greed is expressed through more and more people eagerly participating in ever-increasing prices. Therefore, an uptrend could be considered an accumulation of greed over time.

Often, but not always, an investor who creates supply – that is, the seller – is motivated by the fear of losing value in his investment. Likewise, a downtrend would then be the accumulation of anxiety over time. We also spoke of volume as the force that sustains price. A rising volume trend would represent a buildup in energy or fuel. A decrease in volume would then mean the loss of fuel – nonworking energy or entropy. In this way, a healthy downtrend would represent more and more investors selling at ever-decreasing prices.

From this logic, we can use volume and price trends to build a Market Positioning System (MPS). In building an MPS, the first step is to establish the coordinates. For the price trending axis, we will employ the Trend Thrust Indicator Index, and for volume, the VPCI Index. Trend (TTI Index) is plotted on the horizontal axis, and volume (VPCI Index) on the vertical axis, highest to lowest, according to each individual stock's rankings. These two coordinates plot the movements of securities along the plane of our MPS map.

The components from a broad market index such as the S&P 500 can be tracked according to our MPS coordinates. One could also plot a narrower market sector, such as financials or technology, or chart the course of a market-style index, such as the S&P 500 Growth Index or the S&P 500 Value Index. One could also plot industries rather than individual issues through the Morningstar industry groups. The possibilities are nearly endless, but our study focuses on the individual securities within the broad market, as represented by the S&P 500.

To track the components of the S&P 500 with the MPS, each individual security of the S&P 500 is plotted according to its position relative to the VPCI and the TTI. In our MPS map, the equator is the horizontal center, where a security's volume is neither bullish nor bearish when compared to other market components. Securities above the equator are experiencing relatively bullish volume factors. Conversely, securities below the equator are experiencing relatively bearish volume factors.

The vertical center position, or the prime meridian, represents the vertical center of the price trend. Stocks to the left of the prime meridian are in more robust upward trends relative to the market. Conversely, stocks to the right of the prime meridian are experiencing falling trends relative to the composite average.

THE FOUR PHASES OF VOLUME ANALYSIS

The crosshairs of the equator and the prime meridian form four quadrants. Securities in the upper-left corner are in a relatively high state of upward trend with confirming volume. Securities in the lower-left corner are in a heightened state of upward trend with volume contradiction. Securities in the lower-right corner are in downward trends with confirming volume. Securities in the upper-right corner are trending down but on contradictory volume. Through this simple MPS, every security, including sectors and ETFs, can be mapped, and dynamically charted according to its relative position in the VPCI and TTI Indexes (see Figure 24).

Market Position VPCI & TTI

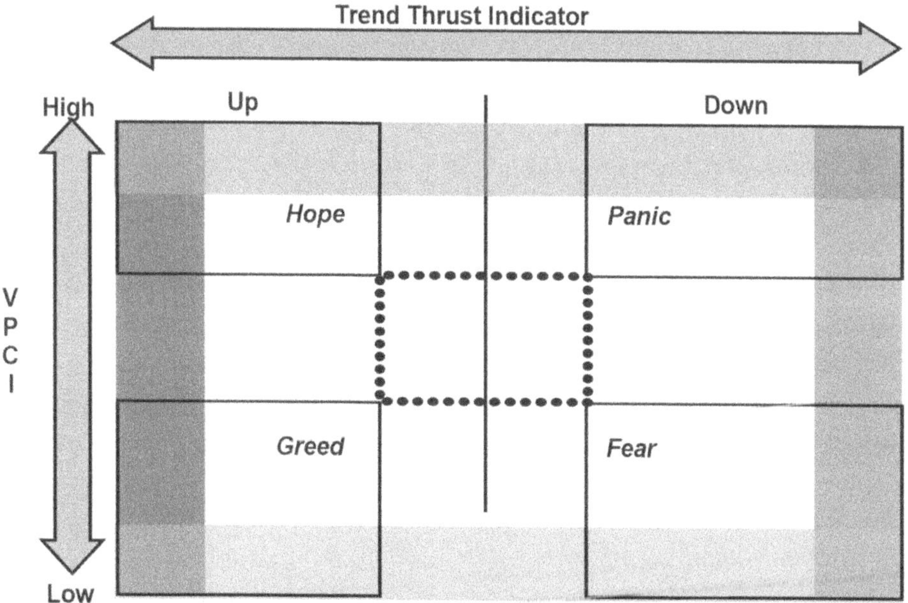

Can a stock's location on the TTI/VPCI MPS impact performance? This Market Position VPCI & TTI study suggests that a stock's MPS location may be the most significant of any investment factor yet devised. We tested the S&P 500 components' performance based on their location within the TTI/VPCI MPS. The test was performed on individual members of the S&P 500 Index from January 1, 2000, to April 30, 2010. The test results were formulated using Worden Brother's StockFinder software and were not optimized in any way. Excluding dividends, the S&P 500 benchmark was down 2.04% during the test period. In the test model, once a stock entered and closed the week within an MPS zone, we tracked its performance until it closed the week outside the zone. Dividend yields were excluded from performance. Volume is most useful during such extremes. As a result, we begin with the acute edges of the TTI/VPCI MPS.

We would expect that an issue moving up vertically across the MPS plane indicates the issue's volume is increasingly bullish. In contrast, an issue moving lower over time indicates that the price trend is becoming increasingly bearish according to volume. Likewise, an issue moving from left to right is an issue that is losing momentum, becoming relatively more oversold. Conversely, an issue moving from right to left gains relative momentum and becomes more overbought. We will track the issues from their locations and movements across the MPS plane in the MPS analysis. In most analyses, a symmetrical path, from high to low or low to high, confirms the relationship. However, because volume is most useful in extremes, we would expect outperformance on the outer tails of the curve.

TTI Most Overbought Index. This represents the issues in the top 10% of the S&P 500 Index according to their TTI scores. The most overbought index comprises the stocks making up the highest 10% weekly TTI readings within the S&P 500 Index. These stocks are purchased when they reach the highest 10% and are sold when they reach the bottom 50% of the S&P 500 Index. The return of the most overbought index was 0.62% during the course of the test period, with an outperformance of 2.66%.

TTI Most Oversold Index. According to their TTI scores, this represents the issues in the bottom 10% of the S&P 500 Index. Conversely, the most oversold index comprises the stocks with the lowest 10% weekly TTI readings within the underlying index. These stocks are purchased when they reach the bottom 10% and sold when they reach the top 50% of the S&P 500 Index. The most oversold index returned 0.99% during the course of the test period, beating buy and hold by 3.03%

HOPE

We will start in the upper-left quadrant (see Figure 25), where stocks show overbought conditions (top 10% TTI) with bullish volume (top 10% VPCI). This quadrant comprises stocks that are strongly up-trending with very high confirming volume. This includes stocks located highest above the equator and furthest left from the prime meridian.

The uppermost-left corner comprises the stocks that overlap with the most overbought (TTI) and most bullish volume (VPCI) index. Traders sold these stocks when they fell below the equator (the bottom half of the VPCI index/weakening volume confirmation) or shifted to the left of the prime meridian (the oversold side of TTI on a weakening trend). This strategy yielded a return of 9.4%, significantly outperforming the index, which lost -2.04% over the same period.

Stocks originating in the upper-left corner (Top 10% TTI & VPCI), which fell downward via a relatively falling VPCI ranking, returned an average of 7.48%. These are stocks maintaining a high trend (overbought) which began on very high-volume confirmation, but over time, the volume confirmation weakened. However, when these upper-left corner stocks (top 10% TTI & VPCI) moved horizontally to the right, losing price momentum (TTI), they returned an average of only 1.06%. This suggests that stocks originating in the upper-left corner that continued moving up and to the left experienced better returns. Conversely, issues moving to the right from a weakening trend were less profitable than those that experienced weakening volume confirmation.

Hope On The Move

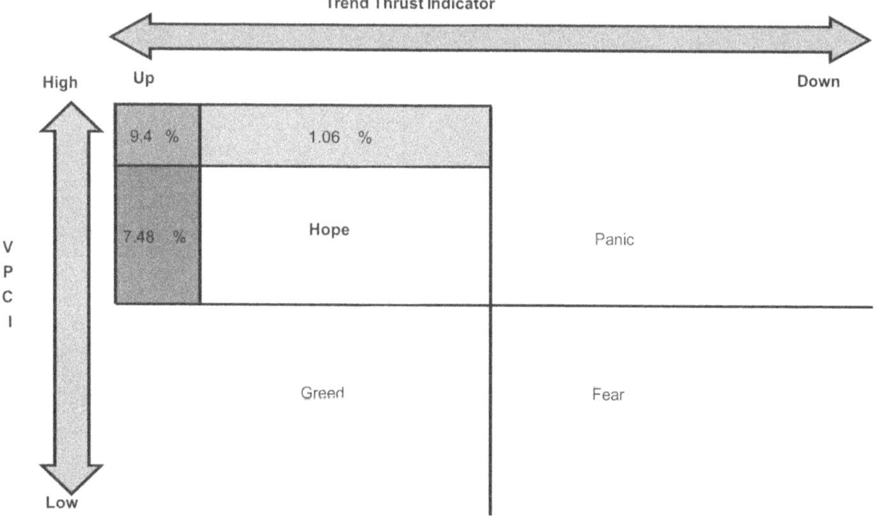

POISONED BY GREED – THE FEAR OF MISSING OUT

Moving downward, the next quadrant (See Figure 26) in our MPS map is the lower-left quadrant, where stocks are overbought, but with bearish volume. The stocks to the right of the prime meridian and beneath the equator identify this on the MPS map. In the very lower-left corner are the stocks overlapping the most overbought index with the most bearish volume index.

Stocks purchased upon first reaching this corner and held until moving both above the equator (bullish volume) and to the right of the prime meridian (bearish trend) experienced a gain of 1.57%. The stocks originating from this corner were sold upon moving up (bullish volume) and experienced a 1.65% return. However, stocks moving to the right on a weakening trend experienced a 0.56% loss. This further demonstrates that stocks moving to the right during the study tended to be more bearish than those moving up or to the left. More importantly, it demonstrates that stocks experiencing strong upward trends with volume contradiction vastly underperform stocks with strong uptrends and volume confirmation.

Hope On The Move Top, Greed In Motion Bottom

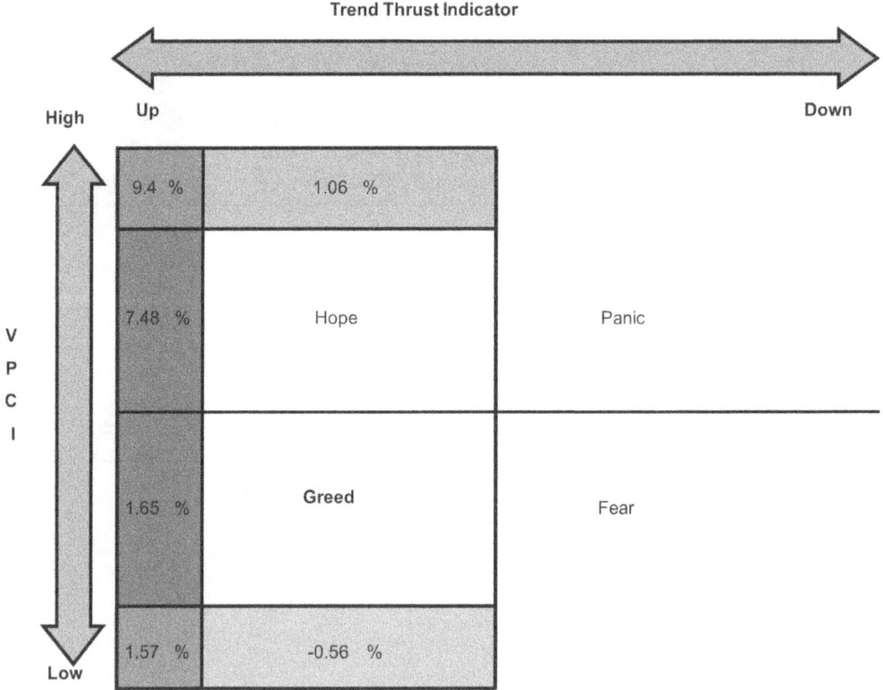

MOTIVATED BY FEAR

Moving to the right on the MPS map (see Figure 27) is the lower-right quadrant, containing stocks that are deeply oversold (bottom 10% TTI) on bearish confirming volume (bottom 10% TTI). The outermost-right corner is where the most oversold and most bearish volume indexes overlap. Stocks purchased upon entering this corner and held until leaving the lower-right quadrant by moving both higher across the prime meridian and up across the equator averaged 4.54%, the third best-performing corner on the map. This may be a shock, because this corner is seemingly the most bearish location on our MPS map.

However, previously we discussed the VPCI V bottom, where stocks become oversold on a price and volume basis and quickly rebound on subtle volume declines. Undoubtedly, many stocks deep in this corner will soon be V-bottom candidates. Stocks in this corner that moved to the left (improving price trend without volume) averaged 1.57%. Stocks moving

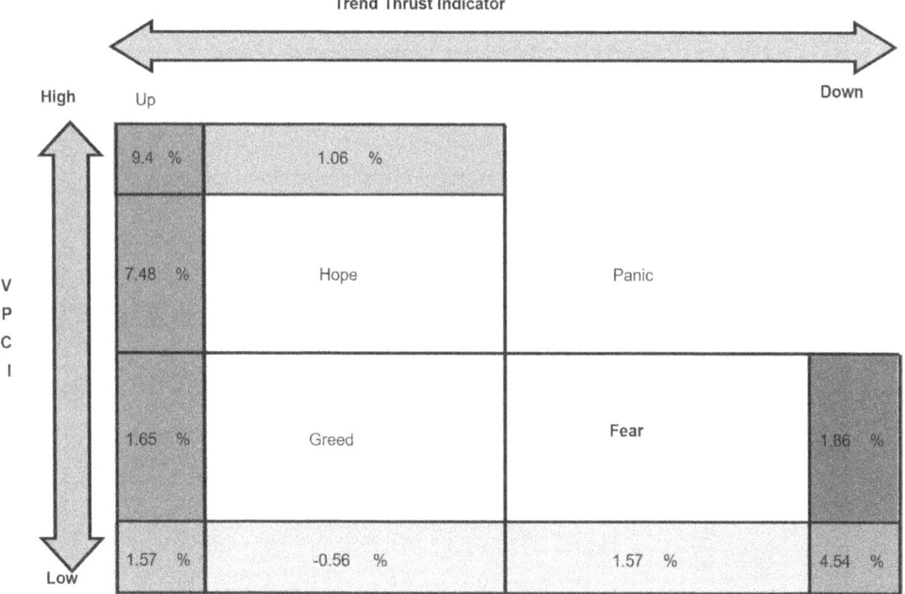

up to the equator on more bullish volume than trend improvement averaged 1.86%.

FEAR IN MOTION, LOWER RIGHT QUADRANT

Capitulation

Finally, moving upward to the uppermost right-side quadrant (see Figure 28), we find deeply oversold stocks with bullish volume characteristics. Stocks purchased when in this corner and sold when crossing both into an uptrend (crossing the prime meridian) and weakening volume (crossing the equator) experienced a 5.11% gain. Stocks that crossed the prime meridian, demonstrating weakening volume while remaining oversold, returned 0.56%. Stocks that crossed the equator, maintaining strong volume but never gaining a strong price trend by being overbought, returned 1.21%. From this, we deduce that bullish volume returns can come from stocks both deeply oversold (bottom 10% TTI) and deeply overbought (top 10% TTI).

Overall, by studying the extremes, we learned that most of the deeply overbought/oversold corners, also experiencing high volume confirmation or contradiction, created significant returns above the index. The lone exception was heavily overbought stocks with very weak volume contradiction.

Panic-Inducing, Upper Right Side

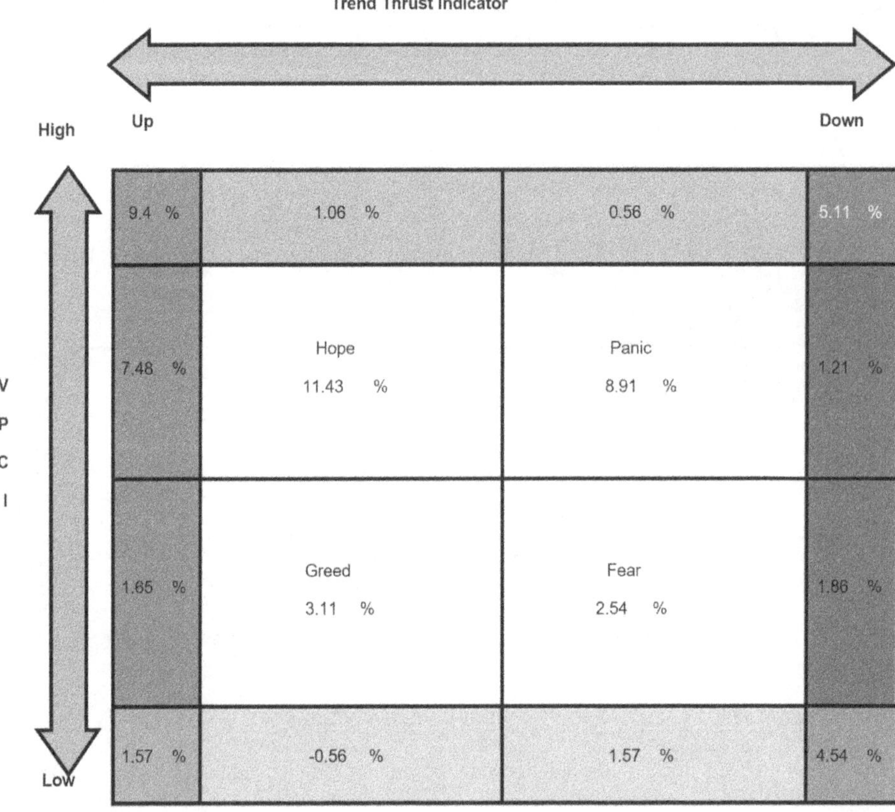

Price Volume Extremes

Now that we have covered the extremes through analysis of the TTI/VPCI MPS corners, let's see if additional insights might be gleaned from examining stocks moving from one quadrant to the opposite (catty-corner) quadrant. The first we explore are stocks located in the most bullish quadrant of a bullish trend with bullish volume. **These stocks in the upper-left quadrant, when held until they have lost both an upward trend (TTI Index) and a bullish confirming volume (VPCI Index) by moving into the opposite corner of a bearish trend and bearish volume, gained on average 11.43% over 13% alpha over its composite index!**

Next, we will examine stocks originating in the lower-left quadrant. These are stocks with bullish trend and bearish volume held until they moved to the diagonally opposite quadrant of bullish volume and bearish trend. Stocks in the quadrant experienced a 3.11% gain.

Moving over to the lower left are oversold stocks with bearish volume. These stocks, beginning in the lower-right quadrant and held until they reached the opposite quadrant of overbought with bullish volume, produced a 4.54% return.

Stocks originating in the bullish volume and down-trending quadrant and later sold upon entering the lower-right corner (uptrend/contracting volume) returned 8.91% (see Figure 29). Thus, these oversold downward trending stocks exhibiting strong volume price contradiction improved upon the S&P 500 Index by 10.95% annually.

Market Position System Employing VPCI/TTI Coordinates

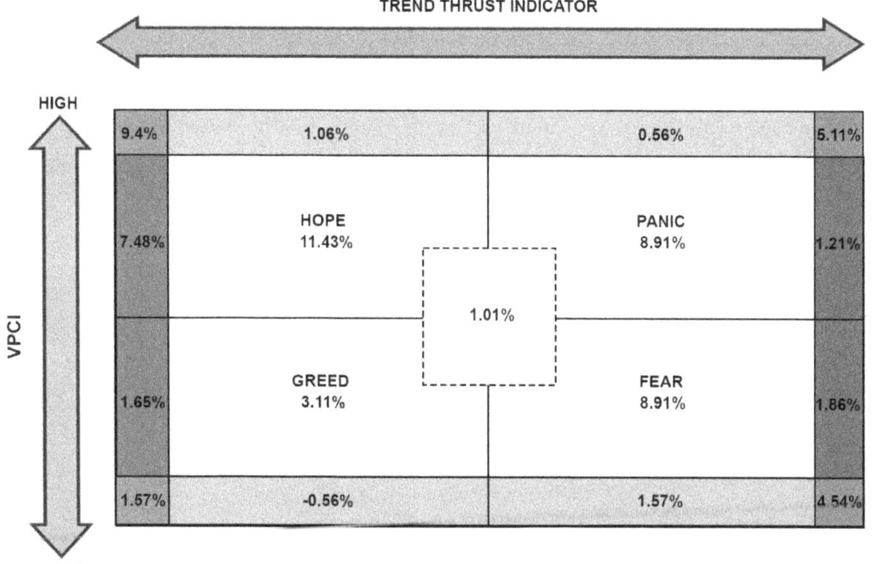

MARKET EQUILIBRIUM

If the market is balanced, basically equal amounts of buying and selling are present. The market has brought in the opposite response. The market is moving and rotating because it has found a fair price to distribute. If the market is imbalanced, either buying or selling is predominant. The market is moving higher or lower to find an opposite response. The market is moving directionally because it is seeking a fair price to distribute. In brief, a balanced market has found a fair price. An imbalanced market is seeking a fair price.

— Market Profile, Chicago Board of Trade

The previous examples illustrated purchasing stocks as they moved across the TTI/VPCII MPS plane. Yet many stocks are not located on the edges but in the middle. We can test how these stocks perform by isolating the stocks in the center of the map. Stocks defined the vertical middle with a VPCI index above 30 and below 70, thus corresponding to the Tropic of Cancer and the Tropic of Capricorn. Likewise, the horizontal middle was defined by a TTI index above 30 and below 70. Stocks located in both middle groups comprised the center of the MPS map. This center represents stocks nearing equilibrium in the price-volume relationship (see Figure 29, dotted space).

These stocks were purchased when they entered the center and then sold when they exited the center. On average, these stocks returned only 1.01%. Thus, purchasing the center stocks resulted in underperformance compared to purchasing stocks on the edges. However, stocks with neither a strong trend nor strong volume contribution/confirmation still slightly outperformed the buy-and-hold approach. My experience suggests that this relative outperformance is likely attributable to active management on the sell side rather than to purchase location on the buy side. Selling stocks as they move down fulfills the money management principle of cutting losses short, while selling stocks as they become overbought is generally prudent in sideways markets. Stocks in the equilibrium or moving toward equilibrium should be viewed in bull markets.

Next, we will continue to build upon the Volume Factor by examining volume's relationship with momentum.

CHAPTER 4:

VOLUME AND MOMENTUM— THE VOLUME FACTOR

"I am always looking for some clue, some easily missed sign that might just be the missing piece in the puzzle."
—Oliver Harris

Some of the data presented in this chapter is hypothetical and back-tested data. This data is not based on any advisory client assets. Past performance of a model is not a guarantee of future results. Actual performance may vary significantly from the hypothetical results shown. Please see the section titled 'Important Information Regarding Hypothetical, Back-Tested Performance' for a full description of this data and the limitations associated with it.

In the realm of physics, momentum is defined as the "quantity of motion of a moving body, measured as a product of its mass and velocity." Yet, in the realm of security analysis, the vast majority of momentum analysis denies this definition's first word, "quantity" or, in market analysis terms, "volume." Instead, momentum analysis tends to focus exclusively on the moving body component: namely, price velocity. Mindful of this oversight, our study of Volume Factor Momentum will duly consider and incorporate the Volume Factor in developing a comprehensive understanding of volume's role in momentum analysis. A challenge associated with momentum strategies is the inclination to allocate resources toward currently successful assets. The uncertainty lies in whether these trends will persist into the future. When examining data from my past two decades of Volume Factor studies, it becomes evident that momentum analysis has focused exclusively on price velocity, overlooking a crucial element. This is where the concepts of volume confirmation and contradiction become very relevant. Taking this into account, our exploration of Volume Factor

Momentum comprehensively integrates the Volume Factor, enriching our understanding of volume's pivotal but largely untapped role in momentum analysis.

NEWTON'S FIRST LAW OF MOTION: INERTIA

"An object at rest remains at rest, and an object in motion remains in motion at a constant speed and in a straight line unless acted on by an unbalanced force."

Newton's Law of Inertia may also be applied in the analysis of security momentum. The Law of Inertia with respect to price momentum could be rephrased as follows:

"A price trend in motion (acceleration) tends to remain in motion at a constant speed and in a straight line unless acted on by an unbalanced force (volume)."

This revised definition conceptually highlights the relationship between price trends and volume in security analysis. It does not imply price trends can continue without volume. In an exchange market, price cannot exist absent volume. Rather, volume is the force behind price momentum and the sustainer of trends. In this context, given the asymmetry between supply and demand, volume serves as the operational force behind price. An exchange (trade) with volume but without price change may not offer much predictive value, whereas a directional motion in securities, combined with volume, indicates force's significance pursuant to Newton's first law of motion. In this way, in the absence of a force (volume) catalyst, price direction and momentum are unlikely to change or have predictive value.

RSI: INTERNAL MARKET MOMENTUM

Price momentum is relative. One form of price momentum relativity is a comparison of a securities price momentum to that of other investments. In market analysis, this type of relative external momentum is called relative strength, or RS. Another type of price momentum is internal relative strength. Internal price momentum contrasts a security's present velocity of price change to its previous velocity. There are many technical indicators by which to measure a security's internal momentum. Of these, one of the most common momentum indicators is J. Welles Wilder's Relative Strength Index, more commonly known as RSI.

Welles Wilder, a mechanical engineer and real estate investor, sold his real estate investments at the age of 38 to focus on trading commodities. He applied his engineering background to develop his investment philosophy, which led to the creation of several technical indicators, including the Average True Range (ATR), the Directional Movement Index (DMI), Parabolic Stops, and the Relative Strength Index (RSI), the latter of which is the topic of discussion here. Wilder documented these innovations in his 1978 book, New Concepts in Technical Trading Systems.

Wilder's RSI is a ratio of the average points gained during "up" periods over past periods, divided by the average points lost during "down" periods across the same period.

RS = Avg. price change (gained) on up days ÷ Avg. price change (lost) on down days

The RS result is then plugged into the oscillation formula below:

RSI = 100 – [100 ÷ (1 + RS)]

This oscillation formula creates an RSI value range between 1 and 99 – hence, the technical term oscillate or oscillator. The RSI oscillator gauges the speed of ascent or descent of a securities momentum relative to its prior momentum. Thus, RSI is a type of speedometer, measuring the momentum of a given security. A high and rising RSI reading implies that the momentum is strong and gaining strength. A low and falling RSI suggests that the momentum is weak and losing strength. Momentum investors typically desire to be long securities with strong and continually strengthening momentum.

Source: Optuma www.optuma.com/volumeanalysis

In Figure 1, we can see a 14-period RSI plotted for the SPDR S&P 500 ETF Trust (SPY). When looking at an RSI graph, several items are worth noting. First, the horizontal lines at the 30 and 70 levels (shown at far right) indicate the predetermined oversold and overbought levels, respectively. It is also important to note that the vast majority of the movement is between the 30 and 70 levels. The crossing of these lines indicates that a security or index may be considered oversold or overbought. However, what is essential for a momentum investor is the RSI line itself. The higher the RSI value – in other words, the closer to 100 – the more momentum the security is experiencing over a given time frame, generally 14 periods.

It is widely established within factor investing that momentum is a strong performance factor. But does Wilder's formula of internal momentum also display factor outperformance? This question was proposed by Richard Tortoriello, who, as an analyst for Standard and Poor's, possessed the background and unique access necessary to build systems and test theories.

In Tortoriello's 2008 book, Quantitative Strategies for Achieving Alpha: The Standard and Poor's Approach to Testing Your Investment Choices, Tortoriello sets out to identify factors driving portfolio alpha. In this work, Tortoriello tests 1,200 strategies in the following categories:

Profitability
Valuation
Cash flow
Growth
Capital allocation
Price momentum
Red flags (risk factors)

Using various techniques, Tortoriello conducted extensive qualitative testing on each of these groups. The testing covered the period spanning from 1992 to 2007 performed on a wide range of securities. Specifically, Tortoriello tested approximately 2,200 U.S. stocks from the Compustat database. According to Tortoriello's findings, price momentum was among the best factor strategies for achieving excess returns. Specifically, Tortoriello's testing reveals that Wilder's RSI, using 28-week relative strength, was among if not the most effective of the thousands of strategies and indicators studied. The results indicate that the top quintile of 28-week RSI stocks outperformed the benchmark by an annualized rate of 6.2%, whereas the bottom quintile underperformed by -3.2%. In addition, the top quintile RSI generated a compounded annualized return of 16.7% compared to the composite universe of 11.1%. Furthermore, the strategy boasted a 78% win ratio over the 15-year study period.

Figure 2: RSI Performance by Quintile

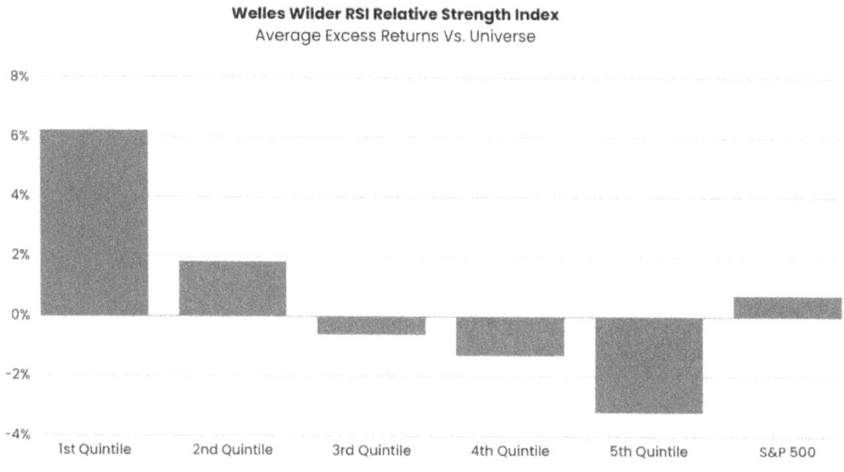

RSI 1992-2007 Source Richard Tortoriello, Quantative Strategies for Achieving Alpha

In Tortoriello's study, notice the symmetrical distribution of RSI returns in Figure 2. The higher the RSI, or the more overbought the momentum, the greater the return. The lower the RSI, or the more oversold the momentum, the weaker the return. To verify RSI's utility in momentum analysis, we conducted our own backtest using the current members of the Russell 3000 from February 10, 2023, back to January 11, 2002. Of note, this test does have survivorship bias. Taking the Russell 3000 index back to January 2002, only 1,152 names were left to test by February of 2023. We then ranked RSI by decile, with each security equally weighted. Our RSI time frame was different: 26 weeks compared to 28 weeks. We chose 26 weeks because it represents approximately one-half or two-quarters of an annual 52-week cycle. Each quarter, the test securities were reranked based on the same RSI criteria.

Our RSI testing results were also symmetrical, but in the opposite way. The oversold, low RSI stocks were the top performers, while the overbought, high RSI stocks were the underperformers. The baseline benchmark, buying and holding the 1,152 equally weighted securities, resulted in a 13.01% return. However, the first decile (highest RSI) only returned a bit over a 10% annual percentage return (APR), whereas the bottom decile (lowest RSI) returned over a 19% APR. Moving from decile 1 toward 10, generally, the returns trended higher as stocks moved from being overbought (high upside momentum) to oversold (strong downward momentum).

Figure 3: 26-Week RSI Deciles 01/11/2002–02/10/2023

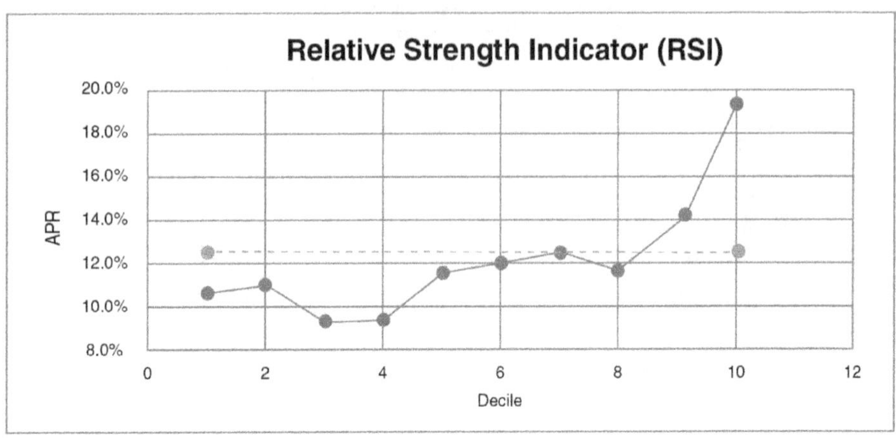

External Momentum: Relative Strength (RS)

Although RSI, the internal momentum of a stock, is thought to be a powerful driver, relative strength (RS) is perhaps the most recognized momentum performance driver among common market factors. Relative strength compares a security's performance relative to that of another security or market. Momentum investors applying relative strength desire to hold long stocks and situate themselves in sectors and markets that are outperforming their peers. Relative strength investing requires one to be invested in those stocks that are rising the most, generally with the least amount of resistance. Again, Isaac Newton said it best, "Every object in a state of motion stays in motion unless acted upon" (Isaac Newton 1st Law of Motion).

However, another physicist, Albert Einstein, believed in a theory called "relativity." Relative strength differs from RSI in that RS is relative to another security or market, whereas RSI represents a security's current momentum relative to its previous momentum. For example, a security that was at $10 at the beginning of the quarter is now at $12. This means the security is up 20%. We do not have all of the data points to calculate the RSI, but we do know the security is up 20% over the quarter.

However, what if the S&P 500 was up 25% over the same time period? The RS of our security would then be weaker or negative relative to the broad composite. Thus, although our stock has strong RSI, or internal strength, it is weak compared to the index. Alternatively, what if the S&P 500 was down 20% during the same time period? Now our security looks very strong relative to the market. Thus, RS, or relative strength investing, is not concerned with the internal strength or momentum of a security but is, rather, entirely concerned with the security's performance relative to a predefined benchmark.

Similar to athletic performance, psychological momentum may also lead to superior market outcomes. Psychological momentum is the perception of moving toward or away from a goal. It is important to note that psychological momentum can be either positive, where almost everything seems to go right, or negative, where nearly everything seems to go wrong. Similarly, investors who own a security perpetually moving higher are less likely to sell. Likewise, an advancing security is more likely to attract new investors, whereas investors holding a security perpetually falling ever lower will be more likely to cut their losses, and potential new investors will lack the urgency to jump on board.

Relative strength is among the strongest known alpha factors. Respected market strategist and technician Michael Carr was an early adopter of relative strength investing, before momentum factor investing grew in popularity. In his book titled Smarter Investing in Any Economy, Carr reviews seven different relative strength techniques in both a bull market cycle, spanning from 1990 to 2007, and a bear market cycle, spanning from 2008 to 2018. In the bull market cycle, all seven RS strategies significantly outperformed buying and holding the S&P 500. The best RS strategy was relative strength using a ratio of multiple moving averages, which returned 21.94% annualized, compared to the S&P 500, which returned 8.7% during the same period. The lowest performing RS strategy, price divided by moving average ratios, outperformed the S&P 500 by over 10% annualized, with an 18.87% annualized return.

Figure 4: Michael Carr's Relative Strength Strategies, 1990–2007

RS Techniques	***Annualized Return***	***Maximum Drawdown***
Normalized rate of change	20.10%	-52.26%
Back-weighted ROC	21.77%	-47.21%
Front-weighted ROC	19.83%	-53.06%
Price/Moving average ratios	18.87%	-55.42%
Ratios of multiple moving averages	21.94%	-42.41%
Averaging different time periods	21.10%	-50.15%
Alpha	20.94%	-53.53%
S&P 500	***8.70%***	***-50.03%***

Source: Smarter Investing in Any Economy, Michael Carr

These RS results are fantastic, but recall, this was in a secular bull market. Could RS provide alpha in a secular bear market as well? Carr kept up his RS studies and testing over the subsequent decade, beginning in the great bear market of 2008 until 2018. Carr's work proves that relative strength still delivers strong outperformance, even in less favorable investment climates. However, this time the worst-performing RS strategy was the ratio of multiple moving averages, returning only 7.6% yet still beating the S&P 500, returning 7%. As you may recall, the RS ratio of moving averages was the top-performing RS strategy in Carr's prior study.

Figure 5: Michael Carr's Relative Strength Strategies, 2008–2018

RS Techniques	Annualized Returns	Maximum Drawdown
Normalized rate of change	9.10%	-53.20%
Back-weighted ROC	9.40%	-58.50%
Front-weighted ROC	11.00%	-45.50%
Price/Moving average ratios	13.10%	-42.40%
Ratios of multiple moving averages	7.60%	-50.10%
Averaging different time periods	8.80%	-51.60%
Alpha	10.50%	-44.30%
S&P 500	***7.00%***	***-56.00%***

Source: Smarter Investing in Any Economy, Michael Carr

During this less favorable decade, the best performing RS strategy was price/moving average ratios, returning 13.1% for a 6% annualized improvement over buy and hold. To summarize, the best performing RS strategy in the bull market cycle was actually the worst in the bear market cycle, and the worst RS strategy in the bull cycle was the best in the bear cycle. During the bear market cycle, the RS strategies beat buy and hold annually by 2.92%, with a 9.92% RS composite return versus a 7% S&P 500 return. In contrast, during the bull market cycle, the composite of RS strategies beat buy and hold by nearly 12% annually, returning 20.65% compared to the benchmark return of 8.7%. Overall, the best-performing RS strategy over both cycles was price/moving ratios, with an average performance of 15.985%. This closely compares to the worst RS strategy, normalized rate of change, returning 14.6%. Overall, the buy and hold strategy returned 7.85% versus the composite of RS strategies returning 15.29% over the entirety of both studies, spanning from 1990 to 2018, nearly doubling the return of the S&P 500.

In Tortoriello's thousands of studies, he, like Carr, found another strong market factor in relative strength. Specifically, similar to his studies on RSI, Tortoriello studied relative strength from 1992 to 2007. He found that a seven-month period of relative strength (RS) was particularly promising. Like this RSI study, Tortoriello tested approximately 2,200 U.S. stocks from the Compustat database. The stock universe returned 11.2% over this time period. However, high RS stocks in the top quintile (highest relative strength) outperformed by 3.3% over buying and holding the testing universe, whereas low RS stocks, those in the lowest quintile, underperformed by 3.4%.

Figure 6: Tortoriello's Seven-Month RS Quintiles, 1992–2007

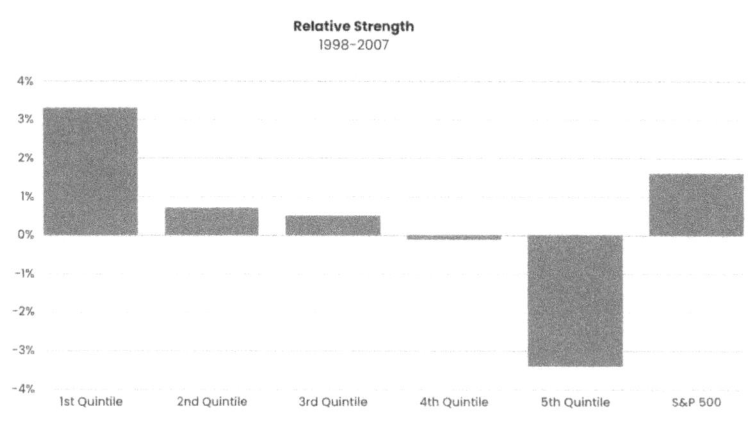

Source: Quantitative Strategies for Achieving Alpha – Tortoriello (Standard & Poor's)

Our own study testing relative strength (RS), conducted from February 10, 2023, back to January 11, 2002, using the same current members of the Russell 3000 as the previous RSI study, also showed strong RS results. As in our RSI study, we again used a 26-week RS representative of two quarters, reallocated each quarter into deciles by RS ranking. Top decile RS (highest RS) stocks retained outperformance of the universe, returning a nearly 17% annual rate of return (APR) compared to buy and hold at approximately 13% APR. However, there was another, even more impressive decile contradicting the results of the Tortoriello study. The bottom decile RS (lowest RS) stocks outperformed the buy-and-hold universe, returning approximately 19% APR. Thus, relative strength outperformed on both extremes: when heavily overbought, but also when heavily oversold.

Figure 7: RS Deciles 26-Week RS, 01/11/2002–02/10/2023

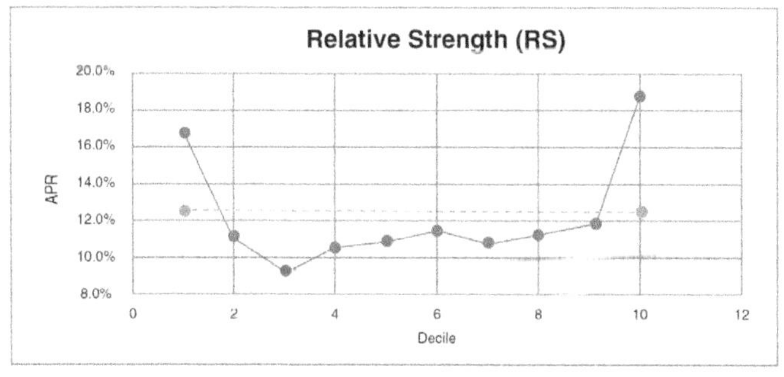

NEWTON'S SECOND LAW OF MOTION: FORCE (VOLUME)

"The acceleration of an object depends on the mass of the object and the amount of force applied."

Momentum

Momentum describes the rate of acceleration or deceleration. In physics, the momentum of an object is measured by the time it takes a constant force to bring a moving object to rest. What does this mean in market analysis? Like traditional physics, in market analysis, momentum refers to the speed of ascent or descent. Momentum investing follows the direction of price motion until it finds a resting point. In Newtonian mechanics, momentum is defined as the "product of the mass and velocity of an object." Force is a vector quantity possessing both magnitude and direction. If m is an object's mass and v is its velocity (also a vector quantity), then the object's momentum is p=m*v (Momentum = Mass * Velocity).

Acceleration

As defined by Newton, "The acceleration of an object depends on the mass of the object and the amount of force applied." This is distinct from Force = Mass * Acceleration. The key difference between velocity and acceleration is that velocity describes the speed and direction of an object's motion, while acceleration describes how quickly an object's velocity is changing.

Newton's second law of motion, which states that force equals mass times acceleration, establishes a connection between an object's mass, acceleration, and applied force. This same concept applies to security analysis as well. Analogous to acceleration, f = m*a describes the F force (volume) being placed on M mass (price trends). Understanding the amount of volume (force) required to move a security (object) a given distance (price change) at a particular speed (momentum) may aid in security analysis.

Our formula could be rephrased in simpler terms as follows: The more volume (force) being applied to price (mass), the stronger the expectation of momentum. In order to gain a more complete understanding of momentum, we incorporate volume data or force into the computation of momentum. The Relative Strength Index can be amended to contain its force properties by incorporating volume into its calculation. This volume-weighted RSI indicator has already been created for us. A volume-adjusted RSI, the Money Flow Index (MFI), was created by Gene Quong and Avrum Soudack in 1989. For the most part, the calculations of RSI and MFI are nearly identical (RSI uses closing price, whereas MFI replaces closing price with Average True Range (ATR)), but MFI volume weights price, whereas RSI uses closing price (absent volume).

Could volume weighting improve the effectiveness of RSI? To test this theory, we reran the former RSI backtest (using the current members of the Russell 3000 from February 10, 2023, back to January 11, 2002 with the same 26-week setting). Each quarter, the securities were reranked, based this time on MFI criteria.

Figure 8: 26-Week MFI Deciles, 01/11/2002–02/10/2023

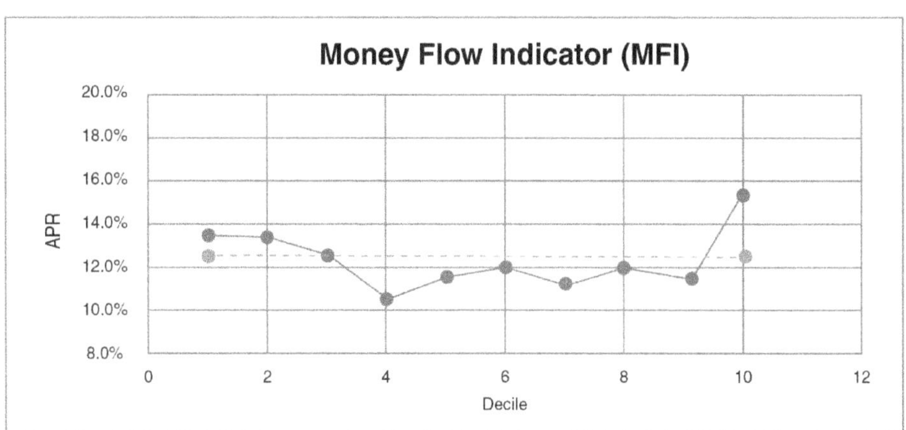

Volume weighting RSI via the MFI turned the unprofitable top deciles one and two from underperformers to outperformers. MFI's top decile's relative performance to RSI showed a significant improvement of approximately 5% effective APR. Overall, MFI's top decile outperformed the benchmark universe by approximately 2% effective APR. Additionally, in the oversold tenth decile, MFI decreased RSI's more than 18% effective APR return to slightly less than 16%.

VPCI: The Most Bullish Volume Index

What if we were more interested in volume's impact on price trends rather than price? The Volume Price Confirmation Indicator (VPCI) is a trend confirmation indicator that unveils the asymmetry between price trends and volume-price trends. Volume is most useful during extremes. The VPCI Most Bullish Volume Index follows stocks in the index with the strongest bullish confirmation. This index is calculated by selecting only the top decile VPCI stocks within the S&P 500 Index. Stated another way, the Most Bullish Volume Index comprises those stocks containing the top 10% highest weekly VPCI readings within the S&P 500. At the beginning of each quarter, new stocks are purchased upon breaking into the top 10% list. Likewise, holdings falling out of the top 50% of VPCI scores are sold at the beginning of the quarter. The sold issues are then replaced with securities with the highest VPCI scores in the top 10% of the S&P 500 Index that are not already included in the holdings.

A test was performed on the individual members of the S&P 500 Index from January 1, 2000, through December 31, 2019. The test results were verified by third-party verification service Ned Davis Research and were not optimized in any way. Excluding dividends, the S&P 500 benchmark annualized return was 6%. In contrast, the annualized return of the most bullish volume index was 8.8% for the period (see Figure 12). This Volume Factor, VPCI's Most Bullish Index, represents an annualized outperformance of 2.8% over the S&P 500 Index over the last two decades.

VPCI: The Most Bullish Volume Index

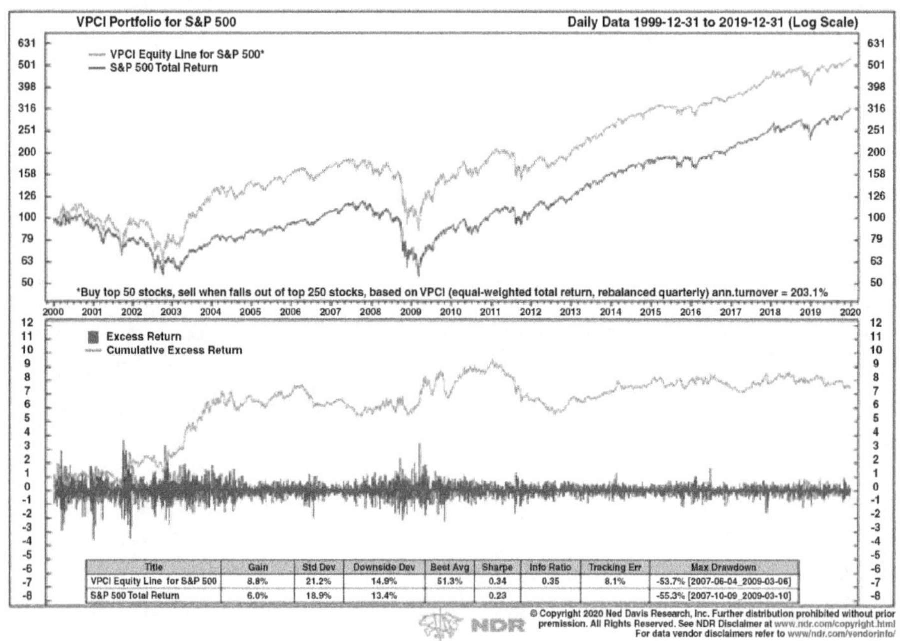

Title	Gain	Std Dev	Downside Dev	Best Avg	Sharpe	Info Ratio	Tracking Err	Max Drawdown
VPCI Equity Line for S&P 500	8.8%	21.2%	14.9%	51.3%	0.34	0.35	8.1%	-53.7% [2007-06-04_2009-03-06]
S&P 500 Total Return	6.0%	18.9%	13.4%		0.23			-55.3% [2007-10-09_2009-03-10]

VPCI RSI

Although Tortoriello tested over 1,200 fundamental and technical indications, he did not test volume, nor did he combine volume confirmation with momentum. One of the problems with relative strength strategies is that they invest in what is working. But how do we know if those trends will continue into the future? This is where volume confirmation comes into play. Volume analysis allows relative strength strategies to be even more effective.

If RSI is the strongest of all investment factors, why not improve upon it by adjusting RSI with volume confirmation? Because volume leads price, adjusting RSI to the Volume

Price Confirmation Indicator (VPCI) allows us to identify positive momentum sooner. Perhaps even more importantly, because volume confirms price, adjusting momentum with the VPCI may provide indications to rotate away from momentum moves that lack adequate capital flows. In this way, VPCI RSI adjusts momentum according to volume price trend asymmetry. VPCI RSI accomplishes exactly that. With VPCI RSI, we adjust RSI by multiplying it by VPCI. VPCI RSI = (1+VPCI) * RSI. Therefore, when VPCI is high, it raises RSI; when VPCI is negative or low, it lowers RSI.

Figure 9: VPCI-RSI

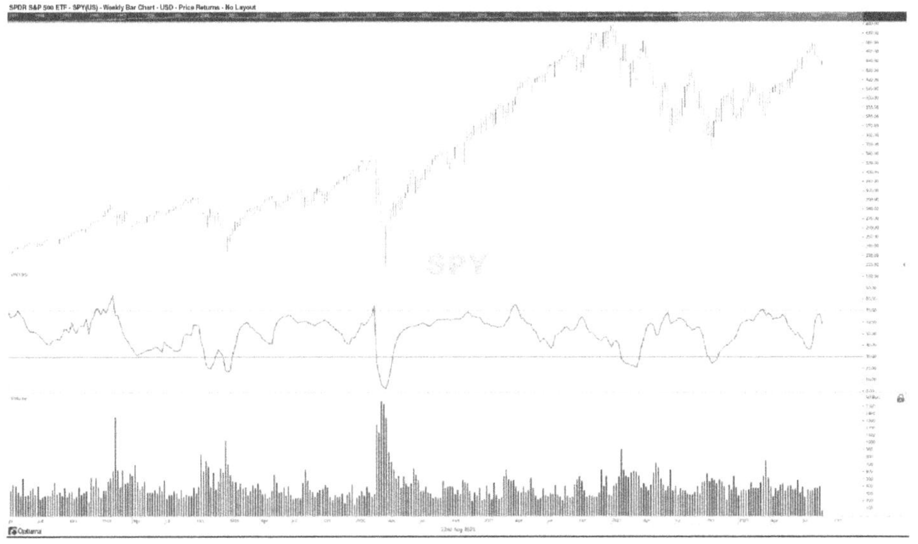

Source: Optuma www.optuma.com/volumeanalysis

The bottom panel of Figure 9 shows the VPCI RSI output. The top panel is SPY's price chart. The Volume Price Confirmation Indicator is directly underneath the price, and below the VPCI is the Relative Strength Index. That leaves us with the panel at the very bottom of the chart, VPCI RSI. Notice that at the end of the chart, between late effective April and early May 2022, RSI is declining, but VPCI RSI is declining much more rapidly, driven by a precipitously falling VPCI.

Figure 10 shows a study trend of purchasing S&P 500 stocks with VPCI-RSI levels above 0.2 and selling members when they drop below 0.2. The test was conducted from January 1, 2000, to May 6, 2002, using weekly data employing a 4% position size per position. Since VPCI-RSI generally oscillates between 0.01 and 0.99, essentially this test eliminates the S&P 500 members with very weak momentum, confirmed by a weak VPCI, and replaces them with members showing strong VPCI-RSI (high RSI confirmed by high VPCI). While on a price appreciation basis, the S&P 500 index returned 6.1% with a Sharpe 22 [risk adjusted] ratio of 0.22, the VPCI-RSI study returned 14.8% with a Sharpe [risk adjusted] ratio of 0.72.

Figure 10: VPCI-RSI > .2

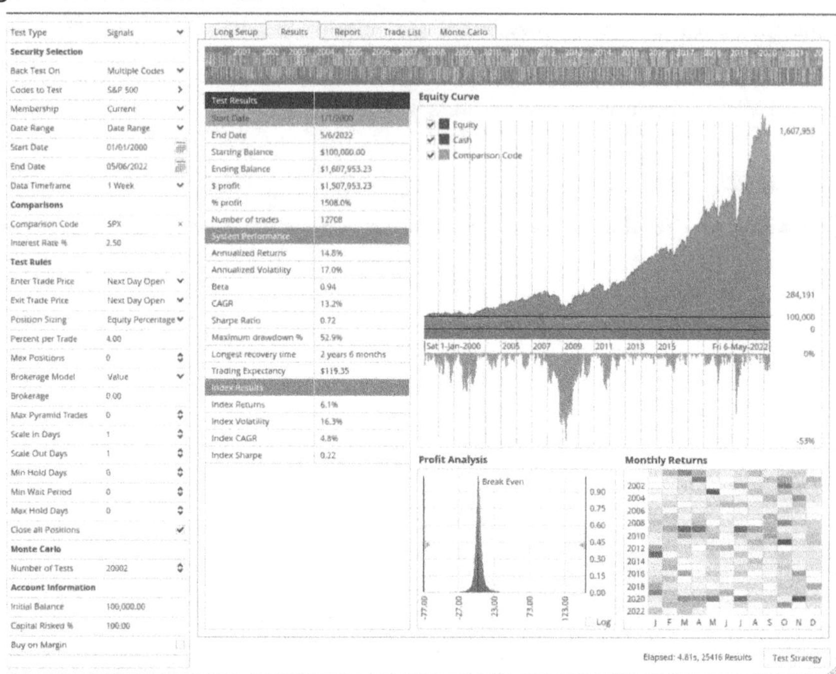

Source: Optuma www.optuma.com/volumeanalysis

Next, we plugged VPCI into our prior January 11, 2002, to February 10, 2023, decile study of RSI. When multiplying the stocks' RSIs by their VPCIs, the VPCI addition brought the performance of the entire scale, deciles 1 – 10, back in line with the benchmark universe. Thus, VPCI improved the overbought, underperforming deciles while weakening the performance of the outperforming, oversold deciles.

Figure 11: Decile Study, 01/11/2002–02/10/2023, RSI, MFI, and VPCI RSI

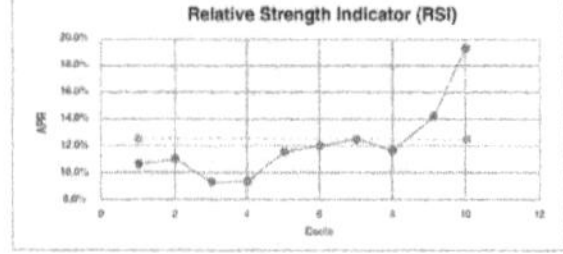

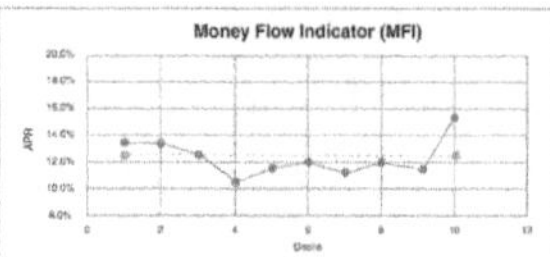

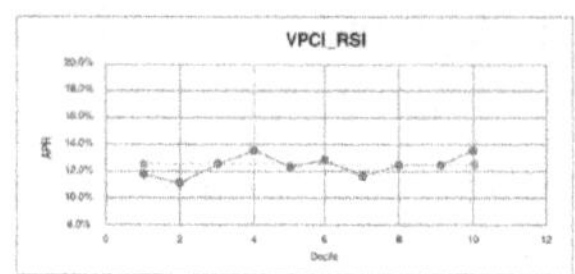

Volume Modified Internal Strength

RSI * MFI * VPCI RSI

Adding the sum of each internal strength indicator, RSI + MFI + VPCI RSI, creates the Volume Factor Internal Strength composite. The Volume Factor Internal Strength composite produced benchmark returns in the top first decile. Then the composite underperformed deciles 2-6. Decile 7 performed in line with the benchmark. Whereas deciles 8-10 showed outperformance with improved performance moving toward deeply oversold (decile 10). Overall, volume-modified Internal Strength did not exhibit the momentum factor, actually demonstrating that weak, oversold internal momentum exceeded strong overbought momentum.

Figure 12: Volume Factor Internal Strength Composite

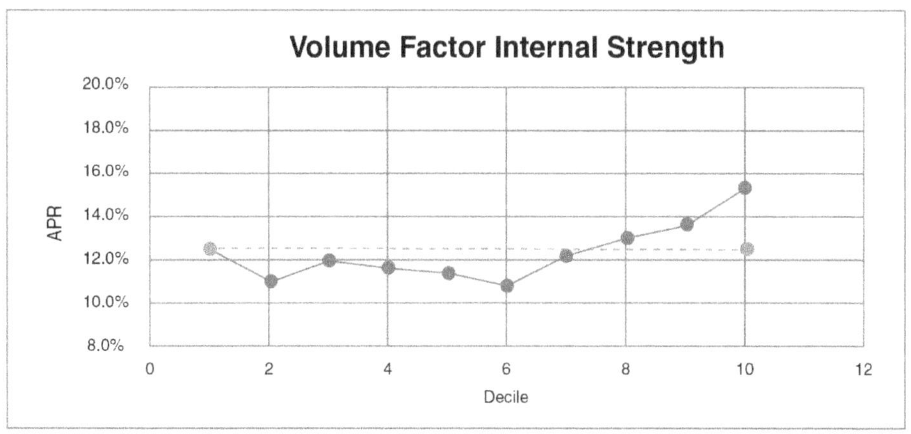

In his book titled Quantitative Strategies for Achieving Alpha, Tortoriello also describes momentum in this way: "Since volume is necessary to push stock prices upward, positive price momentum tells us that an increased number of buyers have entered the market and demand currently outweighs supply." This brings us to another analogy.

NEWTON'S THIRD LAW OF MOTION: ACTION & REACTION (PRICE-VOLUME ASYMMETRY)

"Every action has an equal and opposite reaction"

Newton's third law states that an equal and opposite reaction exists for every action. Similarly, Adam Smith developed a theory in the field of economics, postulating that when demand exceeds supply, the price increases, and when supply surpasses demand, the price decreases. The exchange markets adhere to the same laws of supply and demand as traditional economics, where the assumption is that supply increases as demand rises, and demand rises as available supply decreases, attracting buyers at lower prices. In other words, when demand rises, supply pushes back.

However, the auction market mechanism alters the dynamics of this operation. In the exchange market, supply remains primarily finite. While companies can increase the supply of shares with the help of investment bankers, the directive of every publicly traded company is to boost shareholder wealth, either through dividends or stock price appreciation, including share buybacks. The board of directors will only offer shares (supply) if they deem it necessary to increase the price of the stock or, in response to a crisis, to stabilize it. Consequently, both supply and demand operate under an opportunity cost model, where wealth seeks the best opportunity for growth or, at worst, the best place to preserve capital. Existing shareholders (or short sellers) provide supply in the form of sellers who believe that cash or another opportunity presents greater value than the stock at its current price. Conversely, investors provide demand (buyers) who perceive the stock as the best opportunity for at least a portion of their wealth.

Remember, though, that for every buyer, there is a matching seller. Thus, a rise in volume accompanied by falling stock prices suggests that demand is waning, whereas an increase in volume accompanied by rising stock prices assumes that demand is overwhelming finite supply.

Whenever one object exerts a force on a second object, the second object exerts an equal and opposite force on the first.

Richard Wyckoff's law of effort versus results, which asserts that effort should be proportional to results, is also based on this same principle. In security analysis, the effort (force) is the volume that achieves the result of price change (acceleration). In other words, the size of the executed bids and offers demonstrates investors' commitment. What happens when the movement in price exceeds the movement in volume, or vice versa? To discern this relationship, we observe the price change (acceleration) relative to the volume change (force). Consider this example: A stock breaks out 10% from its previous close on a volume 200% higher than normal. The next day, the stock advances another 5% on 300% higher volume. Finally, on the third day, the stock moves up 2% on 400% higher volume. The high volume on the price breakout is a bullish indication. However, over time, volume (force) expands, while the price change (acceleration) wanes. In Wyckoff's terms, greater effort is producing smaller results. In Newton's terms, when more force (volume) produces less acceleration (price change), the mass (price) is overly expanded (too high). This situation can be an early warning signal that although the stock is still running strong, it might be susceptible to its own crash and burn. Thus, in a bull market, both price momentum and volume momentum should be present.

According to Newton's third law, an applied force creates an equal and opposite force. Much like the material world, the laws of physics apply to economics and are revealed through the volume momentum factor. Force equals mass * acceleration. Force (volume) is the amount of energy required to move an object (price). The strength of that cause should be proportional to the effect. As manifested through trading volume, the asymmetry or imbalance between supply and demand is the external force causing price movements. Thus, price is the object being moved, while volume is the external force, be it buyers' demand or sellers' supply. Demand presses, and supply (sellers) presses back. By examining Newton's third law, "Every action has an equal and opposite reaction," we learned that the difference between demand (buying pressure) and supply (selling pressure) determines the proportional amount of price change reaction. Next, let's employ these physics principles in our volume analysis by studying asymmetry between price momentum (RSI) and volume-weighted price momentum (MFI).

VMI – The Volume Momentum Indicator

The Volume Momentum Indicator (VMI) takes the difference between MFI and RSI to unearth price-volume momentum asymmetry. The VMI is calculated as follows: 1+ (MFI - RSI)/ 100. The VMI measures the asymmetry between price momentum and volume-weighted price momentum.

Figure 13: Volume Momentum Indicator

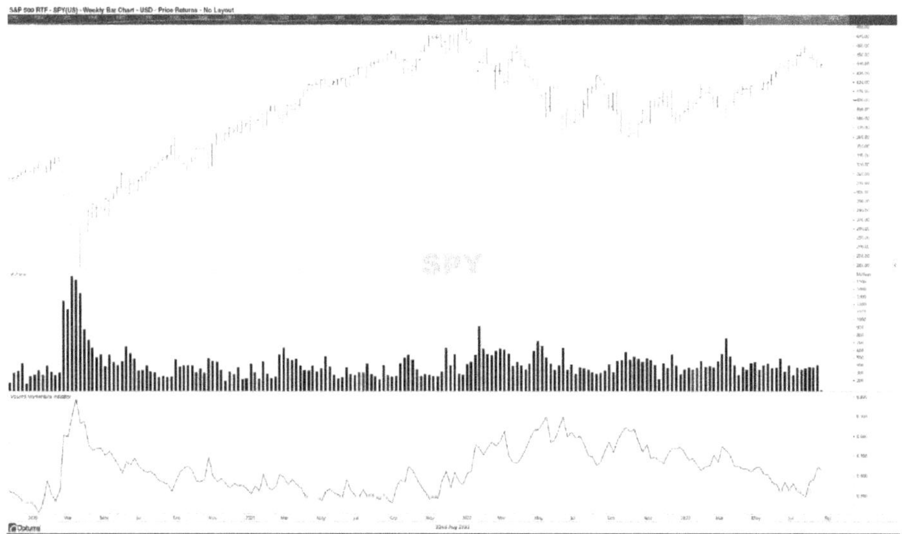

Source: Optuma www.optuma.com/volumeanalysis

When the MFI is greater than the RSI, volume-price momentum is greater than price momentum. Volume analysis seeks to identify issues with greater volume price momentum than price momentum alone. A high VMI represents an opportune time to buy (VMI>RSI), whereas a low VMI may suggest it is time to sell (VMI<RSI).

Here, we buy stocks when VMI equals or exceeds .5 (MFI => RSI) and then sell when VMI is below 0.2. In essence, this model proposes buying S&P 500 components with positive volume price momentum asymmetry, or, in other words, when there is price-volume momentum confirmation. This model then proposes selling the long position when the previous confirmation (>50) has switched to a clear volume-momentum contradiction state (<20), where the volume absent RSI is exceedingly greater than the volume-weighted MFI.

We then tested this model from August 2, 2000, to May 4, 2022, using weekly data on the S&P 500 components with the Optuma software. This VMI model returned 17% compared to buying and holding the S&P 500 at a return of 6.4%. Passively owning the S&P 500 Index produced a Sharpe ratio of 0.34. By applying the Volume Momentum Indicator model to the S&P 500 components, the Sharpe ratio surged to 0.93. Presently, the VMI indicator is also available with the Optuma Software (Optuma.com/volumeanalysis).

Figure 14: Buy VMI => 0.50 Sell VMI < 0.2, 8/02/2000–05/04/2022

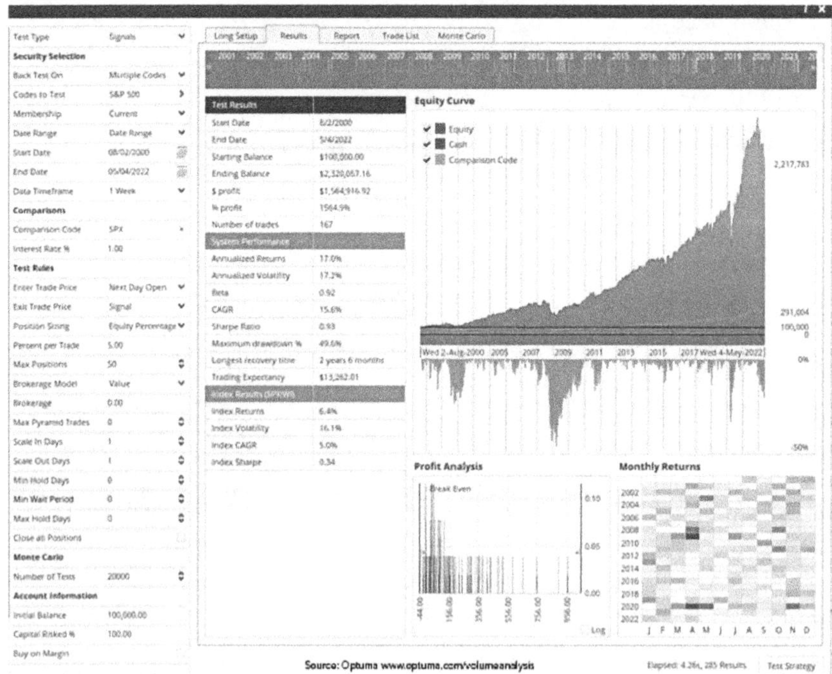

Source: Optuma www.optuma.com/volumeanalysis

Next, let's look at VMI (MFI - RSI) viability within a decile study. We tested the VMI (using the current members of the Russell 3000 from February 10, 2023, back to January 11, 2002, with the same 26-week setting). Each quarter (13 weeks), the securities were reranked based on the same VMI criteria. The top decile, decile 1, represents the top 10% of stocks ranked by the difference between MFI and RSI. Similarly, the bottom decile, decile 10, illustrates the purchase of the bottom 10% of stocks ranked by the difference between MFI minus RSI. Notice that top decile 1 shows dramatic improvement from the benchmark, as well as the other deciles. Over the course of the study, the benchmark universe returned approximately 13% effective APR, whereas stocks in VMI decile 1 returned just under 20% effective APR. This asymmetry between price momentum and volume-price momentum creates the factor volume momentum asymmetry.

Figure 15: Volume Momentum Asymmetry VMI – (MFI-RS), 01/11/2002–02/10/2023

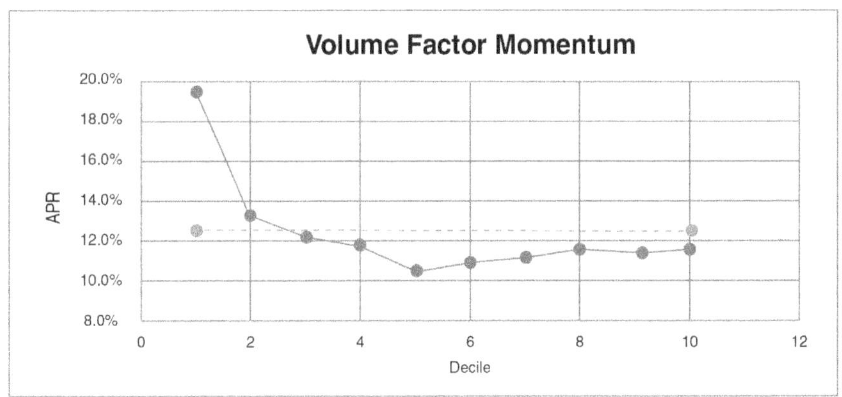

VPMCI = VOLUME PRICE MOMENTUM CONFIRMATION INDICATOR

VPMCI=(1+(VMI)/100) *1+((VPCI RSI-RSI)/100) *VM

The Volume Price Momentum Confirmation Indicator (VPMCI) is the same formula as the original VPCI except it incorporates momentum characteristics instead of trend variables. As opposed to utilizing the asymmetry between SMA (Simple Moving Average) and VWMA (Volume Weighted Moving Average), we employ the asymmetry between our new momentum indicators, VMI and VPCI RSI. With VPMCI, we swap VPC with VMI. Similarly, VPMCI substitutes the VPR with the difference between VPCI RSI and RSI. Like the VPCI, we keep the volume multiplier ratio the same (VM = (short-term average volume / long-term average volume)). Presently, this indicator is only available with the Optuma software.

VPMCI Volume Price Momentum Confirmation Indicator

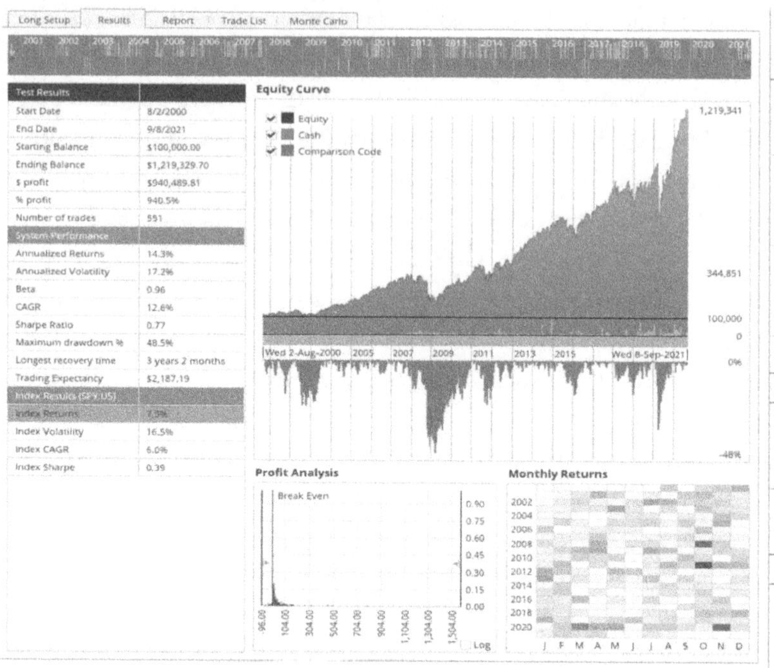

Source: Optuma www.optuma.com/volumeanalysis

The bottom panel in Figure 7 shows the VPMCI in red. Often the volume momentum confirmation aligns with the volume price confirmation trend, but at times the VPMCI will contradict the VPCI trends. Ideally, a bullish setup is one exhibiting both strong VPCI and strong VPMCI.

Purchasing Stocks when VPMCI >.2

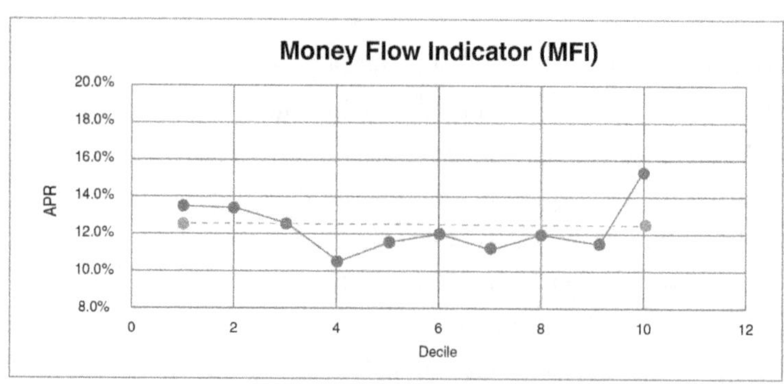

Source: Optuma www.optuma.com/volumeanalysis

Similar to our VMI and VPCI RSI tests, let's see what happens in stocks with poor VPMCI scores from the S&P 500. From August 2, 2000, to September 8, 2021, the S&P 500 Index returned 7.5%, whereas eliminating poor VPCMCI scores under .2 raised the annualized return to 14.3%. Position sizes of 4% were taken.

Buy VPCMCI >. 5 Sell VPMCI < .2

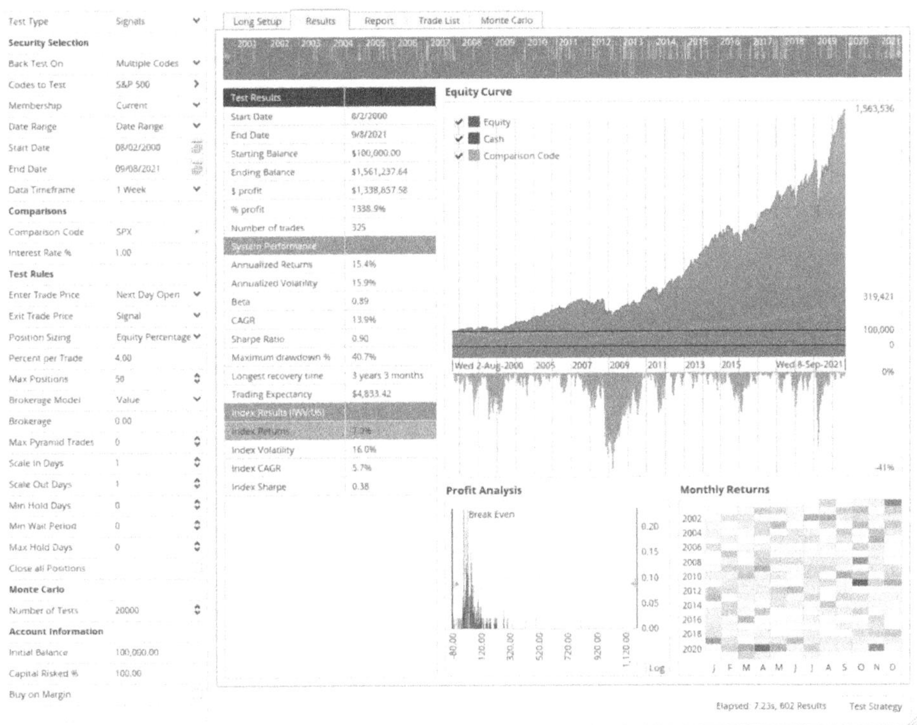

Source: Optuma www.optuma.com/volumeanalysis

Let us amend that model only to purchase stocks with positive volume price momentum – that is, stocks with a VPMCI above .5. We will then sell these stocks when their volume price momentum weakens below .2. Again, a 4% position size is taken. Adding the positive VPMCI component to the prior model improves the return to 15.4% from 14.3%. Our $100,000 investment improves upon the S&P 500 buy and hold return of $320K to $1.2 million. When adding positive momentum asymmetry, as indicated by a VPMCI >.5, this further enhances the return to $1.56 million. Moreover, our risk-adjusted return, or Sharpe ratio, goes from 0.38 with the S&P 500 to 0.89. These improvements are created by purchasing positive price volume (VPMCI >.5) and then selling when the price-volume momentum turns strongly negative (VPMCI<.2). Notice the lack of many yellow shoots within the blue mountain chart in Figure 9. These yellow shoots represent the percentage of cash holdings. Notice that in most all of these volume price momentum tests, the models remain close to fully invested, as observed by the absence of yellow in the blue mountain chart.

THE VOLUME MOMENTUM ASYMMETRY FACTOR

Three distinct aspects of volume momentum principles comprise the Volume Factor. The first principle is internal strength. Internal strength is the present momentum of a security versus its past momentum. Internal strength answers the following question: Is the security's momentum gaining or weakening compared to its past?

The second principle is the relative strength of the security. RS determines if the security's momentum is strengthening or weakening compared to other securities, indexes, and markets. Perhaps a security appreciates and gains internal momentum. However, are comparative securities rising even faster?

The third aspect infuses volume data into the relative strength computation. RSI (Relative Strength Index) is modified to MFI (Money Flow Index). Additionally, RSI may be combined with the VPCI (Volume Price Confirmation Indicator), adjusting RSI to price-volume trend asymmetry. These computations add volume (force) to the momentum (inertia) calculations.

The fourth and final principle is volume-price momentum asymmetry, contrasting price momentum to volume-price momentum. The difference between price momentum and volume-price momentum creates Volume Factor Momentum Asymmetry. For example, the price momentum is strong, but is it stronger or weaker than its volume-price momentum? The wider the asymmetry between volume-price momentum and price momentum, the stronger or weaker the indication depending upon the direction of asymmetry. For example, when volume-price momentum confirms the price, the asymmetry between price and volume is above 0.5, as indicated by the Volume Momentum Indicator. In contrast, if volume is contradicting an upward-rising price momentum, then the asymmetry between price and volume momentum is below 0.5, a bearish indication. In this way, strongly negative Volume Momentum Indicators contradict the bullish price momentum, whereas strongly positive Volume Momentum Indicators confirm the bullish price momentum.

Next, let's combine the law of action versus reaction, or, in other words, Volume-Price Momentum Asymmetry, to our volume-modified internal relative strength study. Remember that previously, this strategy was ineffective in adding alpha to the benchmark. We will adjust this internal relative strength formula with volume-price momentum asymmetry, creating Volume Factor Internal Momentum. In this revised formula, we will subtract RSI from both the VPCI-RSI and the MFI: that is, VPCI-RSI minus RSI plus MFI minus RSI. Specifically, Volume Factor's Internal Strength mathematical formula is as follows: ⟦VF⟧_Mom=MFI+⟦VPCI⟧_RSI-2*RSI. We then retest the survivor biased Russell 3000 universe with the identical process employed in our earlier studies, but this time with a start date of April 10, 2023, using the revised Volume Factor Internal Momentum formula. The results of the study are listed in Figures 16 and17 below.

Figure 16: Original Volume-Modified Internal Relative Strength Study, 01/11/2002–04/10/2023

	EW BM	1	2	3	4	5	6	7	8	9	10
Final Account ($K)	123.584	121.292	93.145	111.134	104.006	99.895	89.212	116.029	135.337	150.800	208.105
Best Month	20.0%	18.6%	16.3%	14.9%	16.5%	21.1%	18.1%	20.2%	27.5%	30.2%	33.6%
Worst Month	-19.8%	-20.6%	-18.8%	-19.5%	-20.8%	-22.1%	-21.0%	-21.8%	-22.4%	-20.5%	-22.6%
Best 12 Months	97.8%	114.9%	96.1	98.5%	101.6%	92.3%	89.9%	95.9%	88.5%	116.5%	135.2%
Worst 12 Months	-32.5%	-48.5%	-47.7%	-41.4%	-43.6%	-44.3%	-45.0%	-39.8%	-40.4%	-40.4%	-32.8%
Worst Drawdown	-57.1%	-60.0%	-60.1%	-56.8%	60.6%	-56.2%	-59.5%	-54.4%	-57.3%	-58.9%	-56.8%
Current Drawdown	-13.1%	16.2%	-16.5%	-11.3%	-7.0%	-8.4%	-11.7%	-9.5%	-12.9%	-17.7%	-23.3%
Effective APR	12.6%	12.5%	11.1%	12.0%	11.6%	11.4%	10.8%	12.2%	13.0%	13.6%	15.3%
Average Annual Return	15.7%	15.2%	14.1%	14.6%	14.5%	14.2%	14.2%	15.2%	16.4%	17.7%	20.4%
Standard Deviation	18.7%	18.2%	17.6%	17.7%	17.5%	18.9%	18.9%	19.8%	20.5	22.2%	23.8%
R-Squared	1.00	0.78	0.89	0.94	0.95	0.97	0.97	0.96	0.94	0.92	0.88
Correlation	1.00	0.88	0.94	0.97	0.97	0.99	0.98	0.98	0.97	0.96	0.94
Sharpe Ratio (1% Risk Free)	0.68	0.67	0.60	0.66	0.68	0.61	0.62	0.64	0.72	0.64	0.68
Information Ratio	0.00	-0.01	-0.25	-0.16	-0.25	-0.33	-0.45	-0.03	0.15	0.24	0.40
Beta	1.00	0.86	0.89	0.92	0.91	1.00	1.00	1.04	1.06	1.14	1.19
Upside Capture	1.00	0.93	0.90	0.95	0.93	0.96	0.96	1.02	1.05	1.11	1.19
Downside Capture	1.00	0.87	0.91	0.95	0.93	1.00	1.02	1.04	1.05	1.09	1.14
MTD	-0.43%	-2.20%	-0.61%	-0.26%	-0.04%	0.26%	0.44%	0.44%	0.15%	0.23%	-2.16%
QTD	-0.43%	-2.20%	-0.61%	-0.26%	-0.04%	0.26%	0.44%	0.44%	0.15%	0.23%	-2.16%
YTD	1.22%	-1.14%	-0.21%	3.99%	2.65%	2.11%	3.46%	3.27%	0.97%	0.29%	-3.09%
1-Yr	-6.07	-11.65%	-10.15%	-3.58%	0.67%	-2.31%	-5.00%	-1.86%	-4.82%	-6.85%	-14.48%
3-Yr (ann.)	20.88%	23.46%	19.81%	22.32%	23.27%	22.02%	19.50%	20.77%	18.09%	23.21%	15.14%
5-Yr (ann.)	9.68%	8.19%	8.94%	11.39%	13.10%	9.39%	7.79%	9.11%	10.50%	9.59%	7.51%
10-Yr (ann.)	11.66%	11.46%	9.32%	11.75%	11.70%	10.70%	11.83%	11.56%	13.21%	12.95%	11.05%
2003	60.34%	64.91%	67.06%	53.67%	45.89%	64.33%	50.44%	64.01%	52.78%	62.82%	73.51%
2004	23.45%	27.97%	23.54%	24.02%	21.86%	16.93%	24.53%	21.16%	28.23%	21.47%	24.28%
2005	9.46%	14.01%	9.14%	7.58%	10.86%	6.41%	8.27%	12.34%	8.99%	5.66%	11.20%
2006	21.09%	32.98%	22.61%	19.62%	18.57%	15.87%	15.62%	14.01%	20.17%	21.59%	30.11%
2007	-0.57%	18.15%	11.12%	5.48%	-0.28%	5.33%	-7.13%	-1.66%	-9.76%	-14.06%	-10.17%
2008	-31.82%	-34.15%	-38.47%	-33.81%	-35.00%	-34.37%	-33.36%	-33.09%	-26.00%	-29.29%	-23.56%
2009	45.57%	13.99%	33.72%	31.95%	37.08%	45.05%	50.61%	51.37%	45.03%	64.90%	88.92%
2010	26.70%	18.38%	17.95%	32.42%	28.14%	24.09%	20.79%	22.27%	24.83%	42.84%	36.36%
2011	-2.32%	-5.03%	3.44%	-4.27%	-1.19%	-2.95%	-1.91%	-2.49%	1.26%	-8.08%	-2.85%
2012	18.93%	9.46%	10.70%	12.67%	20.88%	16.84%	15.54%	18.12%	23.16%	26.34%	36.54%
2013	39.55%	40.32%	38.19%	43.23%	42.62%	35.04%	45.36%	37.21%	43.34%	38.88%	31.21%
2014	9.96%	9.17%	7.95%	4.75%	5.86%	9.80%	10.28%	11.53%	11.48%	12.45%	16.30%
2015	-2.84%	5.34%	-2.37%	-0.96%	-6.80%	-1.85%	-0.15%	-3.42%	-3.50%	-7.93%	-6.63%
2016	25.26%	21.12%	15.16%	21.20%	18.47%	22.64%	24.54%	33.16%	28.36%	36.97%	31.47%
2017	15.84%	16.01%	7.82%	12.62%	15.47%	12.60%	16.98%	12.97%	20.06%	21.79%	21.89%
2018	-9.48%	-11.15%	-9.21%	-4.27%	-6.13%	-10.56%	-5.87%	-10.52%	-11.60%	-11.91%	-13.87%
2019	26.58%	19.47%	25.85%	29.86%	27.40%	26.53%	23.25%	25.57%	36.50%	25.39%	25.47%
2020	18.05%	18.61%	21.74%	15.94%	30.86%	6.50%	8.22%	11.45%	11.65%	19.96%	25.12%
2021	31.52%	30.19%	30.41%	33.01%	22.60%	34.79%	30.80%	29.33%	22.50%	29.37%	30.39%
2022	12.25%	16.14%	-15.11%	-13.56%	-8.13%	-8.06%	-11.99%	-9.45%	-9.98%	-14.30%	-16.97%

IRS = RSI + MFI + VPCI_RSI

Figure 17: Price/Volume Asymmetry Volume Factor with Internal Momentum Formula, 01/11/2002–04/10/2023, VFIM = MFI + VPCI_RSI – (2*RSI)

Note that adding Volume Factor Momentum (volume-price momentum asymmetry) to our volume- modified internal relative strength equation dramatically improved our for-

	EW BM	1	2	3	4	5	6	7	8	9	10
Final Account ($k)	123.584	450.59	143.819	115.936	106.489	84.024	90.063	95.93	101.191	98.452	99.162
Best Month	20%	31.30%	26.00%	22.90%	23.50%	20.30%	16.70%	18.00%	15.20%	17.90%	13.80%
Worst Month	-19.80%	-20.50%	-21.30%	-24.00%	-22.40%	-20.40%	-21.20%	-18.80%	-18.80%	-21.00%	-18.80%
Best 12 Months	97.80%	219.70%	127.00%	116.00%	105.30%	85.70%	90.10%	83.30%	76.10%	71.90%	76.60%
Worst 12 Months	-32.50%	-49.50%	-47.20%	-44.80%	-45.60%	-44.90%	-41.10%	-34.10%	-34.90%	-38.70%	-41.60%
Worst Drawdown*	-57.10%	-66.70%	-64.20%	-59.90%	-61.10%	-61.80%	-56.40%	-48.60%	-48.00%	-50.80%	-54.60%
Current Drawdown*	-13.10%	-15.90%	-15.60%	-9.10%	-11.10%	-7.70%	-10.90%	-17.40%	-17.20%	-12.90%	-19.20%
Effective APR	12.60%	19.60%	13.40%	12.20%	11.80%	10.50%	10.90%	11.20%	11.50%	11.40%	11.40%
Average Annual Return	15.70%	27.30%	17.50%	16%	14.60%	12.90%	13.80%	13.60%	13.90%	13.80%	13.90%
Standard Deviation**	18.70%	25.60%	22.00%	20.20%	19.70%	18.50%	18.20%	18.00%	16.90%	17.20%	16.70%
R-Squared	1	0.87	0.95	0.96	0.97	0.97	0.97	0.97	0.95	0.93	0.88
Correlation	1	0.93	0.98	0.98	0.99	0.98	0.98	0.98	0.97	0.97	0.94
Sharp Ratio (1% Risk Free)	0.68	0.63	0.65	0.64	0.62	0.62	0.66	0.7	0.69	0.74	0.63
Information Ratio	0	0.74	0.26	0.01	-0.16	-0.58	-0.49	-0.41	-0.29	-0.27	-0.22
Beta	1	1.28	1.15	1.06	1.04	0.97	0.95	0.95	0.88	0.89	0.84
Upside Capture	1	1.32	1.12	1.03	1.01	0.95	0.93	0.95	0.91	0.91	0.87
Downside Capture	1	1.14	1.14	1.05	1.04	1.01	0.97	0.99	0.91	0.91	0.85
MTD	-0.43%	-0.61%	-0.25%	-0.92%	0.41%	0.44%	0.23%	-1.16%	-1.16%	-0.07%	-1.26%
QTD	-0.43%	-0.61%	-0.25%	-0.92%	0.41%	0.44%	0.23%	-1.16%	-1.16%	-0.07%	-1.26%
YTD	1.22%	2.30%	0.49%	2.43%	3.76%	4.99%	1.43%	-1.56%	-0.99%	0.05%	-0.63%
1-Yr	-6.07%	-9.84%	-9.16%	-5.20%	-2.79%	-0.95%	-6.27%	-7.10%	-6.97%	-4.65%	-7.83%
3-Yr (ann.)	20.88%	32.81%	23.26%	22.49%	21.47%	22.01%	20.43%	15.06%	15.54%	18.31%	16.22%
5-Yr (ann.)	9.68%	15.60%	9.37%	11.53%	9.07%	10.06%	10.22%	7.04%	6.18%	8.82%	-7.50%
10-Yr (ann.)	11.66%	16.11%	12.11%	11.61%	10.90%	11.71%	10.76%	9.46%	10.44%	12.16%	10.18%
2003	60.34%	142.93%	67.81%	62.90%	56.80%	42.85%	47.88%	48.10%	43.42%	38.08%	63.87%
2004	23.45%	29.44%	24.28%	24.99%	20.51%	20.54%	19.97%	23.20%	23.18%	22.94%	24.75%
2005	9.46%	11.37%	13.36%	7.67%	7.08%	7.30%	11.19%	7.65%	8.64%	10.60%	9.25%
2006	21.09%	31.99%	25.42%	24.72%	23.27%	20.37%	17.32%	17.30%	20.30%	18.85%	11.86%
2007	-0.57%	-7.13%	-6.50%	-3.33%	-3.76%	-3.80%	-0.20%	0.05%	4.99%	7.48%	6.44%
2008	-31.82%	-32.21%	-33.43%	-32.88%	-34.49%	-34.49%	-32.26%	-22.83%	-30.63%	-29.28%	-36.41%
2009	45.57%	110.29%	61.94%	62.52%	48.88%	34.66%	32.07%	32.57%	34.04%	25.79%	20.83%
2010	26.70%	40.97%	33.42%	28.13%	21.50%	18.47%	28.98%	26.81%	23.85%	21.23%	23.87%
2011	-2.32%	-4.22%	-2.75%	-7.05%	-3.47%	-4.04%	-3.50%	-2.54%	-1.67%	-0.93%	6.94%
2012	18.93%	23.41%	15.42%	17.57%	22.17%	18.04%	23.28%	18.47%	19.28%	13.55%	17.62%
2013	39.55%	40.50%	40.08%	30.41%	42.12%	38.27%	39.97%	38.42%	44.76%	38.65%	42.17%
2014	9.96%	10.52%	13.87%	8.06%	10.64%	11.38%	5.71%	9.18%	7.61%	10.68%	11.50%
2015	-2.84%	-13.14%	-6.20%	-0.78%	-4.50%	-4.98%	0.85%	-2.62%	0.91%	4.99%	-2.66%
2016	25.26%	53.95%	40.21%	24.76%	22.27%	25.48%	13.84%	22.60%	22.15%	16.58%	14.14%
2017	15.84%	16.54%	10.26%	11.65%	15.35%	16.64%	14.44%	13.20%	18.52%	22.12%	19.83%
2018	-9.48%	-13.39%	-10.93%	-9.57%	-9.90%	-11.73%	-9.24%	-9.88%	-8.89%	-6.26%	-5.07%
2019	26.58%	29.11%	28.28%	28.15%	29.36%	26.06%	27.05%	26.59%	21.55%	30.08%	19.19%
2020	18.05%	47.35%	26.64%	19.23%	11.13%	16.04%	14.94%	13.48%	11.90%	4.16%	15.49%
2021	31.52%	44.32%	22.32%	31.70%	30.16%	29.77%	33.75%	26.12%	27.96%	37.59%	30.30%
2022	-12.25%	-16.24%	-13.32%	-9.33%	-12.59%	-9.05%	-10.28%	-13.01%	-13.34%	-10.35%	-15.14%

merly unproductive top decile system. Applying the volume-price asymmetry adjustment vaults the returns to 19.6% compared to the benchmark's effective APR of 12.6% and the 12.5% original internal strength. Moving away from the top decile toward the middle deciles, the returns drop until bottoming out at decile 5. After decile 5, the returns improve slightly but still underperform the benchmark.

If volume-price asymmetry can fix a broken system, can it also improve a winning system? Early in this study, we demonstrated how relative strength (RS) extremes added alpha to both the first decile (overbought) and the last decile (oversold). We will apply the same volume-price asymmetry concept to this successful external relative strength system. Once again, we will employ the identical process of subtracting RSI from both the VPCI-RSI and MFI formulas (Volume Factor Momentum). The result of this calculation is the asymmetry between price momentum and volume-price momentum. Combining volume-price asymmetry with external relative strength creates our Volume Factor External Momentum equation.

[(RS+C)*(1+MFI/RSI (1+(VPCI_RSI)/RSI (1+RSI/100)))]*((MFI+VPCI_RSI+RSI)/100)

Infusing volume-price momentum asymmetry into relative strength boosted the already outperforming top decile from over 16% effective APR to over 18%. One might expect outperformance in the RS top decile, as top decile Volume Factor Momentum (volume-price momentum asymmetry) outperformed in isolation. In contrast, in the oversold deciles, 5 through 10, Volume Factor Momentum underperformed in the oversold deciles. However, applying Volume Factor Asymmetry Momentum to the deeply oversold stocks in decile 10 largely maintained RS's strong outperformance of over 19% effective APR.

Figure 18: Volume-Modified External Relative Strength with Volume Asymmetry

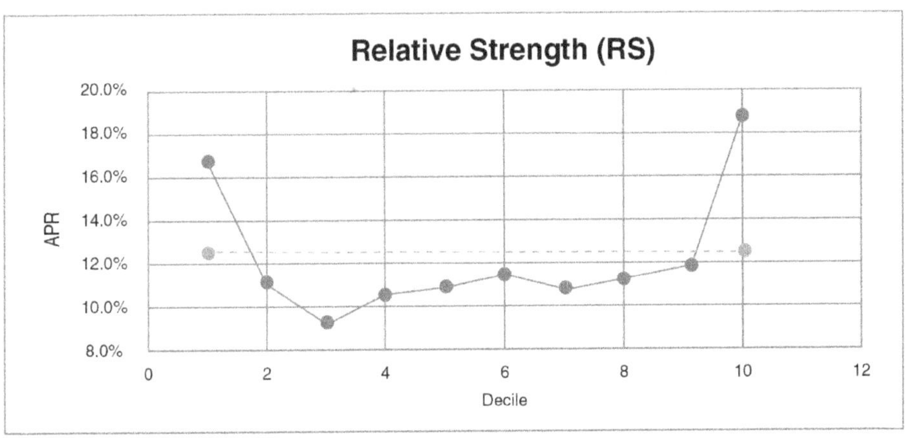

Next, we will compile all of the principles we've covered into one master formula.

VF=[VPCI_RSI*(1+((MFI+VPCI_RSI)/100))*(1+((RSI+VPCI_RSI)/100))*(1+((RSI+MFI)/100))]+[(RS+C)*(1+MFI/RSI (1+(VPCI_RSI)/RSI (1+RSI/100)))]*((MFI+VPCI_RSI+RSI)/100)

That is, RSI (Relative Strength Index) represents internal relative strength, and RS (relative strength) exemplifies external relative strength, MFI-volume-weighted internal relative strength, VPCI-RSI for internal volume-trend adjusted relative strength, and VMI (MFI/RSI), indicating volume-price momentum asymmetry.

A $10,000 investment in this system's top decile stocks beginning on January 11, 2002, would have grown to $259,631 by February 10, 2023. This compares to the benchmark growth of $131,964, which equates to an effective APR of 16.69% compared to the benchmark return of 13.01%. This all-encompassing volume system also displayed favorable upside/downside capture ratios, with an upside capture of 1.09 paired with a favorable downside capture of 0.97.

Figure 19: Volume Factor RS+ IRS+VM Top Decile Russell 3000

```
********************* RESULTS SUMMARY ***********************
GROSS-OF-FEES
VF: Buy Decile 1, Rebal Frequency 13 Wks.
11-Jan-2002 to 10-Feb-2023:          Model        EW Universe
--------------------------------------------------------------
Final Account ($k):                  259.631        131.964
Best Month:                           19.42%         20.00%
Worst Month:                         -20.86%        -19.89%
Best 12 Months:                      162.23%         98.03%
Worst 12 Months:                     -50.17%        -42.30%
Worst Drawdown*:                     -62.99%        -57.14%
Current Drawdown*:                   -10.03%         -7.49%
Effective APR:                        16.69%         13.01%
Average Annual Return:                20.68%         15.67%
Standard Deviation**:                 20.87%         18.74%
R-Squared:                             0.81           1.00
Correlation:                           0.90           1.00
Sharp Ratio (1% Risk Free):            0.67           0.68
Information Ratio:                     0.40
Beta:                                  1.00
Upside Capture:                        1.09
Downside Capture:                      0.97
----------------------------------------------------------
 *Derived from daily data.
**Derived from monthly return data.
```

Figure 20: Russell 3000 Volume Factor RS+ IRS+VM Top Decile $10K Growth, 01/11/2002–02/10/2023

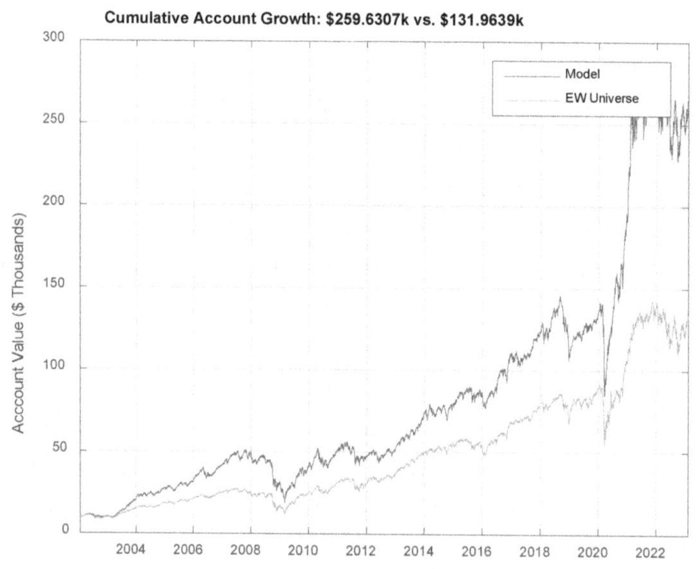

Figure 21: Russell 3000 Volume Factor RS+ IRS+VM Top Decile Yearly Returns

Year	Model	EW Universe	
2003	106.57%	60.40%	X
2004	34.80%	23.47%	X
2005	12.76%	9.35%	X
2006	33.65%	21.13%	X
2007	16.84%	-0.63%	X
2008	-34.87%	-31.84%	
2009	27.26%	45.52%	
2010	25.70%	26.91%	
2011	-7.41%	-2.25%	
2012	10.03%	18.88%	
2013	43.05%	39.64%	X
2014	7.14%	9.97%	
2015	7.42%	-2.81%	X
2016	27.57%	25.25%	X
2017	13.34%	15.87%	
2018	-9.87%	-9.38%	
2019	23.26%	26.57%	
2020	41.49%	18.13%	X
2021	48.58%	31.59%	X
2022	-13.73%	-12.37%	

X = Outperform annually 50.00% of the time.

Although the top decile of high momentum/overbought stocks performed very well, there was an even more impressive decile. That decile was once again the tenth decile, containing deeply oversold stocks with elements of volume contradiction. Over the course of the study, the tenth decile stocks produced an annual percentage return of 19.25% versus the benchmark universe of 13.01%. A $10,000 investment in this all-inclusive model grew to $410,119 compared to the equally weighted universe, which grew to $131,964. The risks of this model were elevated with a 1.26 beta and a 1.13 downside capture. However, the upside capture was 1.29, and the model outperformed 70% of the time on an annual basis.

Figure 22: Volume Factor RS+ IRS+VM Bottom Decile Russell 3000

******************** RESULTS SUMMARY ********************

GROSS-OF-FEES

VF: Buy Decile 10, Rebal Frequency 13 Wks.

11-Jan-2002 to 10-Feb-2023:	Model	EW Universe
Final Account ($k):	410.119	131.964
Best Month:	38.52%	20.00%
Worst Month:	-22.59%	-19.89%
Best 12 Months:	154.85%	98.03%
Worst 12 Months:	-32.88%	-42.30%
Worst Drawdown*:	-56.94%	-57.14%
Current Drawdown*:	-16.93%	-7.49%
Effective APR:	19.25%	13.01%
Average Annual Return:	23.49%	15.67%
Standard Deviation**:	25.73%	18.74%
R-Squared:	0.84	1.00
Correlation:	0.92	1.00
Sharp Ratio (1% Risk Free):	0.70	0.68
Information Ratio:	0.62	
Beta:	1.26	
Upside Capture:	1.29	
Downside Capture:	1.13	

*Derived from daily data.

**Derived from monthly return data.

Figure 22: Russell 3000 Volume Factor RS+IRS+VM Bottom Decile $10K Growth, 1/11/2002–02/10/2023

Figure 23: Russell 3000 Volume Factor RS+ IRS+VM Bottom Decile Yearly Returns

Year	Model	EW Universe	
2003	79.87%	60.40%	X
2004	24.66%	23.47%	X
2005	9.93%	9.35%	X
2006	29.10%	21.13%	X
2007	-9.97%	-0.63%	
2008	-22.11%	-31.84%	X
2009	103.68%	45.52%	X
2010	35.82%	26.91%	X
2011	-3.50%	-2.25%	
2012	40.79%	18.88%	X
2013	32.65%	39.64%	
2014	15.02%	9.97%	X
2015	-8.41%	-2.81%	
2016	38.58%	25.25%	X
2017	24.63%	15.87%	X
2018	-13.18%	-9.38%	
2019	28.04%	26.57%	X
2020	51.69%	18.13%	X
2021	32.52%	31.59%	X
2022	-19.93%	-12.37%	

X = Outperform annually 70.00% of the time.

VOLUME FACTOR MOMENTUM

In review, our all-inclusive volume momentum model provides value at both ends of the extremes: strong momentum as well as weak momentum. However, among the models included in the all-encompassing momentum model, Volume Factor Internal Strength was a large detractor in the first decile results. Since we have evidence that Volume Factor Internal Strength is not a beneficial model, we will not include internal strength in the Volume Factor Momentum algorithm. Similarly, solely focusing on decile 1 excludes the informative properties of the deeply oversold stocks with volume contraction in decile 10. However, eliminating the decile 1 overbought stocks also reduces opportunity.

To capture the volume benefits offered at both ends of the extremes, we will substitute relative strength (RS) with absolute relative strength (ABS RS). Absolute relative strength is the absolute value of relative strength, where positive relative strength is unadjusted and negative relative strength is its inverse. For example, the absolute value of +5 is +5, whereas the absolute value of -5 is also +5. In this way, absolute values have practical uses, such as determining how far something traveled that went 5 feet one way and 5 feet back. By substituting RS with ABS RS, we not only draw from the most positively momentous (overbought) issues, but also the most negatively momentous (oversold) issues. Additionally, by employing ABS RS to Volume Factor External Momentum, we not only apply volume analysis to the overbought issues, but simultaneously incorporate the oversold issues as well. This ABS RS approach exploits the "U-shaped" informational properties originating from both volume and external relative strength, as informational value is often discovered on the tails of their curves.

In this way, Volume Factor Momentum combines both the qualities of ABS relative strength of Volume Factor External Momentum combined with Volume Factor Momentum Asymmetry. We tested the Volume Factor Momentum model from January 11, 2022, to April 10, 2023, using the same database and process earlier employed, specifically, a 26-week Volume Factor Momentum in the surviving members of the Russell 3000. Each security was equally weighted. The model was reranked and reconstructed quarterly employing the Volume Factor Momentum algorithm ABS(RS)+(VP-CI-RSI)+(MFI-RSI) ranking.

Figure 24: Volume Factor Momentum by Decile Chart, 01/11/2002–04/10/2023

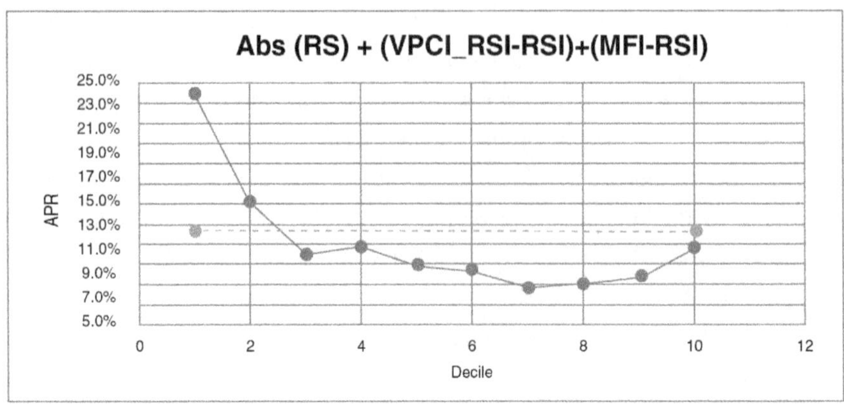

The results of combining the positive characteristics of absolute relative strength with volume analysis were quite impressive. Over the course of the study, the equally weighted benchmark universe grew from $10,000 to $123,584, whereas employing the Volume Factor Momentum model grew the model to $1,053.143! In terms of effective annual percentage return, Volume Factor Momentum returned an astounding 24.5% compared to the universe's effective APR of 12.6%. On an average annual return (AAR) basis, Volume Factor Momentum produced a 31.7% AAR, more than doubling the universe's AAR of 15.7%. The Volume Factor Momentum model also posted a high information ratio of 0.9, which is quite unusual given the 20-year plus time frame of the study. Although Volume Factor Momentum's down capture was high at 1.26, the upside capture of 1.55 more than made up for the extra risk assumed.

Figure 25: Volume Factor Momentum by Deciles, 01/11/2002–04/10/2023

	EW BM	1	2	3	4	5	6	7	8	9	10
Final Account ($K)	123.584	1053.143	201.219	112.835	117.281	90.034	78.349	59.962	63.474	71.010	90.758
Best Month	20.0%	35.9%	31.3%	23.7%	19.8%	16.4%	17.2%	14.6%	14.9%	16.2%	14.5%
Worst Month	-19.8%	-19.8%	-21.2%	-22.2%	-20.4%	-20.8%	-19.9%	-20.1%	-20.2%	-20.2%	-16.2%
Best 12 Months	97.8%	212.8%	145.2%	129.8%	111.1%	82.2%	83.6%	71.5%	68.8%	70.8%	56.4%
Worst 12 Months	-32.9%	-50.9%	-46.0%	-44.8%	-42.6%	-38.1%	-40.4%	-42.2%	-43.0%	-41.1%	-32.9%
Worst Drawdown	-57.1%	-65.5%	-61.1%	-61.3%	-57.8%	-53.6%	56.0%	-56.3%	-56.5%	-55.6%	-47.4%
Current Drawdown	-13.1%	-24.1%	-16.6%	-9.7%	-9.8%	-10.7%	-12.8%	-9.6%	-15.9%	-13.1%	-12.8%
Effective APR	12.6%	24.5%	15.2%	12.1%	12.3%	10.9%	-10.20%	8.8%	9.1%	9.7%	10.9%
Average Annual Return	15.7%	31.7%	19.9%	16.4%	15.5%	13.8%	12.6%	11.2%	11.7%	11.8%	13.3%
Standard Deviation	18.7%	29.2%	22.9%	20.6%	19.0%	18.0%	17.6%	17.2%	16.5%	16.6%	15.5%
R-Squared	1.00	0.84	0.94	0.96	0.97	0.97	0.97	0.96	0.94	0.93	-0.89
Correlation	1.00	0.92	0.97	0.98	0.99	0.98	0.98	0.98	0.97	0.97	0.95
Sharpe Ratio (1% Risk Free)	0.68	0.69	0.66	0.55	0.68	0.66	0.62	0.59	0.58	0.64	0.73
Information Ratio	0.00	0.90	0.50	0.00	-0.07	-0.48	-0.72	-0.94	-0.77	-0.61	-0.31
Beta	1.00	1.43	1.19	1.08	1.00	0.95	0.93	0.90	0.86	0.86	0.78
Upside Capture	1.00	1.55	1.18	1.05	1.01	0.93	0.91	0.86	0.83	0.85	0.82
Downside Capture	1.00	1.26	1.14	1.09	1.02	0.97	0.97	0.95	0.90	0.90	0.79
MTD	-0.43%	-1.21%	-0.72%	-0.84%	-0.17%	-0.99%	1.11%	-0.45%	8.74E-04	-0.29%	-0.87%
QTD	-0.43%	-1.21%	-0.72%	-0.84%	-0.17%	-0.99%	1.11%	-0.45%	8.74E-04	-0.29%	-0.87%
YTD	1.22%	-0.12%	2.91%	3.32%	4.91%	0.38%	3.89%	0.79%	-2.05%	0.10%	-1.83%
1-Yr	-6.07%	-17.68%	-9.86%	-1.35%	-4.55%	-4.07%	4.20%	-0.63%	-7.17%	-4.89%	-5.68%
3-Yr (ann.)	20.88%	34.91%	24.84%	21.31%	24.09%	17.79%	17.80%	17.61%	13.93%	17.16%	15.80%
5-Yr (ann.)	9.68%	19.59%	9.92%	9.11%	12.20%	7.33%	8.10%	7.16%	4.38%	7.49%	8.57%
10-Yt (ann.)	11.66%	19.67%	11.53%	9.77%	13.01%	9.40%	10.25%	10.25%	8.83%	11.11%	11.08%

Throughout the 20 full years of the study, Volume Factor Momentum outperformed the benchmark universe 14 out of 20 times, a beat rate of 70%. In the course of the study, the benchmark universe finished the year up 14 times. Of these 14 occurrences, only once did the benchmark universe outperform Volume Factor Momentum (2014 +9.96% -vs- +9.5%). In the years when the market was down, the equally weighted benchmark universe outperformed Volume Factor Momentum by 1.15% per down year. When the benchmark universe was up, Volume Factor Momentum outperformed by 23.65%. There was one year (2007) when the benchmark was down and the Volume Factor Momentum model was up. There were no years when the Volume Factor Momentum model was down and the benchmark universe was up.

Figure 26: Russell 3000 Volume Factor Momentum Top Decile Yearly Returns

Year	EW BM	VFM Decile 1
2003	60.34%	167.53%
2004	23.45%	39.03%
2005	9.46%	16.95%
2006	21.09%	38.58%
2007	-0.57%	7.68%
2008	-31.82%	-32.74%
2009	45.57%	88.82%
2010	26.70%	35.89%
2011	-2.32%	-5.85%
2012	18.93%	31.20%
2013	39.55%	48.18%
2014	9.96%	9.50%
2015	-2.84%	-9.30%
2016	25.26%	47.62%
2017	15.84%	23.93%
2018	-9.48%	-10.44%
2019	26.58%	33.04%
2020	18.05%	73.56%
2021	31.52%	49.56%
2022	-12.25%	-17.80%

CONCLUSION

One challenge associated with momentum strategies is their inclination to allocate resources toward currently successful assets. However, the uncertainty lies in whether these trends will persist into the future. This is where the concept of volume confirmation becomes very relevant. In this study, we examined volume's role in market momentum, applying the laws of motion.

1. Law: An object at rest remains at rest, and an object in motion remains in motion at a constant speed and in a straight line unless acted on by an unbalanced force.
   Analogy: Volume is the unbalanced force causing price change.
2. Law: The acceleration of an object depends on the mass of the object and the amount of force applied.
   Analogy: Price acceleration (momentum) is powered through volume.
3. Law: Whenever one object exerts a force on another object, the second object exerts an equal and opposite on the first.
   Analogy: The difference between momentum and volume-adjusted momentum exposes the asymmetry between price momentum and volume.

The First Law of Motion, inertia, states "An object at rest remains at rest, and an object in motion remains in motion at a constant speed and in a straight line unless acted on by an unbalanced force." In momentum analysis, the object is price, and with unbalanced force, is volume. We then studied two types of momentum indicators: internal (RSI) and external (RS) momentum. Neither of these indicators directly contains volume data (absence of external forces). We found inconsistencies, with internal momentum acting as a consistent market factor, but we found large agreement that external momentum was a strong market factor in upside momentum and possibly in downside momentum as well.

Next, we turned to Newton's Second Law of Motion, Force: "The acceleration of an object (price) depends on the mass of the object and the amount of force (volume) applied." Force is a vector quantity with magnitude and direction. Likewise, volume is the quantity associated with price change. To account for the law of force, we amended internal (RSI) and external strength (RS) to include volume data. Amending these momentum indicators with volume demonstrated improved performance in the top decile results.

After covering Newton's First and Second Laws of Motion, we then moved on to the third, Action and Reaction: "Whenever one object exerts a force on another object, the second object exerts an equal and opposite force on the first." In an exchange, every buyer is matched with a seller, and every seller is matched with a buyer. Buyers exert demand, or buying pressure, and sellers offer resistance. The difference between the forces of demand (buying pressure) and supply (selling pressure) is the catalyst for price change. Calculating the difference between price momentum and volume-weighted momentum exposes the force being exerted upon price momentum. Not only did price-volume momentum asymmetry produce strong results on its own, but it also demonstrated improved results when infused with other momentum strategies.

Finally, utilizing the information discovered, we infused the positive properties of price-volume momentum asymmetry with absolute relative strength, forming Volume Factor Momentum. Fueled by integrating volume analysis into momentum analysis, Volume Factor Momentum showed very strong returns against the benchmark universe (24.5% -VS-12.6%), with a high information ratio (0.9) and a high success rate (70%), especially during up markets (100%).

When examining the data from over two decades of Volume Factor studies, it becomes evident that momentum analysis focused solely on price velocity overlooks a crucial element. Taking this into account, our exploration of Volume Factor Momentum comprehensively integrates the Volume Factor, enriching our understanding of volume's pivotal but largely untapped role in momentum analysis.

CHAPTER 5:

RISK MANAGEMENT—MATH ALWAYS WINS

"If you're gonna play the game, boy, you gotta learn to play it right.

You got to know when to hold 'em, know when to fold 'em
Know when to walk away, know when to run
You never count your money when you're sittin' at the table
There'll be time enough for countin', when the dealin's done

Now, every gambler knows, the secret to survivin'
Is knowing what to throw away, knowing what to keep
'Cause every hand's a winner and every hand's a loser."

– Don Schiltz The Gambler

Some of the data presented in this chapter is hypothetical and back-tested data. This data is not based on any advisory client assets. Past performance of a model is not a guarantee of future results. Actual performance may vary significantly from the hypothetical results shown. Please see the section titled 'Important Information Regarding Hypothetical, Back-Tested Performance' for a full description of this data and the limitations associated with it.

Thus far, we have added a remarkable amount of alpha (return above the benchmark) through volume factors. Although the evidence presented in this book builds our case that volume is indeed a powerful market factor, perhaps even the king of all factors, this book's mission is the achievement of financial outcomes. Additionally, a much more effective way to build wealth exists beyond merely focusing on the top line. Risk management is the true and narrow path to successful financial outcomes. *"Risk Management is the missing piece of the puzzle that helps safeguard investments against market volatility."* Investors do not like fluctuations; they fear corrections, but it is bear markets that destroy financial plans. For this reason, risk management is mission one in all of our Volume Factor models.

In the end, investing is all about creating desired financial outcomes. For financial advisors, outcomes are the contrast between a successful client-advisor relationship generating recurring revenue and the failure of their client's financial plan. These outcomes determine if a retiree can enjoy their retirement, is forced back into the labor market, or dies forgoing many of their life's dreams and aspirations. In the case of endowments, financial outcomes dictate the advancement or the abandonment of their mission and its intended impact. In the case of an estate, financial outcomes mean the difference between leaving a legacy to their loved ones or becoming a burden to their would-be heirs. Make no mistake about it: Monetarily consistent, planned financial outcomes are the end game—not financial returns.

The advancement of successful investment and financial planning outcomes begins and ends by preserving capital and minimizing drawdowns as the A1 top priority. Over the long haul, equities are by far the best option to grow wealth. Over a full market cycle, if the owners (equity) cannot make more than the lenders (debt), our economy cannot survive, as it lacks the incentive to undertake the risk needed to create wealth through work. Thus, equities are the *de facto* investment vehicle for long-term financial plans. Yet, equities are volatile. Over the short and intermediate term, declines in equities can easily blow up the most conservative plans in the withdrawal phase (for example, when retirees are pulling money out of their retirement funds). Managing risk and volatility is an art of survival. Below are four founding principles that are helpful in delivering successful financial outcomes.

FOUNDING PRINCIPLES

Wealth is primarily built through capital preservation.

Lower volatility develops a more tolerant and rational investor.

Low drawdowns lead to more sustainable withdrawal strategies.

Markets are efficient in the mean but often irrational during extremes.

The art of survival begins with the endgame in mind. With investing, that endgame is knowing your exit. Risk management is the path to successful financial outcomes. The key to preserving wealth is surely determined by the decision regarding which investments to purchase (asset allocation). But, more importantly, deciding when to sell or exit positions (post-modern asset allocation theory) determines the outcome of investing. Yet, it is much easier for most investors to form a purchasing decision than to develop a selling discipline. Fear can be a greater motivator than greed. Even the best of investors will sometimes sell out of panic at exactly the wrong time.

Why are exits difficult? The first reason is lack of emphasis. Most investors carefully plan their entries but fail to plan their exits. The second is lack of control. After an investment is placed, the market dictates the conditions, not the investor. The third is lack of discipline. Investors tend to only be content when exiting at or near the high.

But consider this thought: The key to investing is protecting one's downside. This is especially true when employing a momentum, deep-value strategy, or other high volatility strategies. Likewise, the art of surviving is knowing your exit, especially when employing high alpha strategies like the Volume Factor. Observing Figure 1 below, was point "A" a good entry?

Figure 1: Exits Determine Outcomes

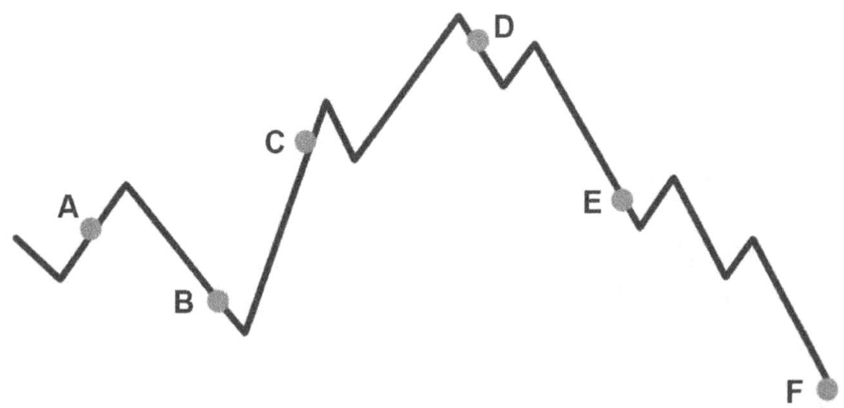

It all depends on your exit, be it point B, C, D, E, or F. **Exits, not entries, determine the outcome of a trade and, ultimately, the sustainability of a portfolio and the outcome of a financial plan.**

Consider this analogy. Perhaps you play golf? In most sports, when an athlete makes a mistake, they want to make up for it. That is, the emotion caused by the desire to win provides increased energy to play better, run faster, and hit harder. However, like investing, golf is a game of skill. These same emotions to win often work against our better judgment, positioning the most skilled player in a trouble spot. First, the golfer makes a lousy shot. Now the player feels the urge to catch up. So, instead of playing their game, they try to make up for it by attempting a more difficult shot. The player may have made the shot before, but that shot was the exception, not the rule. The cost of not making the shot is that the ball ends up in the trap. The player pays the price for going against the odds. Now they are way behind in strokes. So, they try another shot similar in difficulty, once again going against the odds. Now, they are in the water with no hope of recovery, out of contention.

Similarly, the markets are also a game of skill. Markets overachieve, becoming overbought because of the emotion of greed. Investors typically feel comfortable with winners and are reluctant to sell. Meanwhile, others see their success and want in late in the game, further driving up the price. But markets overcorrect because investors lose rationality. After all, when they are losing money, they sell—often when they should buy. **An advisor's role is to provide objectivity and a game plan because their clients' default is to become emotional, not rational, or strategic.**

Unfortunately, most advisors have been trained to keep their clients invested, even throughout the most vicious of bear markets. This always keep your seatbelt buckled approach is held primarily for two reasons. One, the advisor is not skilled enough to know when to exit or reenter. We will repair that problem shortly. Two, clients fear missing out on an ensuing rally.

On the chance that one makes it through with enough capital to survive, when the new bull market is reborn, holding on could indeed have merit. We will address those occurrences as we advance deeper into this chapter. Let us first, though, address this fear of missing out. To do this, let us review the common statistics taught to advisors, then ultimately relayed to their clientele. The chart below (Figure 2) is an advisor's go-to slide when convincing clients to buckle up and stay invested. The slide shows what happens when an investor misses the best days of the stock market. The chart below is from 2000–2020.

Figure 2: Missing the Best Days of the Stock Market

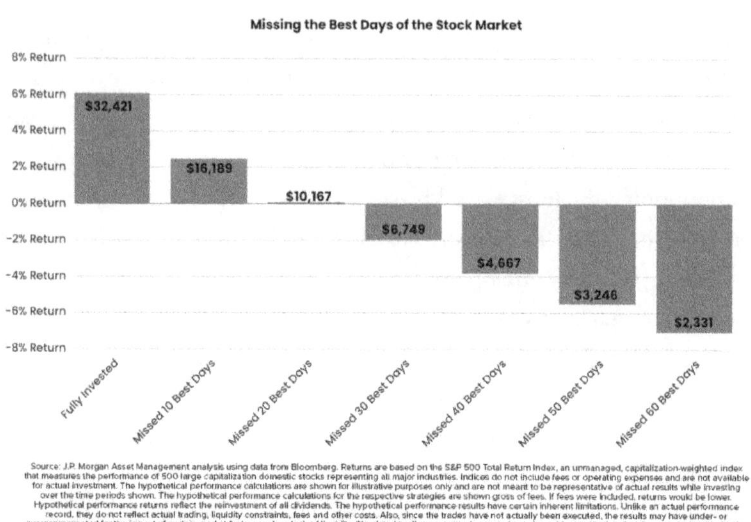

The opportunity cost of missing out is indeed strong motivation to stay invested, but it neglects the whole story. Below is the untold story of missing the worst days in the market.

Figure 3: Missing the Worst Days in the Stock Market

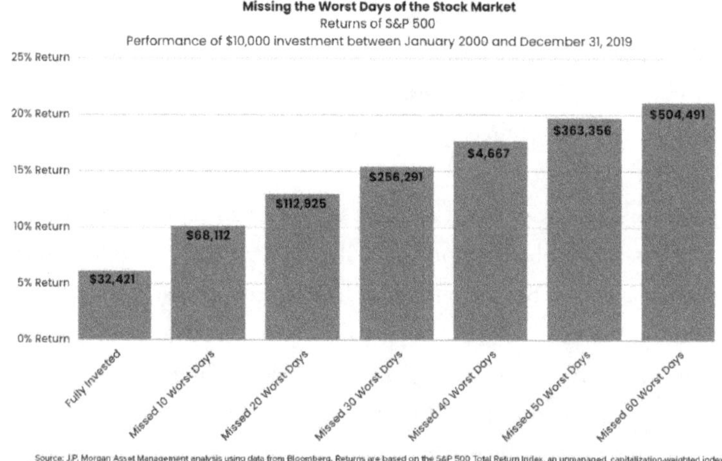

However, a fair presentation would include missing both the best and worst days. Research from Michael Batnick of Ritholtz Wealth Management demonstrates this point by showing what happens if you miss the 25 best days of the S&P 500 returns but also miss the corresponding worst days:

Figure 4: Missing the Best and Worst Days

Although fair, this exercise is not realistic, as nobody knows the worst or best days in advance. Figure 4 illustrates that the fear of missing out is generally not a rational motive to always remain invested. Rather, I like to think of investing as akin to planting a garden. The gardener sows' seeds, hoping to bear much fruit. However, as the garden is cultivated, inevitably, weeds pop up. The good gardener will recognize the problem and pull the weeds. Yet, the typical investor does not recognize their failing investments as weeds, but instead sees them as potential flowers. The investor recognizes their investment (weeds) is now at a tremendous discount, whereas the flowering investment has profits. With these thoughts in mind, the investor picks their flowers using the proceeds to water their weeds. This practice is called averaging down. The problem with the investor's approach is that it goes against the laws of mathematics, and over time, math always wins. Like the good gardener, investors need a game plan to cultivate a portfolio.

Figure 5: The Law of Incremental Returns (Compounding)

Laws of Multiplication		
If you make...	You need...	To make...
10%	9%	20%
20%	8%	30%
30%	7%	39%
40%	6%	49%

This is part one of "our game plan:" maximize returns when the markets are up. Returning to our physicist, Einstein once said, *"Compound interest is the world's eighth wonder. He who understands it, earns it … he who doesn't … pays it."* Let us now put that into practice. If one makes 10%, they only need 9% more to get to 20%. If one earns 20%, they only need 8% more to make 30%. After making 30%, only 7% more is required to achieve approximately 40%. And after earning 40%, one only needs to compound 6% more to reach nearly a 50% return. The moral of the story? When your investments are up, allow your returns to compound. In other words, pull your weeds and water your flowers."

Figure 6: The Law of Reverse Compounding

The Law of Reverse Compounding	
If you lose...	You need this % to break even
10%	11%
20%	25%
25%	35%
35%	50%
50%	100%

Defense is the more difficult part of the game plan. Unfortunately for investors, compounding laws also work in reverse. If you lose 10%, you'll need 11% to get back to even.

However, if you lose 20%, you'll need a 25% return to break even. If you lose 25%, now you will need approximately 35% to return to even. If you lose 35%, you'll need over a 50% return to break even. And if you lose 50%, you'll need to double your capital to break even.

If you are an advisor, never forget that your clients' capital is precious. Investors rightfully expect their advisors to have a plan to protect them. To protect clients' capital, forget about being right. Don't think about capital outcomes in terms or being right or wrong. Instead, follow what you believe is the best financial decision to meet your clients' objectives, regardless of gains and losses. Remember, it is in our inherent nature to take credit for wins and avoid admitting mistakes. Maximize gains, not wins. The best mistakes are always the realized ones. Strive for excellence, not perfection. Perfection is impossible and unattainable, leading to frustration, failure, and less money. Make your exit your priority by employing a great defensive game plan.

Here are some keys to building a stellar defense. First, plan your exits. Know your floor before you buy. If the market signals you are wrong, tune in to the market's message. Employ technical analysis and understand essential support levels, accessing risk versus reward. Remember why you bought and determine whether that reason is still valid. When overweighted, trim but don't outright abandon your winners. Don't let pride or fear control you; rather, tie your decisions to objective indications. Below are some famous last words, potentially on our own tombstones. Clients find excuses when left to their own devices. Unfortunately, excuses often lead to graveyard mistakes.

Figure 7: Graveyard Mistakes

FAMOUS LAST WORDS

- Losses are real

- Your Cost Basis is not the Market's Concern

- Would you still buy it today?

- Be Wise! Admit your mistakes - capital is precious

- Don't get knocked out, some never come back

Risk management, not excuses, keeps your clients in the game and out of the grave.

Figure 8: High Volatility -VS- Low Volatility

The Tortoise & The Hare				
Month	***Hare***	***Monthly Return***	**Tortoise**	**Monthly Return**
	High Volatility	*$100,000.00*	Low Volatility	$100,000.00
1	10	*$110,000.00*	4	$104,000.00
2	-8	*$101,200.00*	-2	$101,920.00
3	10	*$111,320.00*	4	$105,996.80
4	-8	*$102,414.40*	-2	$103,876.86
5	10	*$112,655.84*	4	$108,031.94
6	-8	*$103,643.37*	-2	$105,871.30
7	10	*$114,007.71*	4	$110,106.15
8	-8	*$104,887.09*	-2	$107,904.03
9	10	*$115,375.80*	4	$112,220.19
10	-8	*$106,145.74*	-2	$109,975.79
11	10	*$116,760.31*	4	$114,374.82
12	-8	*$107,419.49*	-2	$112,087.32
13	10	*$118,161.44*	4	$116,570.81
14	-8	*$108,708.52*	-2	$114,239.40
15	10	*$119,579.37*	4	$118,808.97
16	-8	*$110,013.02*	-2	$116,432.79
17	10	*$121,014.33*	4	$121,090.11
18	-8	*$111,333.18*	-2	$118,668.30
19	10	*$122,466.50*	4	$123,415.04
20	-8	*$112,669.18*	-2	$120,946.74
21	10	*$123,936.10*	4	$125,784.60
22	-8	*$114,021.21*	-2	$123,268.91
23	10	*$125,423.33*	4	$128,199.67
24	-8	*$115,389.46*	-2	$125,635.68

So, what is our defensive game plan? The key to any risk management strategy is keeping volatility and drawdown low. Here, we have **two investors: the tortoise and the hare.** Both investors average a 1% monthly return, but the fast hare returns it on high volatility, a 10% monthly return followed by an 8% monthly loss. At the same time, the tortoise achieves its 1% monthly return on low volatility, with a 4% gain followed by a 2% loss. And we all know who wins the race. Within two years, the hare's $100,000 grew to $115,389 compared to the tortoise's $125,635. Who would have thought that *The Tortoise and the Hare* is among the greatest investment books of all time? Low drawdowns and low volatility not only deliver a more comfortable ride, keeping clients and investors in the game, but also yield greater returns over time. Most importantly, lower volatility delivers a higher probability of delivering successful client outcomes.

Low volatility strategies work by keeping drawdowns low. The Sharpe ratio uses volatility to measure risk-adjusted returns. My preferred risk-adjusted return is the Sortino ratio. The Sortino ratio only uses downside deviation, removing upside volatility from the calculation. I view upside volatility as good because upside volatility allows upside compounding to be more robust. It is the drawdowns that blow up portfolios and financial plans, especially in the distribution phase. Next, let us review a real-life scenario.

Figure 9: Neglecting Risk Management

The Cost of Neglecting Risk Management			
Year	**SPX**	**Withdrawal**	**1,000,000**
2000	-9.10%	50,000.00	859,000.00
2001	-11.89%	50,000.00	706,864.90
2002	-22.10%	50,000.00	500,647.76
2003	28.68%	50,000.00	594,233.53
2004	10.88%	50,000.00	608,886.14
2005	4.91%	50,000.00	588,782.45
2006	15.79%	50,000.00	631,751.20
2007	5.49%	50,000.00	616,434.34
2008	-37.00%	50,000.00	338,353.64
2009	26.46%	50,000.00	377,882.01
2010	15.06%	50,000.00	384,791.04
2011	2.11%	50,000.00	342,910.13
2012	16.00%	50,000.00	347,775.75
2013	32.39%	50,000.00	410,420.31
2014	13.69%	50,000.00	***416,606.86***
2015	1.38%	50,000.00	372,356.03
2016	11.96%	50,000.00	366,889.81
2017	21.83%	50,000.00	396,981.86
2018	-4.38%	50,000.00	329,594.05
2019	31.49%	50,000.00	383,383.22
2020	18.40%	50,000.00	***403,925.73***

The laws of reverse compounding are exaggerated in the distribution phase, also known as "dollar cost averaging in reverse." Here, we have a retiree whose advisor selected one of the top-performing investments over the past two decades, the S&P 500. Historically, this index has returned over 10%. In this scenario, it is January 2000. An advisor's client retires with $1 million, requiring $50,000 a year to supplement their lifestyle. Believing the S&P 500 to be a solid and diversified investment option, the advisor invests the $1 million into the S&P 500. The figure of $50,000 equates to a 5% distribution, which is half the historical rate of return of the S&P 500 Index. By the end of 2002, following three consecutive down years, the investor has just over half their money left. Now, that 5% annual distribution is a 10% annual distribution. Then, after five years of positive returns, 2008 arrives, knocking their portfolio down to under $340,000. This equates to a nearly 15% annual distribution. By 2020, despite a decade of ensuing bull markets, the client's portfolio only returns to just over $400,000, a 12.5% distribution rate.

Figure 10: Neglecting Risk Management with Fees Included

The Cost of Neglecting Risk Management			
Year	**SPX**	**Withdrawl**	**Market Value**
			$1,000,000.00
2000	-10%	$50,000.00	$850,000.00
2001	-13%	$50,000.00	$689,500.00
2002	**-23%**	**$50,000.00**	**$480,915.00**
2003	26%	$50,000.00	$555,952.90
2004	9%	$50,000.00	$555,988.66
2005	3%	$50,000.00	$522,668.32
2006	15%	$50,000.00	$551,068.57
2007	5%	$50,000.00	$528,622.00
2008	**-37%**	**$50,000.00**	**$283,031.86**
2009	26%	$50,000.00	$306,620.14
2010	15%	$50,000.00	$302,613.16
2011	2%	$50,000.00	$258,665.43
2012	15%	$50,000.00	$247,465.24
2013	32%	$50,000.00	$276,654.12
2014	14%	$50,000.00	$265,385.69
2015	1%	$50,000.00	$219,101.09
2016	12%	$50,000.00	$172,168.51
2017	22%	$50,000.00	$149,045.58
2018	-5%	$50,000.00	$91,593.30
2019	32%	$50,000.00	$70,445.19
2020	**18%**	**$50,000.00**	**$33,407.10**

The first example assumes no investment costs, which is not realistic. Above is the same scenario, this time including a 1% advisory fee. With just a 1% advisory fee, the client ran out of money before the end of the second decade. Was the S&P 500 a poor investment? No. I've often heard advisors say, "I wish we would have just bought the index." These sentiments have merit, as very few broad investments have performed better than the S&P 500 over the last two decades (the NASDAQ did, but with the illustrated distribution, the investor would not have retained the capital to see it through). The investment is not the problem. The issue is a risk management failure. The failure resulted from an absence of risk management applied to the underlying investment, as well as an inappropriate distribution policy.

Figure 11: The Art of Survival—Distinguishing between Fluctuations, Corrections & Bear Markets

ART OF SURVIVAL, CLIENT RETENTION, SUCCESSFUL OUTCOMES

Correction or Bear Market

Fluctuations Daily 0-5%

Corrections Weeks to Months 7-20%

Bear Markets Months to Years >20%

1. Cyclical Bear Markets short painful Months & Quarters usually *Event Driven
2. Secular Bear Markets long grueling brutal Multiple Years Decade(s) *Fundamentally Driven

The advisor's first and foremost job is risk management. When the markets are up, clients don't think they need you. But when they are down, you can become indispensable. Armed with principles from the Volume Factor risk overlay, you will now have the tools and strategies to keep your clients alive and continually in the game.

The art of survival is the path to client retention and successful financial outcomes. As an advisor, you will not be vital by adding 2 or 3% in alpha (although we shoot for that, too), but by reducing volatility and drawdown. The key to minimizing drawdowns is correctly distinguishing between market fluctuations, corrections, and bear markets. Clients do not like fluctuations; they fear corrections, but the bear market destroys financial plans. The key to thriving is surviving while keeping your passengers happy and secure, leading them to successful financial outcomes. Successful financial outcomes are procured by avoiding bear markets, especially during the withdrawal phase. So, how do we dodge bear markets?

Figure 12: Buy & Hold -VS- Following the Trend

Unleveraged Buy and Hold versus Unleveraged Moving Average Timing (October 1928-December 2020)						
Metric	S&P 500	10-Day	20-Day	50-Day	100-Day	200-Day
Annual Return	9.4%	11.7%	10.4%	10.2%	10.7%	10.9%
Annual Volatility	18.9%	12.0%	11.6%	11.6%	12.1%	12.4%
Sharpe Ratio	0.32	0.68	0.6	0.58	0.59	0.59
Sortino Ratio	0.57	1.07	0.93	0.89	0.91	0.9
Max Drawdown	-86.2%	-49.5%	-46.6%	-46.6%	-46.5%	-49.5%
Beta	1	0.4	0.38	0.38	0.41	0.43
Annual Alpha	0.0%	5.3%	5.4%	5.2%	6.4%	5.7%
Avg Trades/Year	0	38	26	15	10	5

Source: Charles Bilello & Michael Gayed Leverage For the Long Run

The most common of the effective tactic to avoid bear markets is to follow market trends. When the trend is up, stay long. When the trend is down, get out. Trend-following systems work because they keep drawdowns low. Figure 12 lists four trend-following moving average strategies tested from October 1928 to December 2020. Notice that all of these simple trend strategies have beaten buy and hold while significantly reducing risk. Although the 100-day moving average has the best risk-adjusted returns (Sortino ratio) and the highest return, the 200-day is the most popular strategy. This is because the 200-day is the most practical, generating on average five turns a year compared to the 100-day, with 10 trades per year.

Trend-following systems work, but they are not without significant drawbacks. First, they are notorious for whipsaws. Second, they almost always miss the initial run-up, which is often the strongest point of investment returns. Solving these common problems is where our volume analysis risk overlay comes into play.

Our first solution to improve trend systems is to employ leading indicators vs. price indicators. Broad market price trends are an effective tool to avoid bear markets. Indexes are used to follow broad markets, not individual securities. Thus far, though, we have only employed volume analysis for individual issues. To avoid bear markets, one needs to learn how to apply volume analysis to broad market indexes.

Unique differences exist between individual securities and indexes when using volume analysis. Through my experience and expertise, I find that these differences, although materially significant, are rarely, if ever, taken into account. Unfortunately, these unique differences are not small matters, but are instead extremely significant factors. The primary problem is not in the theory or process of volume analysis. The problem is with the data used to compile the analysis. In fact, these data issues are so atrocious that I (founder of Volume Analysis.com and VolumeFactor.com) have not used traditional index volume data in over two decades. However, if we can solve this problem, then we've got a great shot at solving the most significant investment problem of them all. That is the inability to correctly position investors in and out of the equity markets.

Figure 14: S&P 500 Volume as Reported by Yahoo Finance

Source: Yahoo Finance

Let us begin with an example in Figure 14. Look at the chart above of the S&P 500 and volume. The closing price on September 10, 2021, is $4,468.73, and the volume is 3.1 billion shares. This data is from Yahoo. By the way, there is nothing special about this date. It is a random date chosen a few days before delivering a presentation for a CMT educational series. Next, let's look at another data source on the same day.

Figure 15: S&P 500 Volume as Reported by IBD

Figure 15 is the same security and day using Investor's Business Daily (IBD) data. According to IBD, the S&P 500 price is identical, but the volume on September 10, 2021, the same day, is reported as 444.4 million shares.

Figure 16: S&P 500 Volume According to MSN

Data from Refinitiv

And when you want to know the correct answer, what do you do? You google it. Here is SPX 500 volume, googled on the same day, September 10, 2021 (source: MSN). The volume is 1.8 billion shares. We could go on and on with more examples, but here is what you will find. The price on the S&P 500 always matches. However, the volume reported is all over the place.

Figure 17: Volume of Shares Traded as Reported in Tapes A, B & C

Trade Date	Nyse Tape A	Nyse Arca Tape A	Nyse American Tape A	Nyse National Tape A	Nyse Chicago Tape A	Consolidated Tape A	Nyse Tape B	Nyse Arca Tape B	Nyse American Tape B	Nyse National Tape B	Nyse Chicago Tape B	Consolidated Tape B	Nyse Tape C	Nyse Arca Tape C	Nyse American Tape C	Nyse National Tape C	Nyse Chicago Tape C	Consolidated Tape C
2021-09-13	851.2	211.2	14.6	53.5	3.4	3,914.80	49.9	297.2	36.5	25.8	3.8	1,884.30	63.2	408.9	10.9	33	3.9	4,723.50
2021-09-10	776	191.1	12.5	47.9	3.7	3,623.20	43.7	279.6	42.4	27.1	1.9	1,992.70	57.1	380.4	9.1	30.3	4.2	4,587.20
2021-09-09	789.8	206	11.9	54.5	3.8	3,735.70	41.1	273.4	34.1	27.2	3.2	1,742.00	57.6	345.1	7.9	27.9	2.2	4,031.20
2021-09-08	822.8	203.4	12.5	46.4	5.1	3,764.00	42.2	285.5	36	27.6	4.3	1,812.20	59.8	332.4	12.7	28.1	3	4,135.60
2021-09-07	811.7	196.7	13.8	48	2.8	3,823.00	35.9	272.3	35.2	25.9	2.6	1,665.00	52.6	326.6	10.6	28.2	3	4,014.30
2021-09-03	705.6	167.7	10.6	41.5	2.1	3,220.20	29.1	234.6	30.9	22.5	1.2	1,493.90	46.7	306.7	8.3	25.9	3.2	3,707.00
2021-09-02	803.2	196.8	13.4	48.7	2.7	3,741.60	33.7	241.5	30.8	22.7	1.2	1,546.90	50.4	343.7	11.6	26	2.7	4,052.20
2021-09-01	831.6	227.5	15.5	51.8	6.9	4,057.30	37.3	276.9	29.6	27.8	2.4	1,637.20	57.3	384.7	8.8	27.9	4.7	4,271.70
2021-08-31	1,282.00	209.6	14.9	52.4	5.2	4,335.80	32.7	248.5	31.5	27	3	1,519.90	55.3	321.8	24	29.9	2.1	4,202.60
2021-08-30	703.6	164.1	11.5	41.7	6.7	3,168.70	29.5	233	33.9	22.2	2.2	1,658.80	50.5	339	8.4	27.2	2.7	4,061.80
2021-08-27	740	176.2	12.8	43.3	1.8	3,334.80	34.1	236.5	22.8	22.9	3.6	1,462.00	51.4	321.2	9.5	26	1.7	4,048.60

We have found multiple various sources, all reporting different S&P 500 volumes. That is a huge problem, as the foundational principle of volume analysis is the relationship between volume and price. This is not an isolated instance. It is reported this way every day, five days a week, 52 weeks a year.

What is the discrepancy, and who is right? Answering the second part of the question first, none of this data is any good, at least for analysis purposes. Here is the crux of the problem. Each stock is listed on an exchange, but each stock may trade on multiple exchanges. This does not muddy the waters in reporting on individual securities volume at all. But it sure does throw a huge wrench into things when tabulating volume data into indexes. When reporting S&P 500 Index volume, most data sources do not provide the volume of the S&P 500 components but, rather, report volume tallies from the exchanges.

At the time of this writing, the five biggest capital-weighted components of the S&P 500 were AAPL, MSFT, GOOGL, AMZN, and META. These five companies accounted for approximately 25% of the price weighting. What do you think was the contribution of these five mega-influential stocks to the volume tallies? Was it 30%, 25%, 20%, 10%, or only 5%? The answer is most likely **zero.** That is because most data providers use a form of NYSE Consolidated tape, also known as Tape A, to report S&P 500 volume. All five of these stocks trade on the NASDQ Tape C, not Tape A. Thus, in most instances, S&P 500 Index volume does not even include any of the top 25% of contributors, nor any other S&P 500 Index member not listed on the NYSE. Additionally, you are likely including volume on securities that are not even stocks, such as exchange-traded funds (ETFs), preferreds, and Closed End Funds (CEFs), many of which are actually bonds—not even equities!

BLUE CHIPS

If you are using volume data in index analysis, you are most likely comparing apples to a basket of mixed fruit that is missing the most important and prominent securities. So, why even use index volume data?

This is merely the first reason I do not use index volume. And, if you can believe it, the second reason is equally egregious. The second reason I do not use traditional index volume is because of the differences between how price indexes and volume data are compiled.

Price indexes are typically weighted, whereas volume is tallied. Generally, this means that in price indexes, the biggest companies have the highest weightings, while the smaller companies have the lowest weightings. However, with volume tallies, the low-priced stocks generally have the highest attribution, and the high-priced stocks have the lowest attribution. In other words, **Blue Chips drive price indexes, whereas penny stocks drive index volume tallies.**

Now let us examine a real-life example of this volume data discrepancy in action. I have coined this the ***blue chip to cow chip phenomenon***. Perhaps the best example I can share with you occurred during the credit crisis of 2008 and 2009.

Figure 20: Citigroup Post-Split

Source: Optuma www.optuma.com/volumeanalysis

Pre-credit crisis, Citigroup was the fifth-largest price component of the S&P 500, but typically its volume only accounted for less than 1% of the S&P 500's daily volume tallies (See Figure 20). That's good, but it gets a lot worse, a whole lot worse.

Post-credit crisis, Citigroup went from *blue chip to cow chip*. As a result, its stock price fell by over 95%, to below a dollar per share, at which point Citigroup had almost no attribution to the S&P 500 Index (Figure 20, chart above, is post-split).

"Do you deal in red or blue chips?"
"Mostly brown."

COW CHIPS HAPPEN

Meanwhile, while Citigroup's price had dropped 95%, what do you think happened to Citigroup's volume? It grew by over 400%. As a result, some index volume methodologies were reporting Citigroup's S&P 500 Volume **accounting for a massive 40% of the volume of the whole index!!!** Even the more reputable data providers still reported Citigroup's volume to be accounting for 10% of the index volume. Nonetheless, this accounting still represented a massive contribution to a stock with virtually no attribution to the underlying price index.

"You never said your 50,000 shares were penny ones!"

Here's the bottom line. Because volume is tallied and price indexes are weighted, small, low-priced stocks are overweighted in volume tallies, and large, high-priced stocks are overweighted in price indexes. The end result is depicted in Figure 21. Therefore, if you are using traditional index volume data in your analysis, as our lady here has just discovered, you too, are on a date with the penny ones! Even if you obtain the right data feeds to tabulate the index volume, the small, low-priced, low-weighted stocks drive the volume data.

If you employ indexes and volume in your market analysis, and you are using the industry standard volume data, then you, too, are likely dealing in brown chips (Figure 22). Our blue-chip data are presently only available through Optuma software.

What is the solution? That is what we will cover next. The most vital component of volume analysis is how volume relates to price. The obvious question is, how do we repair volume tallies to align with price indexes? The answer to that pursuit is **Capital-Weighted Volume**. By capital weighting volume proportionate to the price index components, we can perfectly harmonize volume to its price index.

Here's how to calculate Capital-Weighted Volume, perfectly aligning price indexes to volume:

Table 1: Calculating Capital-Weighted Volume

Capital-weighted Volume

- Step #1: Calculate each component's Capital Weighting
    - Price * Shares Outstanding
- Step #2: Determine each component's Index Weighting
    - Stocks Capital Weighting / Indexes Capital Weighting
- Step #3: Calculate each component's Capital-Weighted Volume
    - Volume * Capital Weighting
- Step # 4: Parse Upside VS Downside Volume by Component
- Step # 5: Add Upside + Downside CW Volume = Capital-Weighted Volume
- Step #6: Subtract Upside-Downside CW Volume and accumulate the running total

Figure 23: Capital-Weighted Dollar Volume

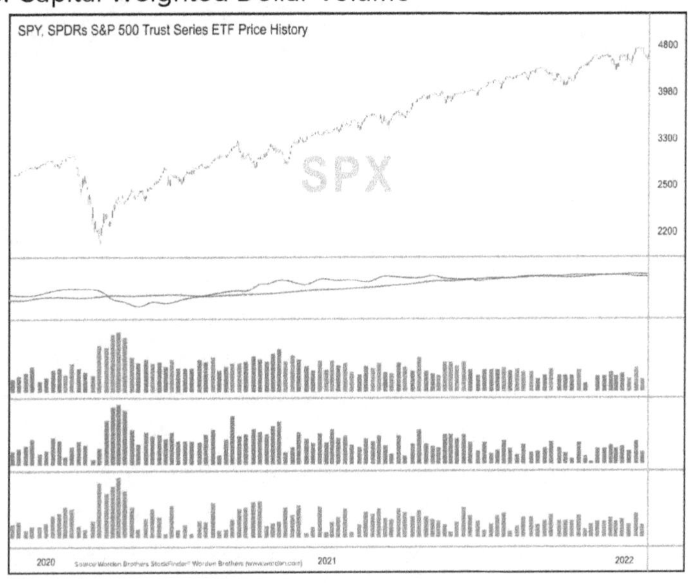

Source: Optuma www.optuma.com/volumeanalysis

See Figure 23 to determine what Capital-Weighted Volume looks like for the S&P 500. By the way, presently **only one platform has this data, and that is Optuma Software**. Starting on the bottom of Figure 23, then moving up, these red bars represent Capital-Weighted Downside Volume. Capital-Weighted Downside Volume reveals, proportionate to market-cap weighting, how many shares in the S&P 500 traded down for the day, week, or otherwise. Moving up a panel, the green bars represent Capital-Weighted Upside Volume. Capital-Weighted Upside Volume identifies, proportionate to capital weighting, how many shares traded up for the time period.

In review, for stocks finishing up, their Capital-Weighted Volume is recorded in the upside volume category, and for stocks which close down, their volume is recorded in the downside volume category. Summing Capital-Weighted Upside Volume with Downside Volume provides us the total Capital-Weighted Volume for the period. This is depicted in the chart with both red and green bars. The volume bars are colored green when Upside Capital-Weighted Volume exceeds downside volume, and red when Downside Capital-Weighted Volume exceeds upside volume.

The flow of shares traded in and out of the S&P 500 is expressed as Capital-Weighted Upside Volume minus Capital-Weighted Downside Volume. The result is depicted in the line chart above: Capital-Weighted Up Volume–Capital-Weighted Down Volume accumulated over time. In this way, Upside Capital-Weighted volume tracks the volume flowing into and out of a market index.

Identically, volume moving out of a market is attributed as Downside Capital-Weighted Volume outflows. When the accumulated trend of these net capital volume flows is moving up, this is indicative of a volume analysis bull market. Conversely, net capital volume flows trending down create a volume analysis bear market. These data are critical in gauging the health of the broad market. Let's look at a few examples.

Figure 24: Capital-Weighted Volume Divergence

Source: Worden Brothers Stock Finder ® Worden Brothers (www.worden.com)

There are multiple, almost exhaustive ways an analyst can employ Capital-Weighted Volume data. We only look at a couple of the more prominent ones. Notice in the chart above (Figure 24) that the price trendline is moving down. What about accumulated Capital-Weighted Volume, the black line in the bottom panel. In which direction is it trending? Up. In this example, Capital-Weighted S&P Volume is diverging from the S&P 500 Price Index. This bullish divergence preempted the eventual uptrend breakout.

Figure 25: S&P 500 Capital-Weighted Volume on April 16, 2010

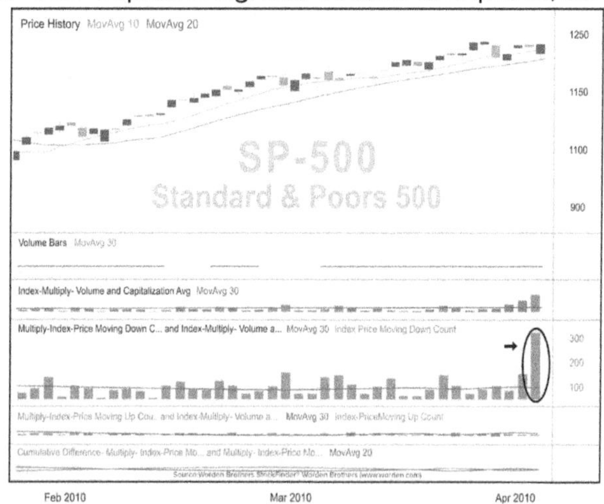

Source: Worden Brothers Stock Finder ® Worden Brothers (www.worden.com)

Detecting Supply and Demand imbalances

We can also employ this data to detect imbalances between supply and demand. This next illustration is a prime example. *Remember that price is the market's testimony, and volume is the market's polygraph, measuring conviction.* The last date on our S&P chart in Figure 25 is April 16, 2010. This day was not a notable day in market history. Nothing big happened; it was a slow news day. Notice in the top panel that price was down a bit that day, 19 points, or -1.6%. Next, moving down to the panel below is Capital-Weighted S&P 500 Volume. It is hard to see because this panel is small to emphasize the panel below it. However, on this day, April 16, 2010, which again was a slow news day, the **Capital-Weighted Volume hit an all-time high.** It was **up a whopping 45%** from its 30-day moving average. This tells us that something big is brewing, but in which direction?

Now, that important question brings us to the enlarged panel below, with the red downside volume bars. This is the Capital-Weighted Downside Volume, and it is absolutely massive. It completely dwarfs upside volume and is up 400% above trend! Friends, if you had this data enabling you to gaze into the market's eyes, you'd see panicked fear on this day.

This example was on the S&P 500. Next, let's look at a couple of the exchanges on the same date to see if they confirm the S&P 500 massive volume distribution day.

Figure 26: NYSE Capital-Weighted Volume on April 16, 2010

Source: Worden Brothers Stock Finder ® Worden Brothers (www.worden.com)

Figure 26 shows the NYSE Index volume with the NYSE Capital-Weighted Volume chart. Our date April 16, 2010, which is circled in each of the panels. Notice that NYSE volume was a bit above average. However, NYSE Capital-Weighted Volume is sticking out like a sore thumb, up a whopping 47% from its 30-day average. Again, another record-setting Capital-Weighted Volume Day, this time on the NYSE.

Figure 27: NASDQ Capital-Weighted Volume on April 16, 2010

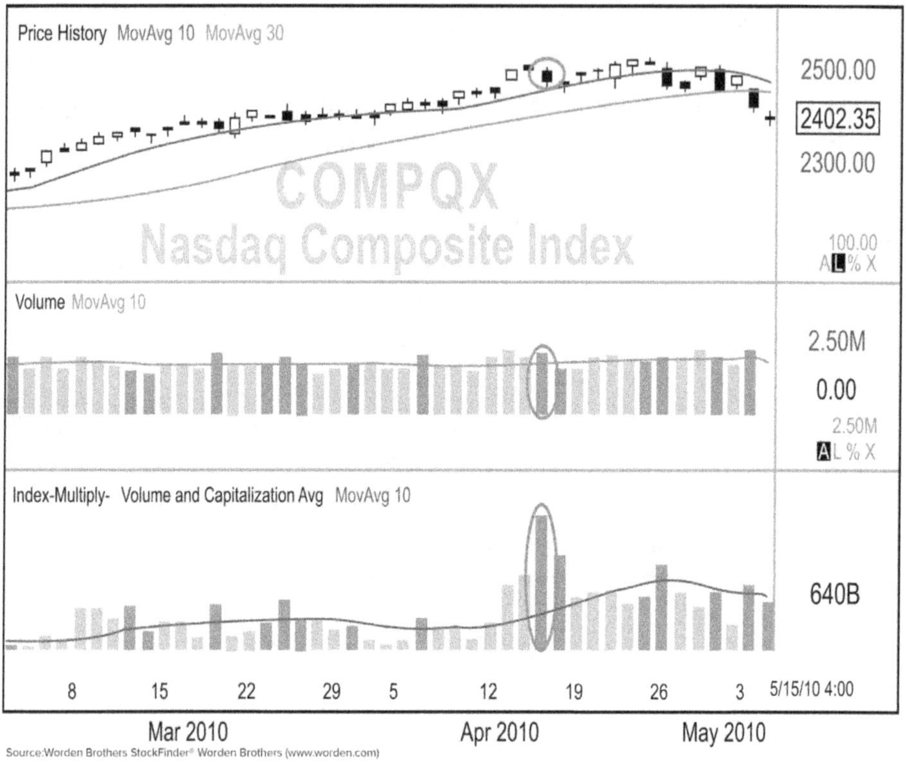

Source:Worden Brothers StockFinder® Worden Brothers (www.worden.com)

Source: Worden Brothers Stock Finder ® Worden Brothers (www.worden.com)

Figure 27 is identical to the last, except we are now looking at April 16, 2010, with the important data circled on the NASDAQ Composite chart. Notice the NASDQ price index closed down just a tad bit from the previous day but near the highs of the day. Notice the NASDQ volume is just barely above trend, whereas the NASDQ Capital-Weighted Volume was **up an extraordinary 55%** from its 30-day moving average, well above all-time highs.

Why am I pointing this out? Yes, it was an extraordinary, record-setting Capital-Weighted Volume Day on what otherwise was a typically slow day on Wall Street. But do you remember what remarkable event succeeded this unknown day? Think about it.

Figure 28: S&P Capital-Weighted Volume April 16 compared to Flash Crash

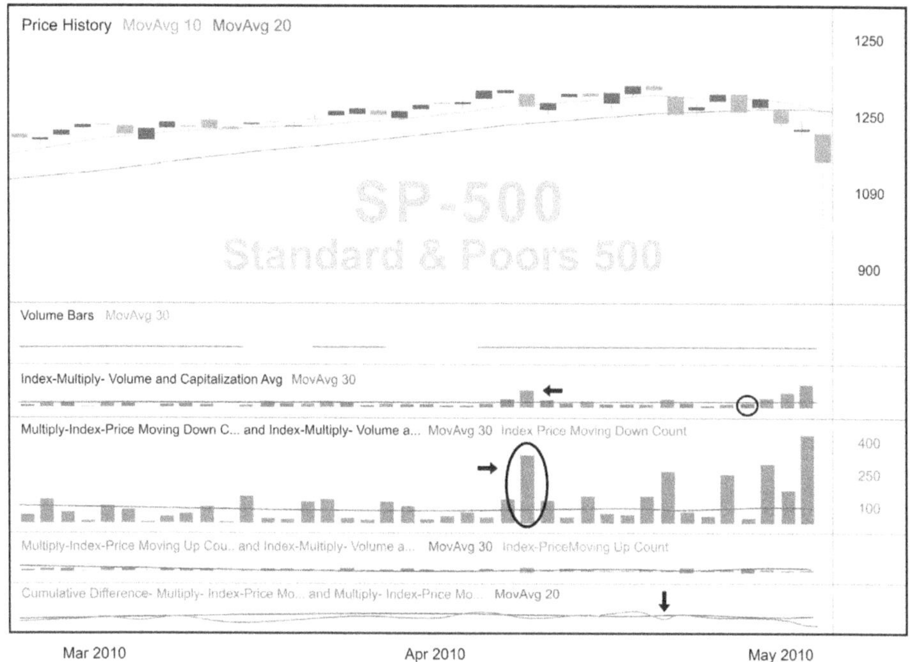

Source: Worden Brothers Stock Finder ® Worden Brothers (www.worden.com)

So, what did these massive downside Capital-Weighted Volume events lead to? The next chart (Figure 28) is again the S&P 500 ending May 6, 2010—aka, the Flash Crash. Please observe that the unremarkable, otherwise hidden events of April 16 were of the same magnitude as the Flash Crash. So, if you had this Capital-Weighted Volume data from April 16, like I did, then you would have known that massive institutional selling was developing underneath the market, an absolutely massive institutional selling program giving way to creating a serious supply / demand imbalance. These conditions were not apparent in the price data, nor in any of the traditional volume data sources, but they were strikingly evident in all of the Capital-Weighted Volume data sets.

Figure 29: NASDQ Volume -VS- NASDQ Capital-Weighted Volume April 16 & Flash Crash

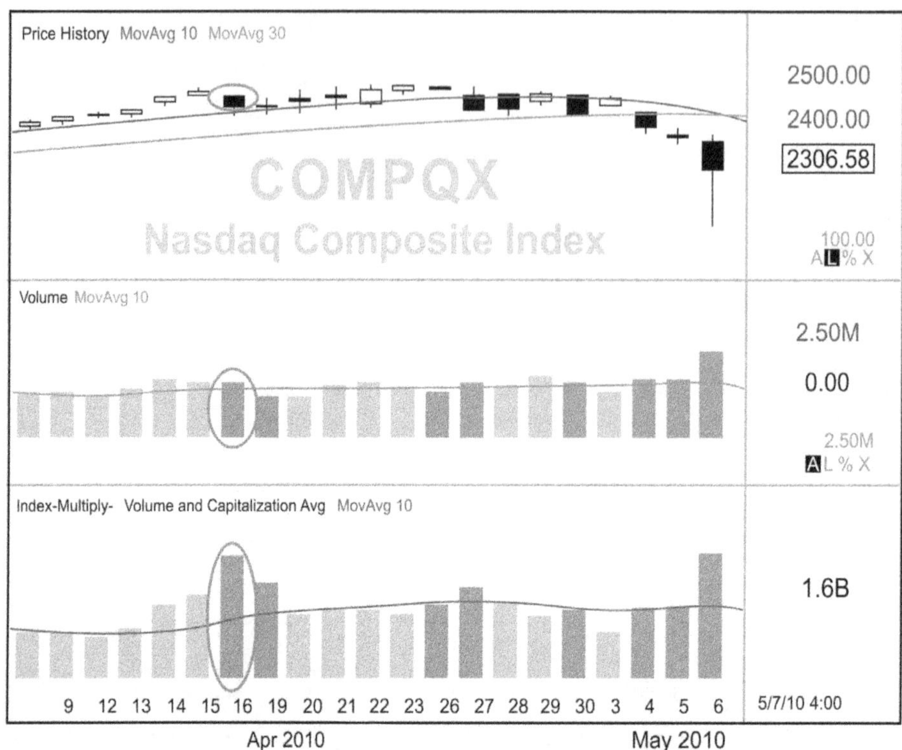

Source: Worden Brothers Stock Finder ® Worden Brothers (www.worden.com)

Notice again in Figure 29 the Capital-Weighted Volume, but this time on the NASDQ Index. The Capital-Weighted NASDQ Volume was again virtually the same on April 16 as it was on the day of the historical Flash Crash.

Perhaps you are wondering why we are discussing index data? **Index data defines whether a market is bullish or bearish.** However, we employ this new and unique volume data analysis, harmonizing price, and volume, to determine our market exposure through a risk overlay.

When accumulated Capital-Weighted Volume is up, it means liquidity is flowing into the market. This is a volume analysis bull market. And when the trend of Capital-Weighted Volume turns negative, or below trend, this means liquidity is now flowing out of the market, or, in other words, a volume analysis bear market.

Figure 30: S&P 500 Capital-Weighted Volume -VS- S&P 500 2000–2022

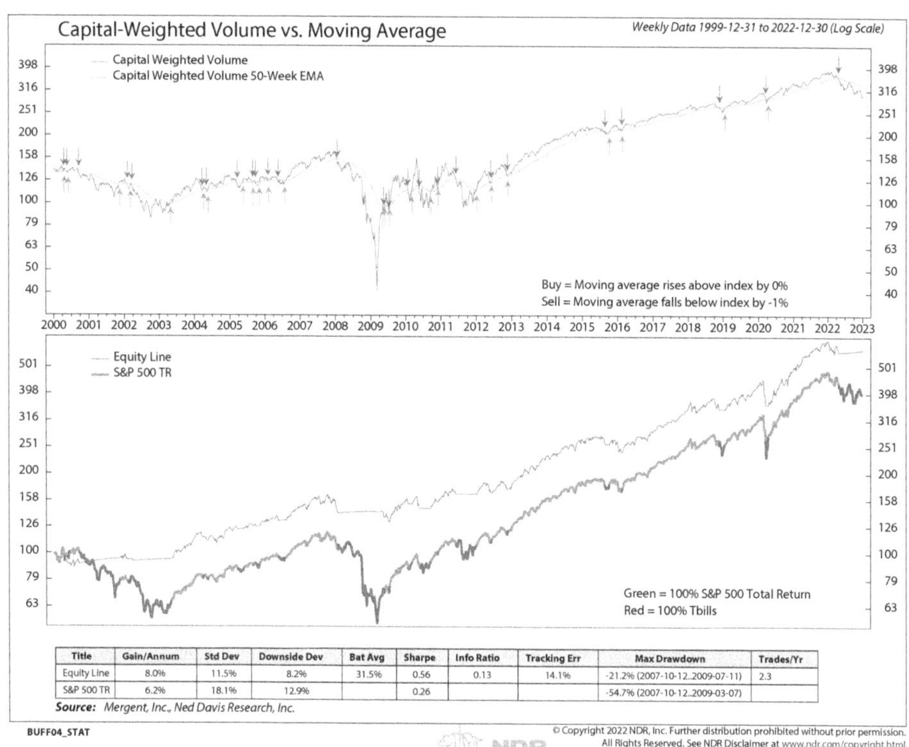

Title	Gain/Annum	Std Dev	Downside Dev	Bat Avg	Sharpe	Info Ratio	Tracking Err	Max Drawdown	Trades/Yr
Equity Line	8.0%	11.5%	8.2%	31.5%	0.56	0.13	14.1%	-21.2% (2007-10-12..2009-07-11)	2.3
S&P 500 TR	6.2%	18.1%	12.9%		0.26			-54.7% (2007-10-12..2009-03-07)	

Source: *Mergent, Inc., Ned Davis Research, Inc.*

Figure 30 employs Capital-Weighted Volume as a risk overlay on the S&P 500 from 2000 to 2022. The analysis was conducted by a respected third-party verification service, Ned Davis Research. Covering the previous two decades, the risk overlay is long (owns) the S&P 500 when Capital-Weighted Volume is above trend and is in cash when Capital-Weighted Volume is below trend. Referencing Figure 30, beginning with the upper panel, the blue line is Capital-Weighted Volume, and the orange line is the trend of Capital-Weighted Volume. The up and down arrows show us trades in (up) and out (down) of the market. Moving down to the lower panel, the green and red line is the S&P 500 (red when the model is in T-Bills, green when in S&P 500). The blue line is the equity line, illustrating the performance of the Capital-Weighted Volume model, being long in the S&P 500 when Capital-Weighted Volume is above trend and out of the market when Capital-Weighted Volume is 1% below trend.

Notice that *going back from 2000 to December 2022*, the market has returned **6.2%**, whereas our model of following the trend of volume flows returned **8.0%**. However, the outperformance comes with significantly less risk, as noted in our standard deviation of only 11.5% compared to the buy-and-hold strategy of 18.5%. With the volume overlay approach, downside deviation, the most critical data point of survival, is down only 8.2%. This compares to the passive buy-and-hold strategy with a downside deviation of 12.9%—a 35% improvement!

Capital-Weighted Volume leads to a significantly higher risk-adjusted rate of return, boasting a Sharpe ratio of .56 compared to the S&P 500 index of .26, **more than doubling the risk-adjusted rate of return**! Most importantly, the low drawdown will massively improve an investor's survival odds, especially in the distribution phase. One last item to point out. Remember the turnover when we studied price trends? The moving average model with the least amount of turnover (200-day MA) was five trades per year. Demonstrating that volume confirms price, this Capital-Weighted Volume model averaged just over two trades per year.

Figure 31: S&P 500 -VS- Low Volatility ETFs Post-Pandemic

2nd Fallacy Trend Systems - Singular Data

Performance

Growth of $10,000 Total Return

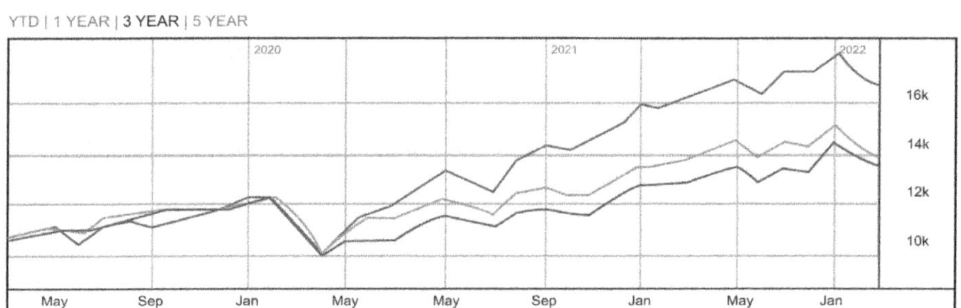

SPLV USMV SPY Comparison S&P 500

The chart above represents the growth of a hypothetical investment of $10,000. The total return is not adjusted to reflect sales charges of taxes; however it does show actual ongoing fund expenses and assumes the reinvestment of dividends and capital gains. If the returns were adjusted to include sales charges, the quoted performance would be lower.

The performance quoted represents past performance and does not guarantee future results. The investment return and principal value of an investment will fluctuate thus an investor's shares, when redeemed, may be worth more or less than their original cost. Current performance may be lower or higher than the performance date quoted herein.

Source: TD Ameritrade

Another common issue in risk reduction strategies is the sole reliance on one data set. Single-factor risk mitigation strategies often lead to extreme bets. Above are two popular ETFs (SPLV Invesco Low Volatility & USMV MSCI Minimum Volatility), both utilizing volatility as a risk mitigation strategy. Unfortunately, both took on the full risk of the decline, and both also severely underperformed during the recovery phase. In contrast, our Volume Factor Risk Overlay uses a four-legged stool utilizing multi-dimensional leading indicators.

- Capital-Weighted Volume
- Capital-Weighted Dollar Volume
- The Advance Decline Line
- VPCI Bottoms

Because the Volume Factor Risk Overlay employs multiple leading indicators, it is not a timing tool but is, rather, a gauge by which to access the health of the market.

Figure 32: Capital-Weighted Dollar Volume -VS- S&P 500 2000–2022

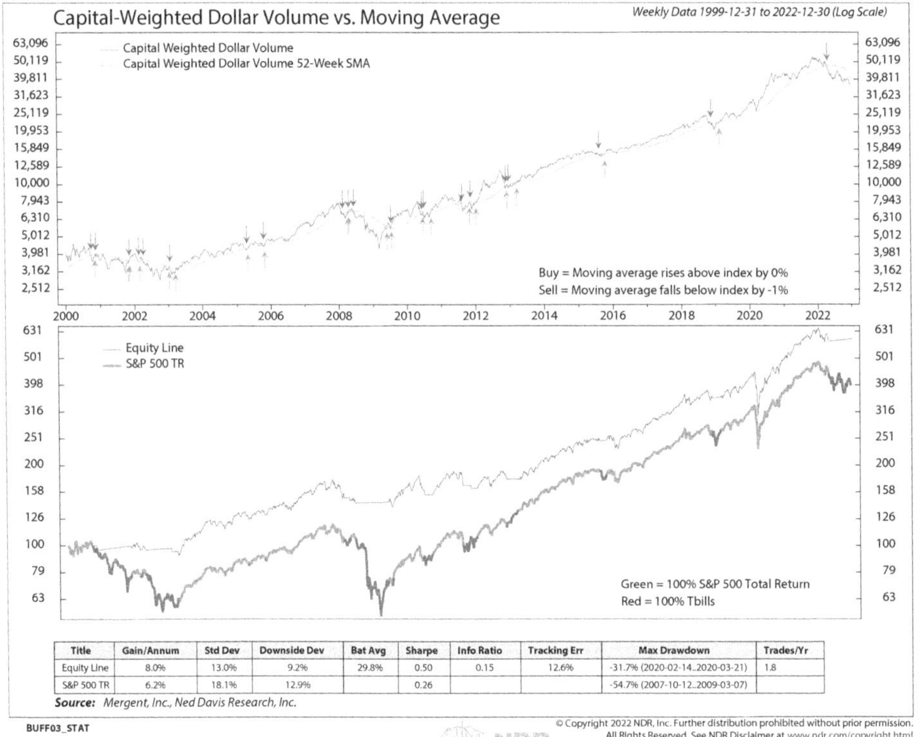

Title	Gain/Annum	Std Dev	Downside Dev	Bat Avg	Sharpe	Info Ratio	Tracking Err	Max Drawdown	Trades/Yr
Equity Line	8.0%	13.0%	9.2%	29.8%	0.50	0.15	12.6%	-31.7% (2020-02-14..2020-03-21)	1.8
S&P 500 TR	6.2%	18.1%	12.9%		0.26			-54.7% (2007-10-12..2009-03-07)	

Source: *Mergent, Inc., Ned Davis Research, Inc.*

BUFF03_STAT

The second fallacy of trends is that they are typically employed in isolation. Trends are a good metric to follow, perhaps the best (especially capital flow trends). However, looking solely at one variable in insolation is like putting all your weight on a one-legged stool. Additionally, isolating your analysis to just one metric, no matter how good it may be, is not gauging, but is timing the market. Multiple leading indicators employed together diversify one risk management approach into a multifactorial approach.

What if there were a way to track every dollar in and out of an index? Could that data be of value? The Capital-Weighted Dollar Volume tracks the trends of money flowing into and out of the capital markets.

Another unique and powerful metric employed by the Volume Factor Risk Overlay is Capital-Weighted **Dollar** Volume (as opposed to just Capital-Weighted Volume). Volume tracks liquidity, whereas Capital-Weighted Dollar Volume tracks all of the money moving into or out of a market index—in other words, Capital Flows. When a stock is purchased within an index, new dollars are coming into the index. Likewise, when a stock within an index is sold, dollars come out of the index. In this way, Capital-Weighted Volume tracks the flow of money into and out of the index.

Table 2: Calculating Capital-Weighted Dollar Volume

Capital-weighted Dollar Volume

- Step #1: Calculate each component's Capital Weighting
  - Price * Shares Outstanding
- Step #2: Determine each component's Index Weighting
  - Capital Weighting / Indexes Capital Weighting
- Step #3: Calculate each component's Capital-Weighted Volume
  - Volume * Price * Capital Weighting
- Step # 4: Parse Upside VS Downside Volume by Component
- Step # 5: Add Upside + Downside CW Volume = Capital-Weighted Volume
- Step #6: Subtract Upside–Downside CW Volume to accumulate CW Volume running total

Notice that the methodology of Capital-Weighted Dollar Volume is exactly the same as Capital-Weighted Volume, except that we consider price changes on each index component member. In this way, Capital-Weighted Dollar Volume accounts for all of the capital flows, dollar for dollar, moving into and out of an index.

Like Capital-Weighted Volume, following capital flows (Capital-Weighted Dollar Volume) improves upon the performance of simply riding out the broad market, while again significantly reducing risk and drawdowns. Dollar volume tracks the capital flowing into and out of a market index, and Capital-Weighted Volume tracks the true volume of shares by capitalization. Capital-Weighted Dollar Volume is useful in uncovering actual money flows within capital trends, whereas Capital-Weighted Volume reveals the liquidity patterns of market participants.

The signals are different, but the overall results appear nearly identical (See Figures 30 & 32), with Capital-Weighted Dollar Volume taking on a bit more risk (Capital-Weighted Volume 11.5 Standard Deviation / Capital-Weighted Dollar Volume 13.0) to receive the same return (8%) as Capital-Weighted Volume.

Figure 33: Pacer Trend Pilot -VS- SPY ETF Post-Pandemic

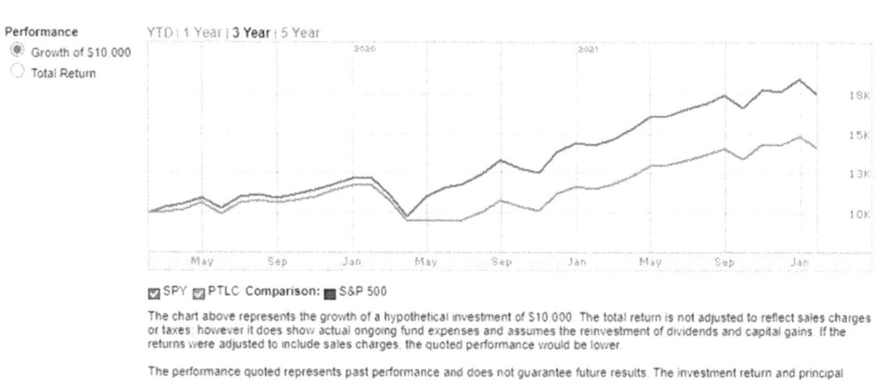

Source: TD Ameritrade

The third fallacy of trend systems is that the reentry is generally late. Above is an example of a large trend following ETF Pacer Trend Pilot Large Cap (PTLC). This strategy primarily employs the 200-day moving average as a signal of being in or out of the market. You can see that this trend system not only was late to exit in 2020, but also missed the enormous initial run.

As a result, this abundantly popular trend flowing ETF (orange line) now is 20% behind buy and hold. An advisor utilizing this strategy for clients now requires a secular bear market for their client to catch up with the buy-and-hold index. That's not an ideal position to be in for an advisor to explain to their client.

Trend-following systems keep drawdowns low. Over the long haul, they should improve risk-adjusted returns. The problem with trend-following systems is that although they have been effective in avoiding secular bear markets, they are notorious for missing the initial run up, which is often the strongest point of investment returns. A holistic approach would emphasize both the defensive side as well as the strategic reentry. When investors are capitulating, running scared out of the market, that's often the ideal time to race back in while prices are severely depressed. By infusing our proprietary VPCI V and W bottom models with our capital flows trend model, we not only position our model to hold the markets when they are trading up and fold when markets are trending down, but we also aim to catch the strongest part of a bull market, it's birth.

Figure 34: Volume Price Confirmation Indicator Signals and Indications

VPCI SIGNALS & INDICATIONS

- Rising/Falling VPCI

- VPCI Crossover VPCI Smoothed

(VPCI Smoothed = VWMA VPCI)

-VPCI Above/Below Zero Line

-VPCI "V" Bottom

To solve the reentry issue, we once again return to the well that never stops giving, volume, and specifically, the VPCI. Do you remember discussing the VPCI in a previous chapter? What we did not cover was the VPCI V Bottom, saving this inspiration for now. By infusing our proprietary VPCI V bottom model with our capital flows trend model, we not only position our models to hold the markets when they are trading up and fold when markets are trending down, but we also position our models to catch the strongest part of a bull market, its birth.

The VPCI V Bottom is an extremely low reading of the VPCI followed by a "V" shaped recovery pattern. These "V" formation conditions often indicate a capitulation bottom may be forming.

Figure 35: VPCI V Bottom Setup Conditions

VPCI "V" BOTTOM SETUP CONDITIONS

1. VA Bear Market: either CW Volume or CW $ Volume below trendline

2. Market Conditions: S&P 500 Index 10% or more below 26 week high (within 20 days)

3. SPY VPCI Condition and Timing:
a. VPCI below 2 standard deviation band (5%)
b. VPCI deeply undersold, VPCI below -4(>1%), signal repeated for 25 days

4. SPY VPCI set up and timing: VPCI crossed above -2 SD from below, signal repeated for 20 days

5. Safeguard: VPCI Time Stop 1 to 3 month duration, reset on W bottom

Source: www.cmtassociation.org

Notice here that I am not using index volume or Capital-Weighted Volume, but ETF volume. **I have found ETF volume to be a superior dataset that is useful in identifying capitulation signals** because of heavy retail participation during panics. With this model, as opposed to following the smart money, we follow the fickle/weak money and do the opposite.

Figure 36: VPCI V Bottom on February 3, 2003

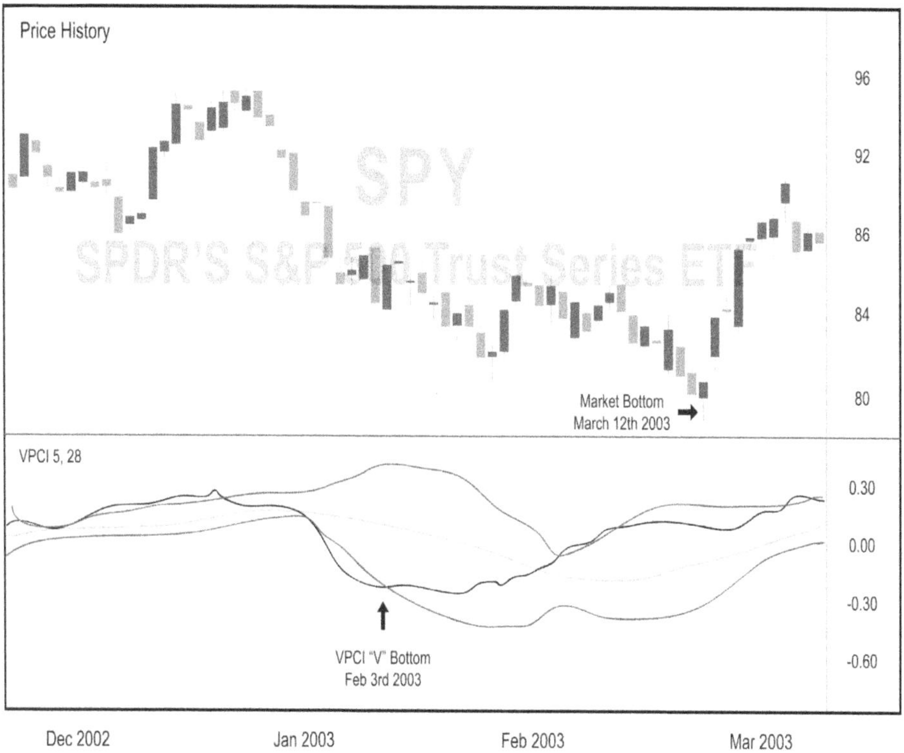

Price History
SPY
SPDR'S S&P 500 Trust Series ETF
96
92
86
84
80
Market Bottom
March 12th 2003
VPCI 5, 28
0.30
0.00
-0.30
-0.60
VPCI "V" Bottom
Feb 3rd 2003
Dec 2002
Jan 2003
Feb 2003
Mar 2003

Source: Worden Brothers StockFinder ® Worden Brothers (www.worden.com)

The VPCI V bottom signal is a rare bottoming or capitulation signal. It occurs by overlaying a standard Bollinger band over the VPCI. In the rare occurrence when the VPCI falls two standard deviations below itself and then crosses back above the two standard deviation line (i.e., the lower Bollinger Band), this event is known as a VPCI V bottom. Here are a few instances of VPCI V bottoms in the past.

The chart above (Figure 36) represents my first observation of a VPCI V Bottom on the SPY—representing the S&P 500 on February 3, 2003, a few weeks before the low cycle forming on March 12, 2003, eventually leading the market into an extended cyclical bull market. If you remember the 2003 bottom, it was a double bottom, with the first bottom occurring in the fourth quarter of 2002. I had recently developed the VPCI indicator at that time, and when I saw how deep the VPCI had fallen and had then quickly risen to cross over its lower Bollinger Band, I thought to myself, this looks very bullish; this could be a capitulation sign. The VPCI did not provide this signal during the first bottom in 2002. And, as it turned out, this signal led to a strong five-year bull market recovery.

Figure 37: VPCI V Bottom on March 9, 2009

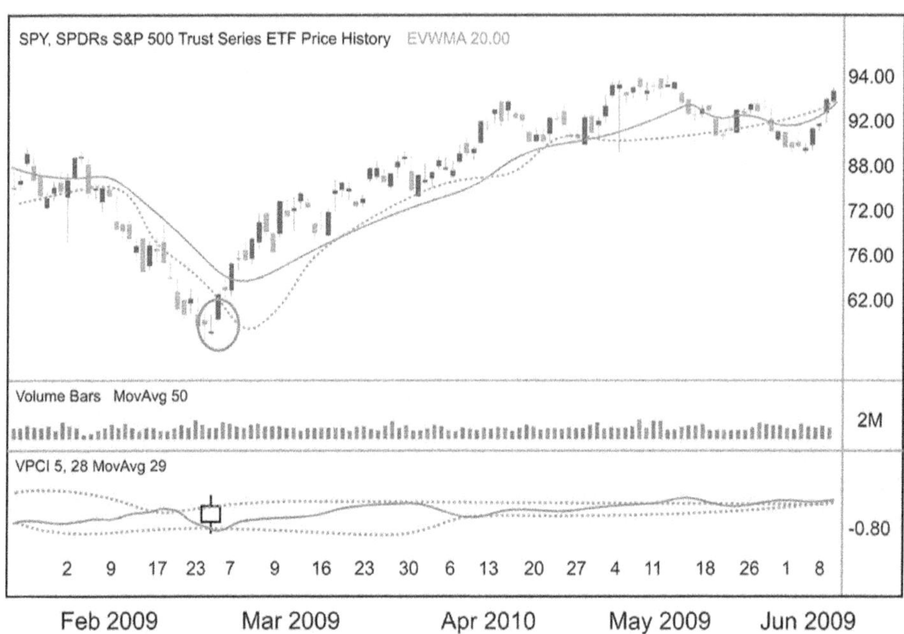

Here is another example, and the best observation of the VPCI V bottom signal yet. Do you know anyone who bought the very low point in March 2009? You do now. The VPCI V signaled a bottom on the close of the day March 8. I still hold a few of those SPY positions as trophies.

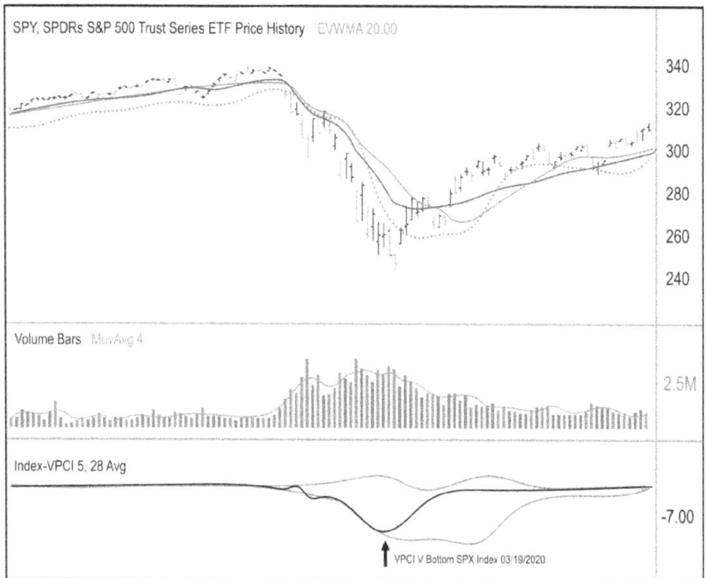

Source: Worden Brothers StockFinder ® Worden Brothers (www.worden.com)

What about the recent pandemic? This time, the VPCI V bottom triggered on the SPY on March 19, 2020, two trading days prior to the actual low. By the way, this signal was called out on Volume Analysis commentaries for clients and subscribers.

Figure 39: S&P 500 Capital-Weighted Volume + Capital-Weighted $ Volume + VPCI V Bottoms -VS- S&P 500 2000–2022

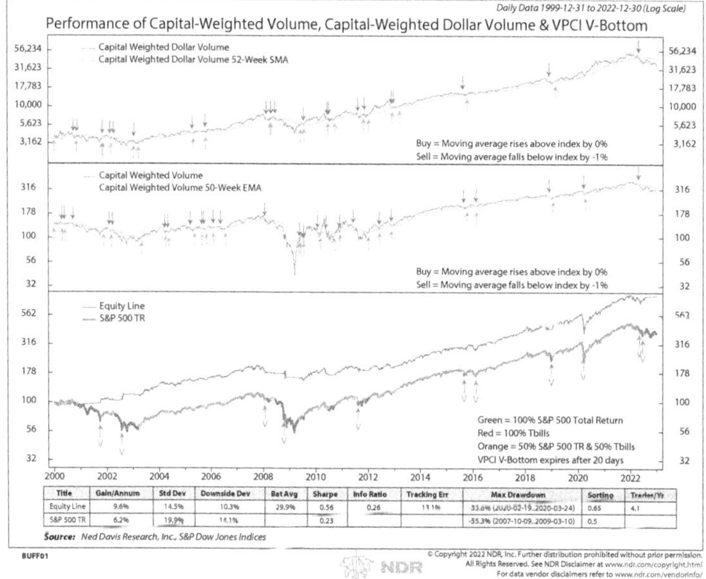

Title	Gain/Annum	Std Dev	Downside Dev	Bat Avg	Sharpe	Info Ratio	Tracking Err	Max Drawdown	Sortino	Trades/Yr
Equity Line	9.6%	14.5%	10.3%	29.9%	0.56	0.26	13.1%	33.8% (2020-02-19..2020-03-24)	0.65	4.1
S&P 500 TR	6.2%	19.9%	14.1%		0.23			-55.3% (2007-10-09..2009-03-10)	0.5	

Source: Ned Davis Research, Inc., S&P Dow Jones Indices

BUFF01

Figure 39 illustrates investments in the S&P 500 utilizing our multi-legged risk overlay stool, infusing Capital-Weighted Volume with Capital-Weighted Dollar Volume and the VPCI V Bottom model. You can see the improvement by utilizing these leading indicators together. The combined model boosted the annual rate of return of the S&P 500 buy-and-hold strategy by more than 3% per year, from 6.2% to 9.6%, meanwhile dropping the risk from a nearly 20% standard deviation to only 14.5%. With more return and less risk, the Sharpe ratio improved from .23 to .56, more than doubling the risk-adjusted returns utilizing our Volume Factor Risk Overlay.

You need to know when to hold them and when to fold them. When liquidity and capital are flowing in the market, it is time to hold them; when they are flowing out, it is time to fold them. Here is an example of following liquidity through our proprietary Volume Factor Risk Overlay. We are long 50% when either Capital-Weighted Volumes are above trend, long 100% when both Capital-Weighted Volumes are above trend and/or if there is a VPCI V Bottom. The VPCI V bottom signal lasted 20 trading days (approximately one month). The red line is the S&P 500 equity line, and the green line is the performance of our Capital-Weighted Volume model vs. passively holding the S&P 500.

Notice that going back to 2000 until recently, the market has returned 6.3%. Our model of following the trend of volume flows returned 9.6%. Here is the point I do not want you to miss: Our model accomplishes this with significantly less risk, as noted in our standard deviation, which is only 14.5% compared to the buy-and-hold standard deviation of 19.8%. Higher returns with less risk lead to significantly higher risk-adjusted rates of return. The Volume Factor risk overlay's Sharpe ratio of .56 compares to the S&P 500 index of .25, more than doubling the risk-adjusted rate of return.

Figure 40: S&P 500 Capital-Weighted Volume + VPCI V Bottoms 2000–2020

Here is where the rubber meets the road. So many believe the primary objective of portfolio management is returns. And if your client's investment objective is aggressive growth and they are never going to spend their portfolio money, that could be true. But most investors are not emotionally suited for aggressive growth, and aggressive growth is rarely appropriate for the life-distribution phase.

Figure 40 is an example of utilizing our Capital-Weighted Volume and VPCI V bottom model, just two of our four legs. In this illustration, an investor retires in 2000 with $1 million **utilizing the endowment method of withdrawals**, taking out 1% each quarter or 4% per year from their remaining principal. In this scenario, the funds are passively invested in the S&P 500. In the volume analysis risk overlay model, the funds are actively invested in the S&P 500 using only the CW Volume with VPCI V bottom.

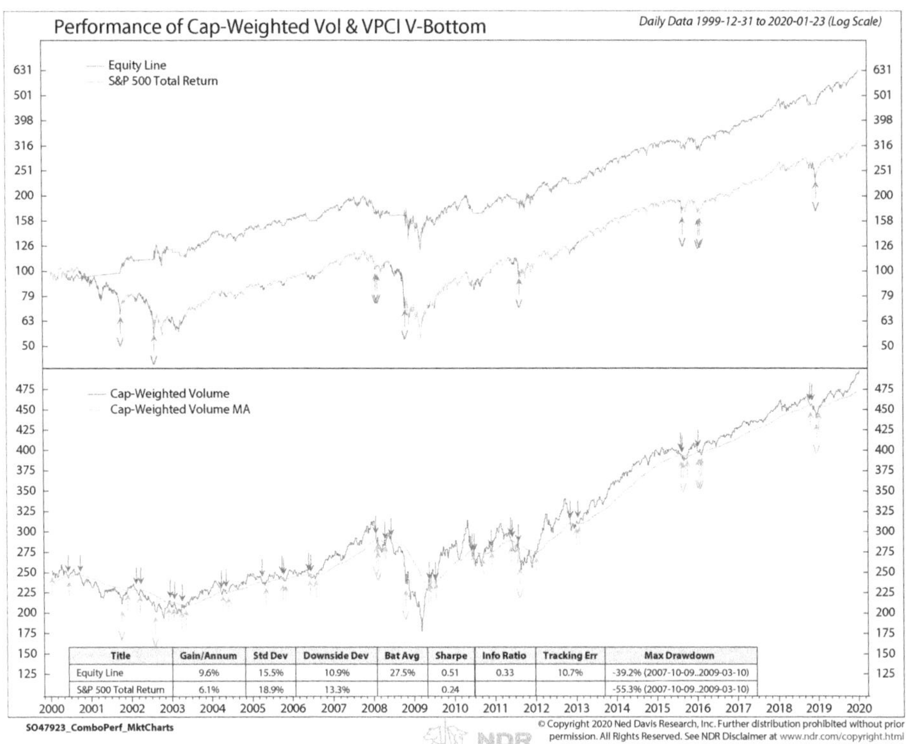

Title	Gain/Annum	Std Dev	Downside Dev	Bat Avg	Sharpe	Info Ratio	Tracking Err	Max Drawdown
Equity Line	9.6%	15.5%	10.9%	27.5%	0.51	0.33	10.7%	-39.2% (2007-10-09..2009-03-10)
S&P 500 Total Return	6.1%	18.9%	13.3%		0.24			-55.3% (2007-10-09..2009-03-10)

	Volume Factor - Rish Management Overlay in the Distribution Phase 2000-2020 1% Quarterly Withdraw S&P 500 - VS - S&P 500 with Volume Factor Risk Management Overlay					
	Applying Tactical Portfolio Construction In The Distribution Phase					
	S&P 500 TR Gross Equity	VPCI & Cap-Wght Vol Gross Equity	S&P 500 TR $ Withdrawn This Period	VPCI & Cap-Wght Vol $ Withdrawn This Period	S&P 500 TR Total Withdrawn	VPCI & Cap-Wght Vol Total Withdrawn
1/1/2000	$1,000,000	$1,000,000	$0	$0	$0	$0
12/31/2020	$1,431,043	$2,744,133	$14,455	$27,718	$673,301	$1,156,817

Source: The Volume Factor, Buff Dormeier, CMT

Source: NDR Presented as supplemental information. All information obtained here is for information purposes only. There is no guarantee that any investment will achieve its objectives. Data quoted as past performance and current performance may be higher or lower.

Once again, here is where the rubber meets the road. As previously stated, so many believe the primary objective of portfolio management is returns, but as a technician, my #1 job is capital preservation. This is because preserving capital leads to successful financial outcomes.

This is an example of utilizing our Capital-Weighted Volume and VPCI V bottom models, just two of our four legs. In this illustration, an investor retires in 2000 with $1 million utilizing the endowment method of withdrawals, taking out 1% each quarter or 4%

per year from their remaining principal. In scenario one, the funds are passively invested in the S&P 500. Additionally, in our volume analysis scenario, funds are actively invested in the S&P 500 employing the Capital-Weighted Volume with the VPCI V bottom dual risk overlay.

Reviewing the last two decades, for an investor who bought the S&P 500 in 2000 and sold quarterly to meet his distribution, his remaining capital would grow to $1.4 million.

However, for the investor who actively applied the Capital-Weighted Volume and VPCI V bottoms to the S&P 500 as a risk overlay, their remaining principal grew to $2.74 million compared to $1.4 million for the passive investor. Note that the S&P 500 buy-and-hold last quarterly distribution was $14,455. That compares to the volume analysis risk overlay's last quarterly distribution of $27,718. Do you think that difference could be important to a retiree or an endowment?

Perhaps even more noteworthy, the S&P 500 passive investor withdrew $673,000 over the course of 20 years. In other words, this person **lived an average lifestyle of less than $34,000 per year** over the two decades. However, the person employing our volume analysis risk overlay withdrew over $1.1 million over the course of 20 years. This indicates that the person employing our volume analysis risk overlay realized a significant improvement in cash flow compared to the passive strategy.

Adding up distributions and remaining capital, our active investor employing the volume analysis risk overlay realized total principal and distributions combined of approximately $3.9 million, compared to the passive approach of $2.1 million in principal and income distributions. Here's the point: Investment returns should not be as important as investment outcomes. Allow me to turn back the page and provide you with yet another example.

Table 4: 1% Quarterly Withdrawals Years Ending 2002, 2008 & 2019 Capital-Weighted Volume + VPCI V Bottoms -VS- S&P 500 Buy & Hold

Applying Tactical Portfolio Construction in the Distribution Phase
Volume Factor-CW Volume Risk+VPCI V Bottom Risk Management Overlay
2000-2020 1% Quarterly Withdraw S&P 500 with Volume Factor Risk Management Overlay

Date	S&P 500 TR: Net Equity After Withdrawl	VPCI & Cap: Wght Vol: Net Equity After Withdrawl	S&P 500 TR: $ Withdrawn This Period	VPCI & Cap: Wght Vol: $ Withdrawn This Period	S&P 500 TR: Total Withdrawn	VCPI & Cap: Wght Vol: Total Withdrawn	S&P 500: TR Total Return Equity Play Withdrawls	VPCI & Cap: Wght Vol: Total Return Equity Play Withdrawls
12/31/1999	$1,000,000	$1,000,000	$10,000	$10,000	$0	$0	$1,000,000	$1,000,000
12/31/2002	$553,111	$1,083,498	$5,587	$10,944	$106,870	$106,981	$659,981	$1,190,367
12/31/2006	$497,702	$1,118,906	$5,627	$11,???	$265,727	$413,576	$763,429	$1,582,575
12/31/2019	$1,431,043	$2,744,113	$14,455	$27,718	$673,301	$1,156,817	$2,104,345	$3,900,931

All information contained herein is for informational purposes only. There is no guarantee that any investment will achieve its objectives. Data quoted is past performance and current performance may be higher or lower. Please refer to the important disclosure information at the end of this presentation for definitions, additional information, and risks.

We have reviewed the end of the story of risk management versus buy and hold. But when you open the book, there are chapters in the buy-and-hold story that look a whole lot worse than the ending. Please reference Table 4.

By the end of 2002, passive assets were just over half of what they started with compared to our volume-oriented risk overlay, which is still above its beginning value despite withdrawing over $106,000. Speaking of income, in 2002, the passive S&P 500 investment strategy saw its quarterly income fall to just $5,500 compared to our volume risk-managed model quarterly withdrawal of just under $11,000.

Then, after five years of positive returns, along comes 2008. And by the end of 2008, over half of the passive strategy capital was depleted, whereas the volume analysis risk overlay continued to grow despite withdrawals. By the end of 2008, the passive strategy quarterly distribution was actually less than half, at $5,000, compared to over $11,000 with the Capital-Weighted volume analysis plus VPCI V bottom risk overlay.

Employing volume factors, with their unique ability to both lead and confirm price trends within a risk overlay, delivers what growth investors want and income investors need: specifically, to be positioned long in the equity markets when they are advancing and repositioned to safety when their trends are declining.

From a real-life perspective, the life dreams of our passive investor retiree were sacrificed on the altar of volatility, whereas our volume-based tactical retiree was able to enjoy the retirement they imagined while forgoing much of the emotional stress of volatile markets. Volume more than moved the needle. It is the game changer of post-modern portfolio theory.

Results are the priority. Do not over-prioritize the fast-racing hare. Rather, choose the steady, armored tank, the tortoise. This is the art of survival. Whether you are a technician, analyst, portfolio manager, financial advisor, endowment manager, or individual investor, risk management is your differentiator. Overall, **risk management provides:**

- Objectivity: Prioritize objective indicators and measurable factors over human emotions
- Decision Points: Minimize the impact of emotion in your methodology
- Discipline: Adhere to a strategy
- Realism: Be prepared to make mistakes because you will
- Excellence: Remember that winning the war entails losing a few battles and retreating to survive another day
- Confidence: Believe in the process, and not in the direction, of forthcoming market movements

Ultimately, investment outcomes are what matters, not investment returns. This is the art of survival. The Volume Factor's low volatility neutralizes the behavioral finance risks of bailing out without a competent reentry plan, as well as reverse compounding risks of large drawdowns. Risk management is the path less taken, but it is the sure path to financial survival, leading to successful investment outcomes for individuals and endowments, as well as client retention for financial advisors.

CHAPTER 6:

BULL RUN, BEAR HIDE—VOLUME FACTOR MODELS FOR GROWTH AND THE ENDOWMENT METHOD OF WITHDRAWAL

"Carefully consider the path of your feet, and all your ways will established"
– Proverbs 4:26

Some of the data presented in this chapter is hypothetical and back-tested data. This data is not based on any advisory client assets. Past performance of a model is not a guarantee of future results. Actual performance may vary significantly from the hypothetical results shown. Please see the section titled 'Important Information Regarding Hypothetical, Back-Tested Performance' for a full description of this data and the limitations associated with it.

When introduced nearly 70 years ago, modern portfolio theory provided evidence that asset diversification may help lower risk within an investment portfolio. Since then, postmodern portfolio theory has shown that risk may not only be mitigated via asset diversification but also through tactical portfolio construction.

Postmodern portfolio theory is a portfolio optimization framework developed by financial economist and Nobel laureate Harry Markowitz in the 1990s. It is an extension of the earlier modern portfolio theory, which considers multiple sources of risk beyond merely market risk.

By incorporating additional factors of risk beyond asset class, postmodern portfolio theory attempts to address the limitations of modern portfolio theory. These factors could include liquidity risk, credit risk, macroeconomic risk, and many more. Postmodern portfolio theory recognizes that traditional measures of risk, such as standard deviations, may not accurately capture all of the portfolio risks in today's complex financial markets.

Post-modern portfolio theory suggests that investors should consider using a combination of diversified assets with low correlations to reduce risk. It also emphasizes the importance of attentive managers who adapt to changing market conditions and new information. Postmodern portfolio theory moves beyond static allocation, recognizing the realities of behavioral finance.

Overall, postmodern portfolio theory is a more sophisticated and nuanced approach to portfolio optimization that considers a broader range of risk factors, encourages active management, and acknowledges the effects of behavioral finance.

Here is an example of behavioral finance. A financial advisor builds an appropriate asset allocation model with their client's goals and risk temperament in mind. Yet, during bull markets, the client is upset that the portfolio is not keeping up with the top-performing benchmarks. Then, during market pullbacks, the client is upset that they are losing money despite outperforming the benchmarks.

Investors with growth objectives are more prone to experience behavioral finance realities while investing. Yet, behavioral finance realities are not commonly considered and accounted for in most growth portfolio strategies. The reality is that growth is always accompanied by drawdowns. For this reason, financial advisors provide clients with a risk assessment to identify their tolerance toward risk. When accompanied by the client's goals, this risk assessment leads to an asset allocation model. Although the advisor builds an appropriate nontactical postmodern asset allocation portfolio, investors are still emotional creatures. Clients are greedy. When the market is up, investors want to track or beat the best-performing indexes—in other words, take on additional risk. Behavioral finance tells us that when the market is hot, investors want *to run with the bulls*. However, when the market is down, clients are gripped with fear and expect their financial advisors to protect them from losing money. Thus, the reality of behavioral finance tells us that clients' risk tolerance is not static but is instead often dependent on their current experience (recency bias).

Behavioral Finance Realities:

- Investors tend to be greedy, desiring to outperform the markets when markets are positive.
- Investors tend to be fearful, desiring flat returns when the markets are negative.
- Emotional investors often enter bull markets late cycle and capitulate near market bottoms.
- A portfolio strategy striving for favorable investment outcomes must be tolerable to investors.

Our Volume Factor approach to postmodern portfolio theory employs tactical asset allocation built on a dual mandate to participate in the strongest performing sectors, with the ability to mediate risk when equity capital flows are reversing. The engine that drives the financial plan is a diversified portfolio. Allocation is diversified among geography, styles, sizes, sectors, industries, themes, and factors.

The goal of the Volume Factor's Bull-Run, Bear-Hide Models is to provide clients with what they want: "To run with the bulls and hide from the bear." In other words, they want the opportunity to participate and hopefully exceed the broad markets during bull market cycles while protecting capital during bear market cycles. This tactical postmodern approach recognizes clients' behavioral finance needs. During bear markets, investors feel the need to act (run from the bear / not be eaten). Sometimes even in bull markets, many investors fear the rally cannot go on forever and want out while they're ahead (protect their homestead). More often, though, during bull markets, clients are acutely aware of all of their neighbors' successes, and they want to make sure they are keeping up with "the Joneses."

Utilizing our time-tested leading volume indicators, our Bull-Run, Bear-Hide Models actively attack this behavioral finance problem. Our Volume Factor models ideally aim to pursue both theories of portfolio management simultaneously. The benefits of modern portfolio theory are achieved through widespread global equity diversification. Contemporaneously, state-of-the-art tactical, factor-based portfolio construction is overlayed with state-of-the-art risk management. By utilizing both modern and postmodern portfolio management concurrently, our Bull-Run, Bear-Hide Models strive to achieve the dual objectives of delivering excess returns throughout bull market cycles while preserving capital during cyclical bear markets.

Next, we will explain how these active models solve this behavioral problem by providing an advisor, individual, or institution with an advanced, data-driven approach following the top performers while gauging the health of the broad market. Not only can this approach address clients' and investors' emotional needs, but the low drawdowns and reduced volatility lead to more sustainable investment outcomes. The goal of the Bull-Run, Bear-Hide Models is to provide investors what they want, "an opportunity to participate and hopefully exceed the broad markets in bull market cycles and to protect capital during bear market cycles."

For example, when the markets are down and investors are gripped with fear, clients expect their financial advisors to protect them from losing money. During bear markets, clients need to feel that their advisors are actively doing something to protect them. In contrast, when markets are up, volume analysis is applied to identify those areas of the markets garnering the strongest capital flows. Thus, much like a football team, our models are split into three separate units: offense, defense, and Special Teams. A Bull-Run offense is employed during volume analysis bull markets, while a Bear-Hide defense is utilized during volume analysis bear markets. Volume Factor Special Teams are employed between market transitions.

VOLUME FACTOR OFFENSE—BULL RUN

Our approach to postmodern portfolio theory is tactical asset allocation, a dual mandate to participate in the strongest-performing sectors with the ability to mediate risk when equity capital flows are reversing.

Our first step is critical. We need to be able to identify when the market is ripe for our offense to be deployed. To determine our risk exposure, we employ our volume analysis tools to gauge the state of the market. Let's review these risk mitigation tools discussed in our previous chapter:

- Capital-Weighted Volume tracks the bullish enthusiasm or bearish anxiety of investors participating in capital markets, expressed through share volume.
- Capital-Weighted Dollar Volume, also referred to as capital flows, tracks the money moving into and out of a market index.
- The Advance-Decline Line tracks the number of stocks moving up versus those moving down, gauging the liquidity of markets.

When all three of these indicators are trending above trend, our Bull Run offensive takes the field. The members of our offensive unit are selected by combining various components used in The Volume Factor security selection process (covered in the Momentum Chapter) and applied to a universe of diversified securities. These securities could represent factors but also styles, industries, sectors, themes, and indexes—both domestically and abroad. The Volume Factor selection process utilizes the Volume Factor security selection ranking system to determine the timeliness. Next, we will unpack the process of building out this diversified Volume Factor model with ambitious growth objectives.

Volume Factor Security Selection Process

There are many ways portfolio managers attempt to deliver alpha. One proven way is through factor investing. Factors are qualities in stocks that have historically provided excess returns over the benchmark. There are five commonly agreed-upon market factors. These five factors are value, momentum, small size, low volatility, and quality. Because momentum can help us to identify important factors or areas of the market, momentum is our first variable in the volume factor methodology. Figure 1 shows the risk /reward of using market factor constructed by First Trust from 1997-2023.

Figure 1: Factor Risk Reward Chart

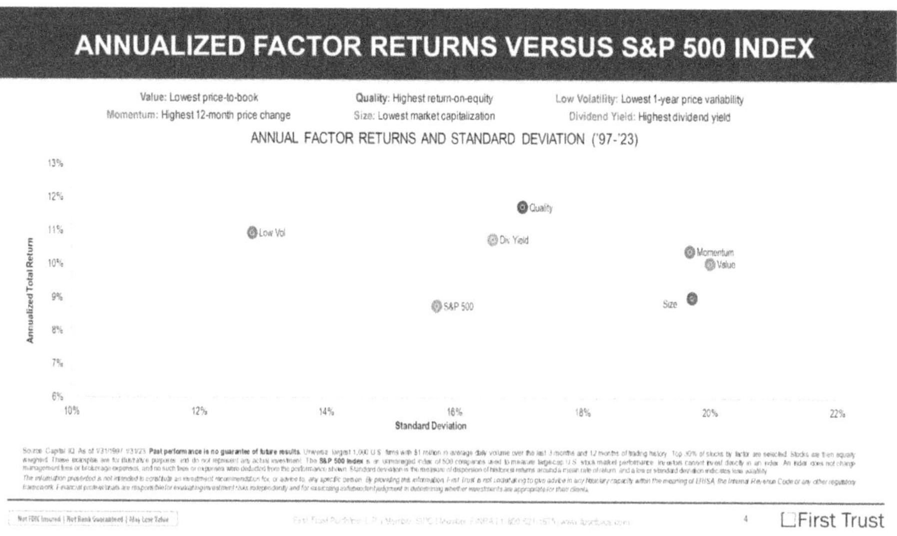

Source: FirstTrust

If factors historically beat indexes, why not invest in these factors? Although factors have outperformed over the course of long investment cycles, they do move in and out of favor. Single factors often remain out of favor for long periods of time, unfortunately, longer than most investors can generally tolerate. However, employing momentum with the Volume Factor can determine which factors, sectors, industries, styles, or regions are presently in vogue. In this way, the Volume Factor approach uses momentum to determine the timeliness of investing in factors and all other market groups and categories. That stated, the Volume Factor widely advances the traditional momentum approach by employing multiple types of momentum, all infused in our volume analysis approach.

In this way, the Bull Run offense adjusts the momentum factor with the unknown factor, the Volume Factor confirming whether or not price momentum is sustainable. The Volume Factor is the factor that "rules them all", both leading price to identify trend momentum earlier while distinguishing between momentum with capital flows to build and continue versus those without capital flows and likely to be topping out.

Volume Factor Defense—Bear Hide

It has been correctly stated, "Defense wins championships." Yet, investment outcomes are not by any means a game. For individual investors, the preservation of their precious hard-earned capital is a vital goal in growing and sustaining wealth. For growth investors, preserving their capital base is fundamental in the building of wealth. With retirees, preserving the capital base is critical in sustaining a recurring revenue stream and passing wealth to the next generation. Endowments must maintain and grow their capital base to support the eternal spending policies of their mission. Perhaps, most importantly for financial advisors, a championship defense is the path to client retention and successful financial outcomes—not only for their clients, but also for their practice. For these reasons, risk management is the top priority for the Bull-Run, Bear-Hide Models. Our defensive models strive to preserve capital by minimizing drawdowns.

The key to maintaining low drawdowns is the ability to distinguish between market fluctuations, corrections, and bear markets. The Volume Factor Risk Overlay analyzes market trends, gauging the market's health and sustainability. Traditionally, the problem with price-based trending systems is that price trends, by definition, lag. Often by the time markets return to a positive trend, much of the gain from avoiding the decline has been lost. To correct for this weakness, Bear Hide employs three price-leading trend indicators to determine equity allocation by employing leading trend indicators such as Capital-Weighted Volume, capital flows, and the Advance-Decline Line. Each empowers our Bull-Run, Bear-Hide Models to potentially identify bear and bull markets before price trend reversals. Although these trend indicators do not fully eliminate the problem of trend lag, they certainly aim to substantially reduce lag.

BULL-RUN, BEAR-HIDE RISK OVERLAY COMPONENTS

CAPITAL-WEIGHTED VOLUME

Capital weighting volume harmonizes index volume with the price index. Capital-Weighted Volume tracks the true volume into and out of the capital markets. From 2000-2020, employing Capital-Weighted Volume as a risk overlay on the S&P 500 reduced volatility from 18.1 to 11.5 while increasing annualized returns from to 6.2% to 8%, more than doubling the Sharpe ratio, from 0.26 to 0.56.

Figure 2: Volume Factor's Bull-Run, Bear-Hide Risk Overlay, Part 1—Capital-Weighted Volume

Capital-Weighted Volume vs. Moving Average

Weekly Data 1999-12-31 to 2022-12-30 (Log Scale)

Capital Weighted Volume
Capital Weighted Volume 50-Week EMA

Buy = Moving average rises above index by 0%
Sell = Moving average falls below index by -1%

Equity Line
S&P 500 TR

Green = 100% S&P 500 Total Return
Red = 100% Tbills

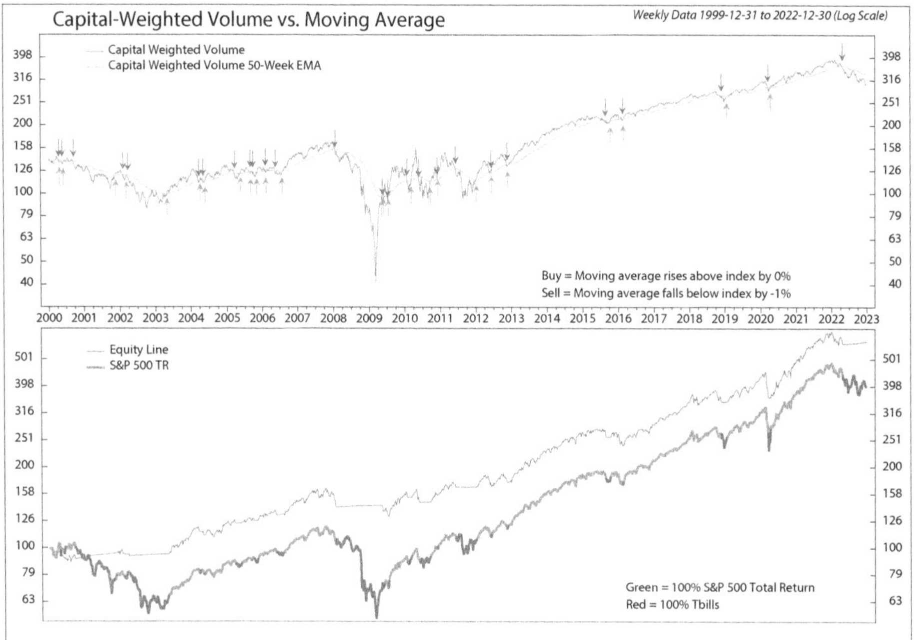

Title	Gain/Annum	Std Dev	Downside Dev	Bat Avg	Sharpe	Info Ratio	Tracking Err	Max Drawdown	Trades/Yr
Equity Line	8.0%	11.5%	8.2%	31.5%	0.56	0.13	14.1%	-21.2% (2007-10-12..2009-07-11)	2.3
S&P 500 TR	6.2%	18.1%	12.9%		0.26			-54.7% (2007-10-12..2009-03-07)	

Source: *Mergent, Inc., Ned Davis Research, Inc.*

BUFF04_STAT

CAPITAL-WEIGHTED DOLLAR VOLUME, AKA CAPITAL FLOWS

Capital-Weighted Dollar Volume tracks the flows of capital. In essence, upside Capital-Weighted Dollar Volume tracks the money moving into a market index as capital inflows. Capital moving out of the market is identified as downside capital outflows. The cumulative net between capital inflows and outflows is Capital-Weighted Dollar Volume. When accumulated Capital-Weighted Dollar Volume is trending higher, it tells us that capital is flowing into the stock market. Conversely, when accumulated Capital-Weighted Dollar Volume trends downward, capital is flowing out of the stock market. Applying Capital-Weighted Dollar Volume as a risk overlay on the S&P 500 over the same period also returned 8% while assuming slightly more risk. Capital-Weighted Dollar Volume produced a 13% standard deviation compared to 11.5% with Capital-Weighted Volume, creating a Sharpe ratio of 0.5% versus a 0.26% buy and hold.

Figure 3: Volume Factor's Bull-Run, Bear-Hide Risk Overlay, Part 2—Capital-Weighted Dollar Volume

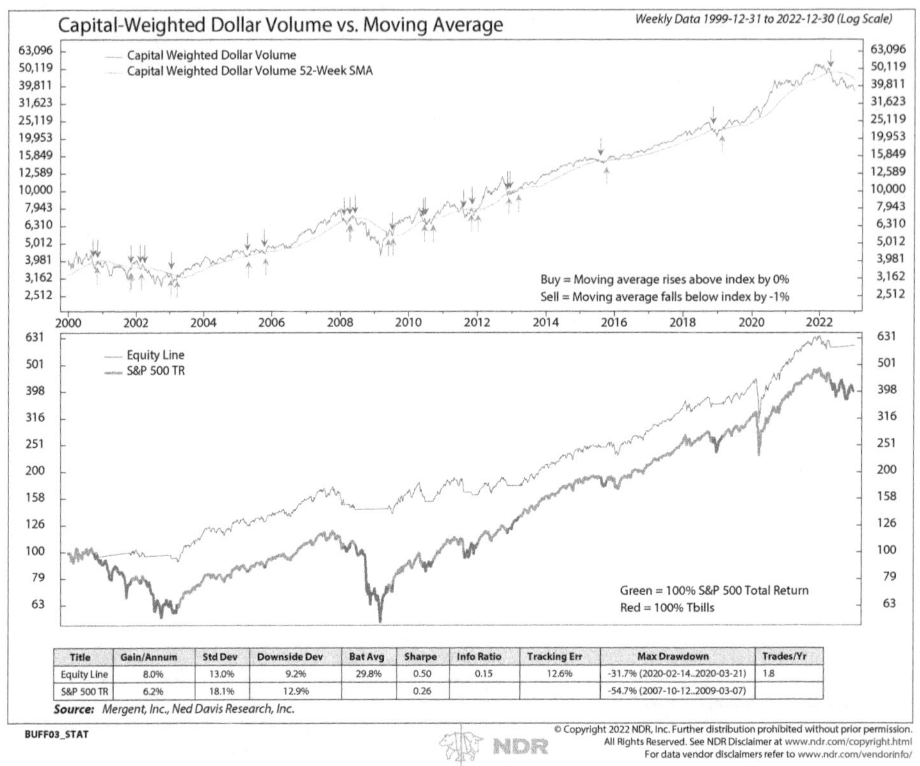

Title	Gain/Annum	Std Dev	Downside Dev	Bat Avg	Sharpe	Info Ratio	Tracking Err	Max Drawdown	Trades/Yr
Equity Line	8.0%	13.0%	9.2%	29.8%	0.50	0.15	12.6%	-31.7% (2020-02-14..2020-03-21)	1.8
S&P 500 TR	6.2%	18.1%	12.9%		0.26			-54.7% (2007-10-12..2009-03-07)	

Source: *Mergent, Inc., Ned Davis Research, Inc.*

BUFF03_STAT

ADVANCE-DECLINE LINE

The Advance-Decline Line is generally the fastest of our three leading indicators. Arguably, there has never been a significant bear market without the Advance-Decline Line first falling below trend. That stated, the Advance-Decline is also known to fall below trend while the market continues to realize higher highs. For this reason, we do not suggest using the Advance-Decline Line as a direct component of our Bear-Hide Risk Overlay. Rather, our Bear-Hide Risk Overlay may employ the Advance-Decline Line as a multiplier, which enhances the signals of our two Capital-Weighted Volume indicators. In this way, the Advance-Decline is applied to confirm the trend of Capital-Weighted Volume and capital flows, allowing the Advance-Decline Line to validate our volume signals while eliminating its weakness of "false" signals when employed in isolation.

Figure 4: Volume Factor's Bull-Run, Bear-Hide Risk Overlay, Part 3—Advance-Decline Line

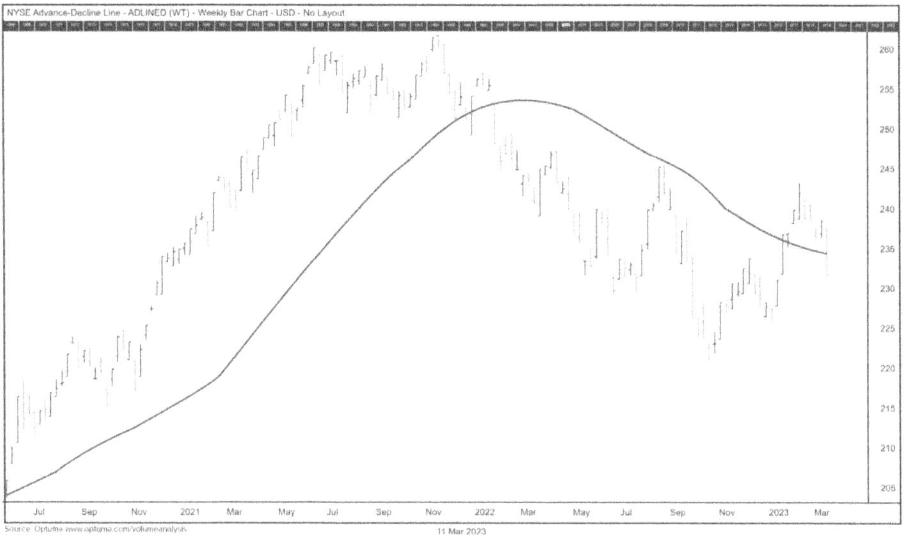

Source: Optuma www.optuma.com/volumeanalysis

By employing three separate indicators, each with its own unique data set, these models gauges the health of the market, not timing it. Additionally, although Capital-Weighted Volume and Capital-Weighted Dollar Volume do an exceptional job of managing risk in isolation, employing the three indicators together prevents our Bear Hide Models from being overconcentrated on any one single indication. Scaling the equity exposure in and out based on the collective readings of these data sets allows for smooth yet decisive repositioning. Otherwise, one single indication could bounce the model equity exposure completely in or out, leading to erratic swings and higher portfolio turnover.

Overall, the Volume Factor Bull-Run, Bear-Hide Models strive to be invested in the top-performing areas during periods of expansion while mitigating downside risk over prolonged periods of contraction. This objective further serves to taper clients' anxieties, whether it be the fear of missing out or the fear of capital loss. Next, we will cover market transitions in Volume Factor Risk Overlays Special Teams.

BULL RUN BEAR HIDE SPECIAL TEAMS:

"Desire without knowledge is not good, and whoever makes haste with his feet misses his way. When a man's folly brings his way to ruin, his heart rages against the LORD."

– Proverbs 19 2–3

VPCI V & W BOTTOMS:

There are critical junctures in the investment landscape when swift transitions from a defensive stance to an offensive posture become imperative. The challenge with relying on trend-based systems lies in the rapid rebounds that characterize market bottoms. By the time markets resume an upward trajectory, a considerable portion of potential gains may have already materialized. Football teams employ special teams during transitions from defense to offense. As an investor, you should employ special teams too. The inherent difficulty lies in discerning when a bear market is primed for a resurgence. To pinpoint market capitulation, we revisit the realm of volume analysis, this time employing the Volume Price Confirmation Indicator (VPCI) to unveil asymmetries between price and volume trends.

To elucidate how VPCI can effectively identify market bottoms, consider this analogy: Is there anyone you know who is consistently right? Probably not, unless, of course, you happen to be married. Conversely, it's more likely that you know someone who perpetually seems to make the wrong decisions at precisely the wrong moments. In the market, these individuals congregate in the SPY—an exchange-traded fund mirroring the S&P 500 index. Our focus, however, is on SPY's volume, a reflection of trading activities driven by the emotions of fear and greed among weak investors.

When the market ascends, these greedy investors, fearing they are missing out, join the fray near its zenith. Conversely, as the market turns bearish, the pain of financial loss compels them to hastily exit. During the critical phase of a capitulation rebound, both the S&P 500 and SPY experience substantial declines, often far exceeding 10% from recent highs. As the market plunges, the volume in SPY surges—a manifestation of these weak investors selling off their positions.

This sets the stage for the sought-after setup, identified by the VPCI plummeting to extreme levels. The trigger to re-enter the market is the deeply oversold VPCI reversing its course. This signal indicates that the majority of weak investors have liquidated their positions, and the selling pressure is poised to dissipate.

In this way, the Volume Factor Risk Overlay employs a proprietary capitulation methodology designed to catch market bottoming formations. *The VPCI V Bottom identifies extreme capitulation points through massive outflows*. During these rare points of massive outflows, the VPCI V Bottom is built to uncover momentum weakness in volume relative to price activity. Historically, these have often been rare dark periods before the coming dawn of a market recovery.

Figure 5: Capital-Weighted Volume Infused with VPCI V Bottoms

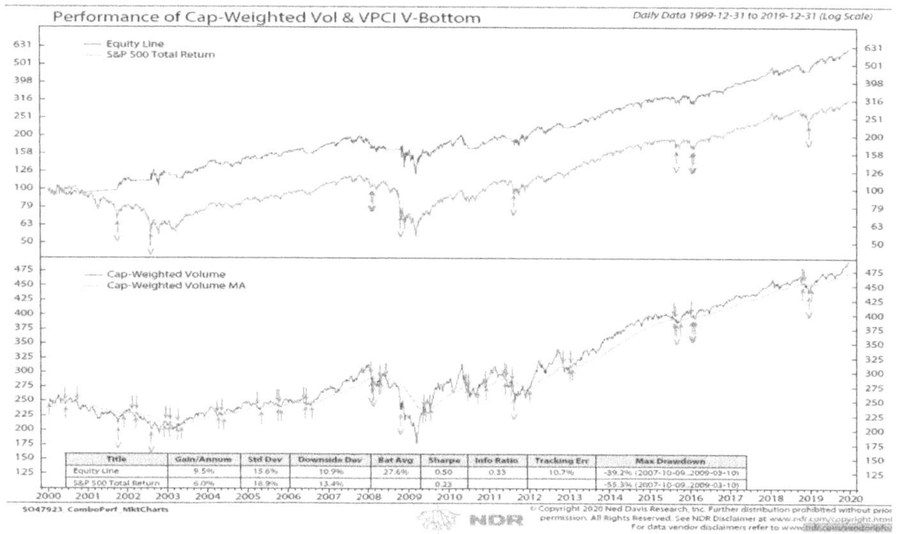

Title	Gain/Annum	Std Dev	Downside Dev	Bat Avg	Sharpe	Info Ratio	Tracking Err	Max Drawdown
Equity Line	9.5%	15.6%	10.9%	27.6%	0.50	0.33	10.7%	-39.2% (2007-10-09..2009-03-10)
S&P 500 Total Return	6.0%	18.9%	13.4%		0.23			-55.3% (2007-10-09..2009-03-10)

Over the past two decades, from 2000-2020, there have been 10 broad market (S&P 500) VPCI V Bottoms.

There are certain set-up perimeters the Bull-Run Bear-Hide Special Teams must meet to uniquely identify points of market capitulation via VPCI V Bottoms. **First**, the S&P 500 needs to have dropped 10% from its highs within the last two quarters. In other words, the S&P 500 is or recently was in a correction phase. **Second**, the VPCI must have fallen at least two standard deviations below its lower 20-day Bollinger band. **Third**, the VPCI must be deeply oversold with a minimum reading of under -4.0. **Finally**, if all these conditions have been met over the past 25 trading days and then, importantly, the VPCI rises back above its lower 20-day Bollinger band, then the VPCI V Bottom set-up is completed. When a VPCI V Bottom occurs, the Bull-Run, Bear-Hide Models (temporarily) revert to full equity.

Often a VPCI V Bottom marks the coming birth of a new bull market. The new bull market should be confirmed by either of the Capital-Weighted Volume(s) returning above their trend. Other times, a VPCI V Bottom could just be a short- or intermediate-term oversold condition. Precautions need to be taken in these situations when the VPCI V Bottom is just a short-term oversold condition, not a new bull market. Otherwise, the Bull-Run, Bear-Hide Models would be stuck in a long position after the oversold condition has run its course, yet the market remains weak. For this reason, I suggest utilizing a gradually fading time stop on the VPCI V Bottom signal. To incorporate the VPCI V Bottom into our risk overlay, we will need to lay down longevity rules. These are the VPCI V Bottom time-stop rules.

Figure 6: Capital-Weighted Dollar Volume Plus VPCI V Bottoms, Expiration 3 Months

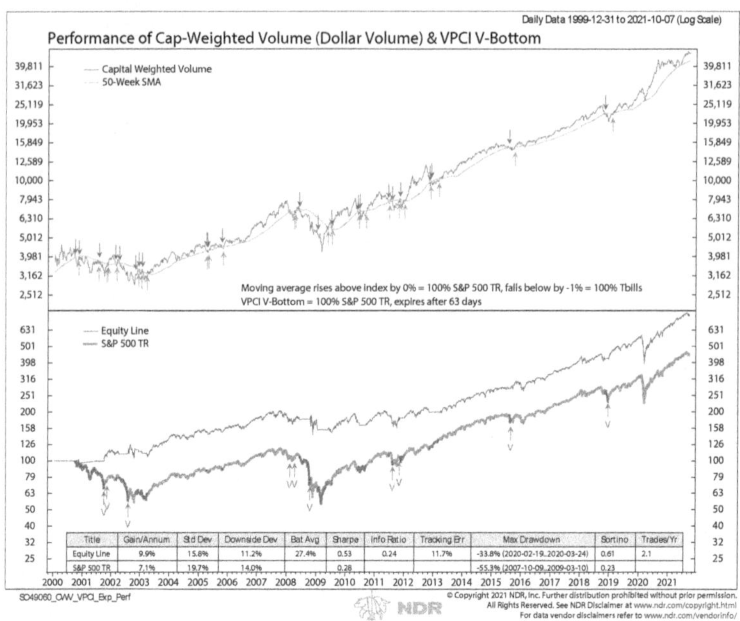

Title	Gain/Annum	Std Dev	Downside Dev	Bat Avg	Sharpe	Info Ratio	Tracking Err	Max Drawdown	Sortino	Trades/Yr
Equity Line	9.9%	15.8%	11.2%	27.4%	0.53	0.24	11.7%	-33.8% (2020-02-19..2020-03-24)	0.61	2.1
S&P 500 TR	7.1%	19.7%	14.0%		0.28			-55.3% (2007-10-09..2009-03-10)	0.23	

Figure 7: Capital-Weighted Dollar Volume Plus VPCI V Bottoms, Expiration 2 Months

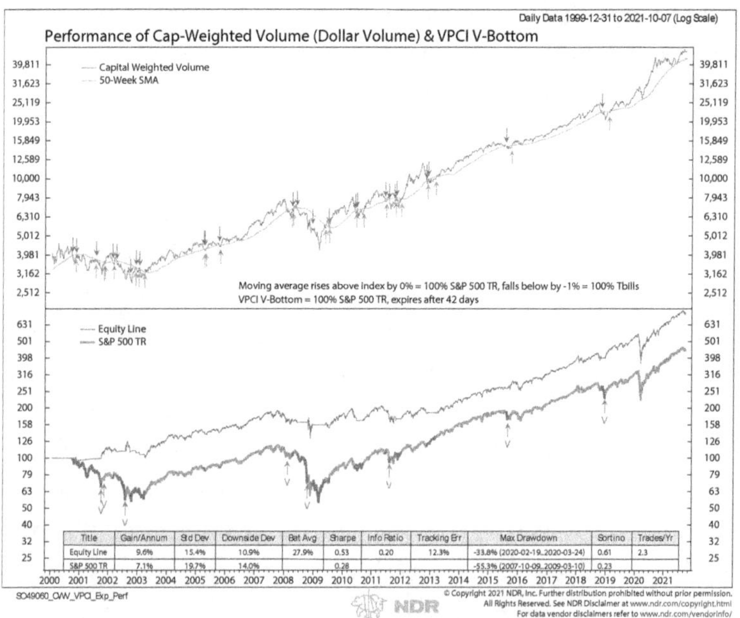

Title	Gain/Annum	Std Dev	Downside Dev	Bat Avg	Sharpe	Info Ratio	Tracking Err	Max Drawdown	Sortino	Trades/Yr
Equity Line	9.6%	15.4%	10.9%	27.9%	0.53	0.20	12.3%	-33.8% (2020-02-19..2020-03-24)	0.61	2.3
S&P 500 TR	7.1%	19.7%	14.0%		0.28			-55.3% (2007-10-09..2009-03-10)	0.23	

Figure 8: Capital-Weighted Dollar Volume Plus VPCI V Bottoms, Expiration 1 Month

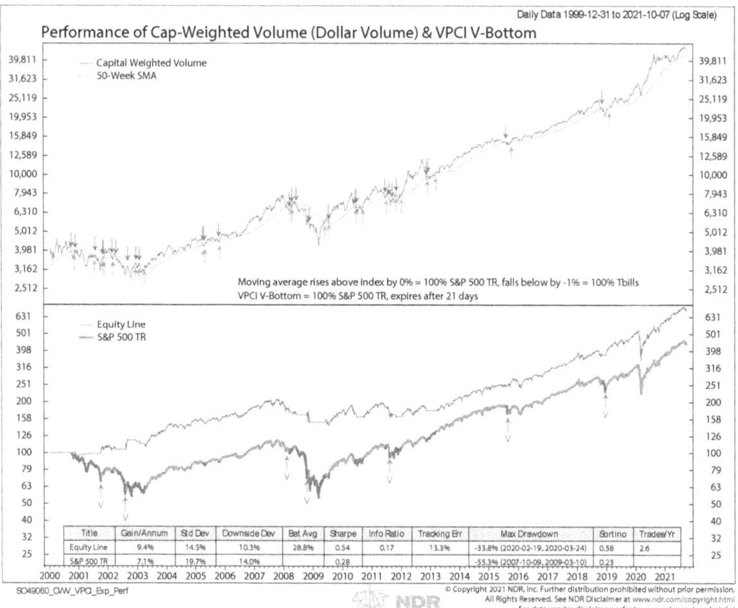

Title	Gain/Annum	Std Dev	Downside Dev	Bat Avg	Sharpe	Info Ratio	Tracking Err	Max Drawdown	Sortino	Trades/Yr
Equity Line	9.4%	14.5%	10.3%	28.8%	0.54	0.17	13.3%	-33.8% (2020-02-19..2020-03-24)	0.58	2.6
S&P 500 TR	7.1%	19.7%	14.0%		0.28			-55.3% (2007-10-09..2009-03-10)	0.23	

Figure 9: Capital-Weighted Volume Plus VPCI V Bottoms, Expiration 1 Month

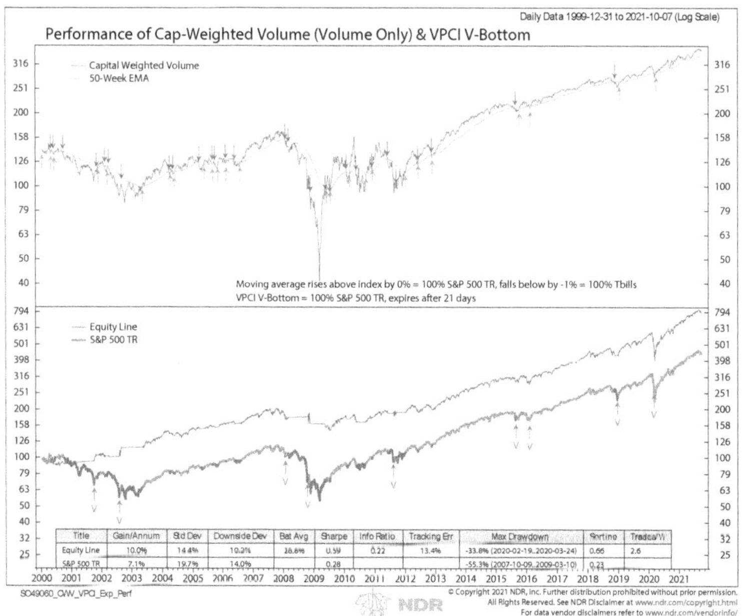

Title	Gain/Annum	Std Dev	Downside Dev	Bat Avg	Sharpe	Info Ratio	Tracking Err	Max Drawdown	Sortino	Trades/Yr
Equity Line	10.0%	14.4%	10.2%	28.6%	0.59	0.22	13.4%	-33.8% (2020-02-19..2020-03-24)	0.66	2.6
S&P 500 TR	7.1%	19.7%	14.0%		0.28			-55.3% (2007-10-09..2009-03-10)	0.23	

Figure 10: Capital-Weighted Volume Plus VPCI V Bottoms, Expiration 2 Months

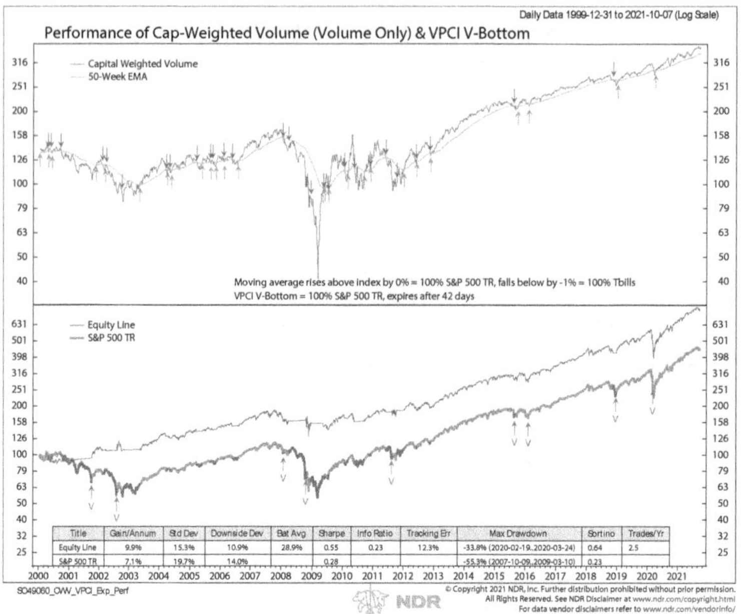

Figure 11: Capital-Weighted Volume Plus VPCI V Bottoms, Expiration 3 Months

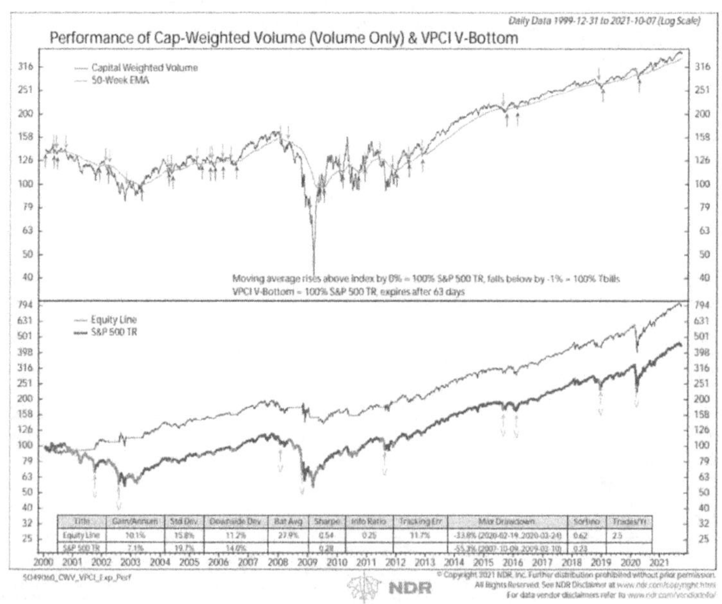

Observing the differences between utilizing a one-, two-, or three-month stop within our Capital-Weighted Volume and Dollar Volume risk overlays, the longer time stop of three months generally has the stronger returns, but with the most risk. With a three-month time stop, Capital-Weighted Volume returned 10.1% annually, with a standard deviation of 15.8%, producing a Sharpe ratio of 0.54, compared to Capital-Weighted Dollar Volume annual return of 9.9% with a standard deviation of 15.8% and a Sharpe ratio of .53. The shorter VPCI V Bottom formation time generally experienced the weakest returns but had the least amount of risk.

Capital-Weighted Volume paired with a one-month time stop returned 10% annually with the lowest standard deviation of only 14.4%, producing a very strong Sharpe ratio of .59. A one-month time stop with Capital-Weighted Dollar Volume returned 9.4% annually while only producing 14.5% of standard deviation, for a Sharpe ratio of 0.54. Overall, the two-month time stop produced a strong median between risk and return. Capital-Weighted Volume with a two-month time stop earned 9.9%, with a standard deviation of 15.3% and a Sharpe ratio of .53. In Comparatively, Capital-Weighted Dollar Volume earned 9.6% with 15.4 units of risk, yielding a Sharpe ratio of .53. Overall, all of the VPCI V Bottom time-stop models significantly increased returns while significantly decreasing risks, generating Sharpe ratios significantly improved over buy and hold.

DEEP VPCI V BOTTOMS PLUS SHALLOW W BOTTOMS

The VPCI V Bottom identifies extreme capitulation points through massive outflows. During these rare points of massive outflows, the VPCI V Bottom is built to uncover momentum weakness between volume and price patterns. Historically, these situations have often been dark periods before the dawn of a market recovery. Because trend data lags and VPCI V Bottoms are so rare, we will next explore employing one other proprietary methodology that is also designed to catch market bottoming formations.

A known but less common form of market bottom is the **W Bottom**. W Bottoms are formed by a V Bottom making a second V Bottom within a defined time window. VPCI V Bottoms are rare occurrences. Two consecutive V Bottoms forming a W Bottom are even rarer. A VPCI W Bottom is formed when two V Bottoms, either shallow (-0.4) or deep (-4.0), occur within a two-month span. Although infrequent, when this capitulation set-up has occurred, it has led to some very nice entry points.

Overall, applying the VPCI W Bottom models to the Volume Factor Overlay improves the the deep VPCI V Bottom models earning 9.69% effective APR. However, the deep V Bottom models risk is slightly lower, at 11.25%, compared to W Bottoms, at 11.92%. Both models, however, significantly reduce the risk of the S&P 500's 15.39% standard deviation.

Additionally, the deep VPCI V Bottoms risk-adjusted returns are marginally better than the W Bottoms, sporting a Sharpe ratio of 0.98 compared to a W Bottoms Sharpe ratio of 0.83, whereas the buy and hold S&P 500 Sharpe ratio is only at 0.50.

Knowing that both deep V and W VPCI Bottoms are effective models for buying during market dips, what if we applied both the deep VPCI V Bottoms with the VPCI W Bottoms within the Bull-Run, Bear-Hide Risk Special Teams Overlay? Would synergies arise by combining both capitulation signals? When both VPCI capitulation signals, V&W, are conjointly run, the effective APR grows to 10.33%, beating either capitulation model applied independently. The conjoined deep VPCI V+W risk is just slightly elevated over either deep V or W capitulation signals run independently at 12.23% (11.25% Deep V, 11.92% W Bottoms). Does the additional risk assumed pay off? The risk-adjusted rate of returns, as measured by the Sharpe ratio in the combined models, improves upon the W Bottom models alone, from .83 to 0.90. But the combo fails to beat the deep V model's Sharpe ratio of 0.98. Overall, combining the deep VPCI V with the VPCI W Bottoms within the Bear-Hide Risk Overlay improves returns while assuming slightly higher risk than the Bear-Hide Deep VPCI V Bottom models.

BULL-RUN, BEAR-HIDE FOUNDING PRINCIPALS

- Wealth is built primarily by emphasizing capital preservation.
- Lower volatility leads to more tolerant investors.
- Lower drawdowns lead to more sustainable withdrawal strategies.
- Markets are efficient in the mean but often irrational during extremes.

Because the Bull-Run, Bear-Hide models keep drawdowns low while generating excess returns, it is an ideal model for those employing the endowment method of withdrawal. The **endowment method of withdrawal** is a withdrawal strategy used to provide a consistent stream of income from a lump sum of assets, such as a retirement fund or an endowment pool. The concept is to spend a portion of the principal while preserving the remaining balance to generate future income. Here's how the endowment method of withdrawal works:

First, determine the length of time used in valuing the assets and setting the distribution. This time frame could be one year, but an average of multiple years or quarters is also a popular option. Second, determine a withdrawal rate. The withdrawal rate is the percentage withdrawn from the assets as determined in step one. Third, determine the desired distribution, such as annually, quarterly, or monthly. Some endowment methods may also include an inflation adjustment.

Benefits of the Endowment Method:

1. Provides a steady stream of income: The endowment method of withdrawal ensures that you receive a consistent stream of income over an indefinite period of time.
2. Preserves the initial investment: Since the withdrawal rate is calculated based on a percentage of the base value of the investment, the endowment method helps to preserve the principal balance for future use.

Drawbacks of the Endowment Method:

1. Limited liquidity: The endowment method of withdrawal may limit your ability to access the full value of your investment. Since a portion of the principal is being used to generate income, you may not be able to withdraw the entire amount at once.
2. Risk of underfunding: Depending on investment performance, the endowment method may not generate enough income to meet your desired withdrawal rate. This risk can be mitigated by investing in a diversified portfolio with a range of assets.
3. Limited flexibility: The endowment method may not be suitable for investors who require greater flexibility in their income stream. Once the withdrawal rate is set, it may be difficult to make changes without affecting the overall strategies.

Overall, the endowment method of withdrawal can be an effective strategy for generating a consistent stream of income from a lump sum. However, it is important to consider the potential drawbacks. All of these drawbacks are accentuated in volatile and violent markets. However, the goals of low drawdown and low volatility in the Bull-Run, Bear-Hide models render it uniquely appropriate for those in need of perpetual income through the endowment method of withdrawal.

SUMMARY

On offense, our Bull-Run, Bear-Hide Models utilize our proprietary Volume Factor analysis, designed to discover emerging trends earlier and identify unhealthy broad market trends before they reverse. When on defense, our risk management overlay strives to be long equities during periods of capital inflows while positioning to defensive assets during times of capital outflows. Our special team's unit is designed to uniquely redeploy capital by swooping in during capitulation bottoms before the price trend reverses.

Furthermore, the Bull-Run, Bear-Hide approach understands behavioral finance realities, providing investors with a data-driven plan. During bear markets, investors need to feel they are doing something to protect themselves. Action often alleviates investors' anxieties, keeping them on board with their long-term financial plan. Similarly, often in bull markets, clients fear the bull cannot go on forever and want to cash out while they're ahead. Providing investors with a defined bear market plan based on objective data points may help keep investors invested during bull market cycles.

Overall, the Bull-Run, Bear-Hide Models strive to be invested in the top-performing areas during periods of expansion while mitigating downside risk over prolonged periods of contraction. These objectives further serve to quell clients' anxieties, whether it be the fear of missing out or the fear of capital loss. Moreover, when the models are applied to investors in the distribution phase, lower drawdowns provide more consistent withdrawals, growing the distribution base over time and leading to high probabilities for successful investment outcomes.

CHAPTER 7:

SECTOR INVESTING

"..they were exactly what the other needed; the missing piece that made everything else magically click into place."

—Jennifer McMahon

Some of the data presented in this chapter is hypothetical and back-tested data. This data is not based on any advisory client assets. Past performance of a model is not a guarantee of future results. Actual performance may vary significantly from the hypothetical results shown. Please see the section titled 'Important Information Regarding Hypothetical, Back-Tested Performance' for a full description of this data and the limitations associated with it.

What makes the Volume Factor Risk Overlay unique and effective is its application of Capital-Weighted Volume and Capital-Weighted Dollar Volume. Previously, we discussed applying the Volume Factor Risk Overlay to the broad market. Capital weighting technology and innovation repair volume index data, producing efficacious financial outcomes in terms of both risks and returns. In this chapter, we expand upon the broad market application of the Volume Factor Risk Overlay by applying it to narrow sector indexes.

Investing in market sectors may offer several advantages to investors. A few key benefits include the following.

1. Diversification: Investing in different market sectors allows for the dissemination of investment risk across a variety of industries. This diversification helps reduce the risk associated with investing in a single company or industry. Should a company within a sector underperform, diversification in other companies in a bullish sector should offset the loss of choosing the wrong company in the right sector.

2. Targeted exposure: Investing in specific sectors allows investors to focus on areas they believe to have strong growth potential. For example, if one has confidence in the technology sector, one can allocate a portion of their portfolio to the Technology Select Sector SPDR Fund (XLK), which contains technology companies, benefiting from their advancements and innovation.
3. Sector trend capitalization: Certain sectors may experience periods of significant growth due to emerging trends or favorable market and economic conditions. Investing in well-positioned sectors early may provide opportunities for higher returns. For instance, energy may be a favorable investment during times of high inflation, and the health care sector may be favorable during economic recessions, whereas technology and consumer discretionary investments may see substantial growth during times of economic expansion.
4. Strategic allocation: Sector investing allows investors to implement a strategic asset allocation strategy based on their own risk tolerance and investment objectives. By allocating funds to different sectors, investors can tailor their portfolios to match their desired level of risk and potential returns.
5. Active management opportunities: Investing in market sectors can be particularly appealing for active investors who closely follow market trends and the economy. According to Ned Davis Research, "Market and sector effects explained about 65% of stock returns vs. 35% for company-specific effects. The implication for investors is that a 360-degree approach that utilizes both top-down and bottom-up analysis has become even more important as broad index and sector ETFs have continued to gain in popularity." Sector investing empowers savvy investors to take advantage of sector-specific data sets, allowing for tactical investment decisions.

Specialized Exchange Traded Fund providers (ETFs), such as Select Sector SPDR ETFs, specialize in providing investors with sector-specific ETFs. According to Rob Anderson, CFA, and Daniel Chin, Ph.D., with Ned Davis Research, sector-focused ETFs have seen a consistent rise in asset value over the past two decades. Figure 1 shows that sector ETF assets rose from $39 billion in February 2009 to $629 billion in April 2022, representing 15.5% of all domestic equity ETF assets.

Figure 1) Asset Growth in ETFs and Sector ETFs

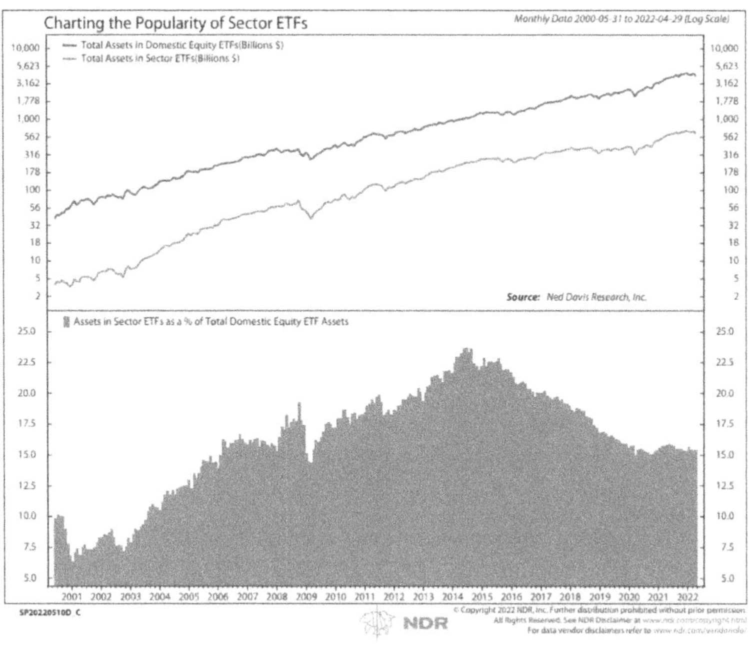

However, index volume in industry sectors is prone to the same paralyzing issues as broad index volume data. In lieu of index volume, many analysts utilize ETF volume or ETF recreation and redemption data. However, setting aside sentimentality, this ETF volume data has not proven to be very valuable in volume or security analysis. Could Capital-Weighted Volume or Capital-Weighted Dollar Volume be helpful in determining when, as well as how, to invest in sector ETFs?

SPDR's Select Sector ETFs are strategically well-positioned to benefit from this innovative type of sector analysis due to their dominance in the ETF sector market. Employing Capital-Weighted Volume's unique and actionable data may empower tactical and strategic investors to make more informed decisions. In this way, the unique and innovative data sets provided by Capital-Weighted Volume Indexes may provide a distinctive vantage point to analysts, financial advisors, and other consumers of sector index strategies.

The key distinction between Capital-Weighted Volume analysis and ETF volume/flows is that the price and volume data are directly derived from the index's internal components as opposed to the ETF. In this way, Capital-Weighted Volume and Capital-Weighted Dollar Volume literally track the liquidity and money flowing in and out of the stocks within an ETF's underlying index. In the broad markets, I previously demonstrated that our unique Capital-Weighted Volume methodologies provided leading data as opposed to coincidental data. Further, these methodologies have proven useful in identifying emerging trends and momentum earlier than price data in broad markets (quicker signals). Simultaneously, the employment of Capital-Weighted Volume data has demonstrated higher probabilities that those momentum trends will continue on into the future (improved reliability).

Additionally, the visible presentation of Capital-Weighted Volume flow trends in sector analysis through Capital-Weighted charts creates a tangible data set that is useful for analysis, especially technical analysis. With Capital-Weighted Volume charts, investors can identify which industry sectors are in bull markets (positive CW Volume flows) and which sectors are in bear markets (negative CW flows). Additionally, this Capital-Weighted Volume data may be contrasted with other data sets to determine relative momentum. The Capital-Weighted momentum analysis represents a trove of new and actionable sector data for analysts as well as investors.

Although most of the Select SPDR ETFs were not started until 1999 (exceptions: Real Estate 2016 / Consumer Staples 2018), most of the industry sectors started in 1992. The lone exception was the real estate sector, which did not commence until September 2016. In this chapter, we will begin by observing the results of testing the 11 sectors and the S&P 500 Index by applying Capital-Weighted Volume and Capital-Weighted Dollar Volume trends. We will start our study by investigating the broad S&P 500 Index.

Figure 2) Capital-Weighted Volumes: S&P 500

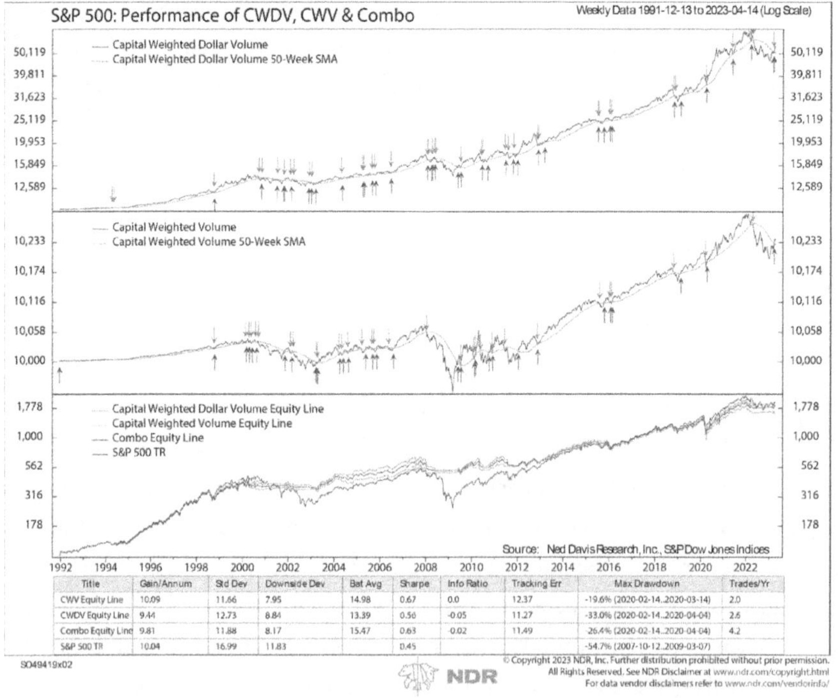

Title	Gain/Annum	Std Dev	Downside Dev	Bat Avg	Sharpe	Info Ratio	Tracking Err	Max Drawdown	Trades/Yr
CWV Equity Line	10.09	11.66	7.95	14.98	0.67	0.0	12.37	-19.6% (2020-02-14..2020-03-14)	2.0
CWDV Equity Line	9.44	12.73	8.84	13.39	0.56	-0.05	11.27	-33.0% (2020-02-14..2020-04-04)	2.6
Combo Equity Line	9.81	11.88	8.17	15.47	0.63	-0.02	11.49	-26.4% (2020-02-14..2020-04-04)	4.2
S&P 500 TR	10.04	16.99	11.83		0.45			-54.7% (2007-10-12..2009-03-07)	

Following the trends of Capital-Weighted Volume and Capital-Weighted Dollar Volume in the S&P 500 produced very favorable results. Since 1992, the S&P 500 earned 10.02% annualized, with a 16.99 standard deviation in risk, a downside deviation of 11.83, and a Sharpe ratio of 0.45. Over the same period of time, Capital-Weighted Dollar Volume earned 9.44% annualized, with a 12.73 standard deviation in risk, a downside deviation of 8.84, and a Sharpe ratio of 0.56. Thus, Capital-Weighted Dollar Volume produced slightly less returns with significantly less risk, creating higher risk-adjusted rates of return.

The trend of Capital-Weighted Volume provided the overall best returns of 10.09% annualized, only to be combined with an ultra-low standard deviation and downside deviation of just 11.66 and 7.95, respectively. These results assisted in producing a very high Sharpe ratio of 0.67. Combing Capital-Weighted Volume with Capital-Weighted Dollar Volume through a 50/50 split produced a 9.81% annualized return, with low standard and downside deviations of 9.81 and 8.17, respectively. Risk-adjusted returns are the key to producing tolerable and successful investment outcomes, especially in the withdrawal phase. These statistics demonstrate that our Capital-Weighted Volume models perform extremely well in the broad market, capturing the trends required to produce exceptional risk-adjusted rates of return.

Independent research further supports Capital-Weighted Volume as a suburb market factor. In the Journal of Applied Business and Economics (JABE Volume 22, Number 3, 2022 ISSN: 1542-8710), Dr. Matt Lutey states: "We show additional risk overlay using the Capital-Weighted Volume, and Capital-Weighted Dollar Volume indicator(s) on the S&P 500 and Center for Research in Security Prices (CRSP) database. We validate the excess returns using the capital asset pricing model, Fama and French 3 and 5 factor models."

Table 1: Capital-Weighted Volume, Dr. Lutey Study (p-value)

Table 5. Daily CWV Center For Research in Security Prices (CRSP) – 2001-2021

	CWV – 250 Day MA	CRSP Share code 10,11
Return	10.05%	9.44%
Risk	12.55%	18.77%
CV	0.80	0.50
t-test	3.68	2.31
p-value	0.0001	0.0104

Statistical analysis supports Professor Lutey's conclusions. A p-value of less than 0.05 illustrates moderate evidence and a p-value of 0.001 illustrates very strong evidence. The p-value from Dr. Lutey's Capital-Weighted Volume study is 0.0001!!!

The Fama and French Factor Model has been widely accepted as the gold standard in factor analysis. Dr. Lutey's paper, "Accumulated Capital-Weighted Dollar Volume &

Volume Price Confirmation Indicator Factor Model," places yet another bold exclamation point on our theory of volume as an investment factor. Table 2 shows Dr. Lutey's findings using a three-factor model comprised of market risk, size, and value.

Table 2: Capital-Weighted Volume / VPCI Model, Dr. Lutey Study (three-factor model)

Table 9. CRSP

CWVA-rf	alpha	Mktrf	Smb	hml
CAPM	6.08***	85.83***		
	(2.66)	(47.54)		
FF3F	5.66***	81.96***	37.23***	29.38**
	(2.52)	(45.52)	(10.19)	(9.54)

** denotes significance at p-value < 0.05 *** denotes significance at p-value <0.01

Table 3 illustrates a five-factor model comprised of risk, size, value, profitability, and quality and employing the same Capital-Weighted Volume model. (Note the technical factor momentum is excluded–typical behavior of academics! I am grateful there are open-minded professors such as Dr. Lutey who are also interested in the technical/behavioral perspectives.)

Table 3: Capital-Weighted Volume VPCI Model, Dr. Lutey Study (five-factor model)

JABE, Volume 22, Number 3, 2022 ISSN: 1542-8710

Table 10. CRSP 5 Factor Analysis

CWVA-rf	alpha	Mktrf	Smb	hml	Rmw	Cma
FF5F	6.23***	79.18***	27.62***	19.55***	(37.57)	26.60***
	(2.78)	(39.72)	(7.30)	(5.58)	(7.72)	(4.14)

** denotes significance at p-value < 0.05 *** denotes significance at p-value <0.01

According to Dr. Lutey's study, "We show that the S&P 500 CWV strategy has alpha (excess return) of 14.33% annualized and 23.06% annualized for the CAPM and 3 Factor model, respectively. We can see that the returns are statistically significant for the 3-factor model… we see that the model holds for both CAPM and the 3-factor model, as well as the 5-factor model. The excess return is statistically significant for all three models with very strong levels of significance. The excess returns range from 6.08% for CAPM, 5.66% for the 3-factor model and 6.23% for the 5-factor model. All returns are annualized." To summarize Dr. Lutey's findings, market returns (CAPM), size and value (Fama French Factor Model 3), and profitability (Fama French Model 5) are statistically significant in improving Alpha with the Capital-Weighted Volume model.

Could understanding the volume and capital flows in sectors provide similar results in sector analysis? If so, could one create strategies following the money to invest in only those sectors garnering liquidity (Capital-Weighted Volume) and capital flows (Capital-Weighted Dollar Volume)? To create a successful system, we do not need all sector strategies to produce higher or risk-adjusted returns. We just need the strategy to capture the big uptrends in the sectors in vogue and, even more importantly, to avoid the big losses of the sectors presently out of favor.

Third-party verification service Ned Davis Research tested our Capital-Weighted Volume models since the inception of each sector. Six of the 11 sectors produced stronger risk-adjusted returns with Capital-Weighted Volume. Capital-Weighted Dollar Volume also produced better risk-adjusted returns in 6 of the 11 sectors. The 50/50 combo model outperformed in 7 of the 11 sectors on a risk-adjusted basis. The sectors that underperformed buy-and-hold were primarily the defensive sectors, such as staples, health care, and real estate. In comparison, the volume trend strategies that outperformed were the more cyclical sectors, such as energy, communications, information technology, financials, industrials, and consumer discretionary. The exceptions were utilities, a defensive sector that exhibited stronger risk-adjusted returns with the volume strategies than buy-and-hold, and materials, a cyclical sector that produced better risk-adjusted returns with buy-and-hold.

Figure 3) Capital-Weighted Volumes, Energy Sector

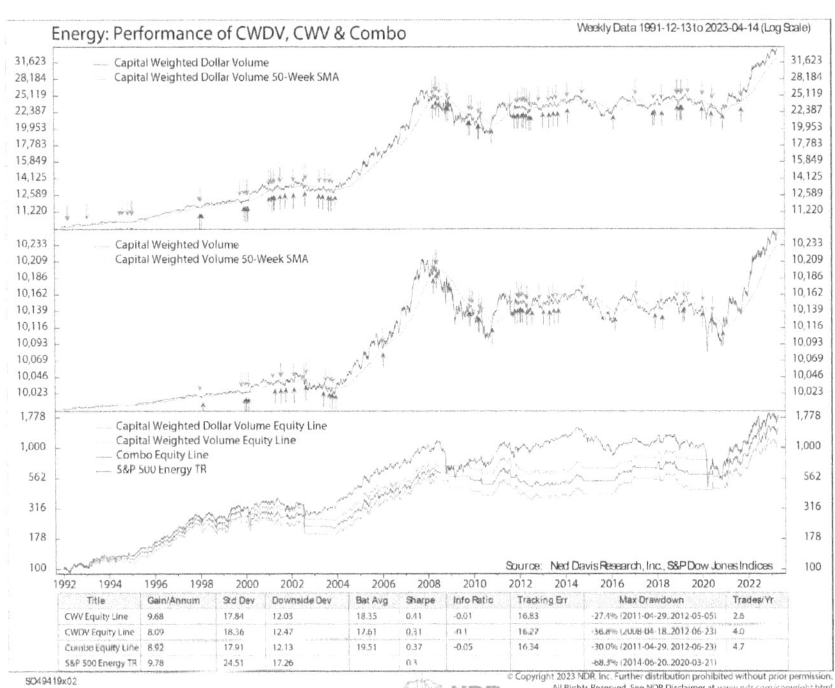

Title	Gain/Annum	Std Dev	Downside Dev	Bat Avg	Sharpe	Info Ratio	Tracking Err	Max Drawdown	Trades/Yr
CWV Equity Line	9.68	17.84	12.03	18.35	0.41	-0.01	16.83	-27.4% (2011-04-29..2012-05-05)	2.6
CWDV Equity Line	8.09	18.36	12.47	17.61	0.31	-0.1	16.27	-36.8% (2008-04-18..2012-06-23)	4.0
Combo Equity Line	8.92	17.91	12.13	19.51	0.37	-0.05	16.34	-30.0% (2011-04-29..2012-06-23)	4.7
S&P 500 Energy TR	9.78	24.51	17.26		0.3			-68.3% (2014-06-20..2020-03-21)	

Figure 4) Capital-Weighted Volumes, Materials Sector

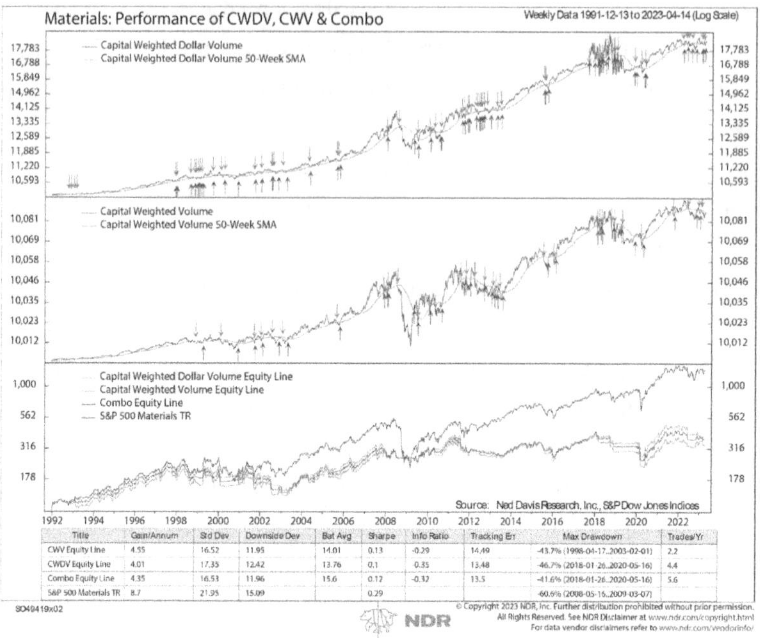

Title	Gain/Annum	Std Dev	Downside Dev	Bat Avg	Sharpe	Info Ratio	Tracking Err	Max Drawdown	Trades/Yr
CWV Equity Line	4.55	16.52	11.95	14.01	0.13	-0.29	14.49	-43.7% (1998-04-17..2003-02-01)	2.2
CWDV Equity Line	4.01	17.35	12.42	13.76	0.1	-0.35	13.48	-46.7% (2018-01-26..2020-05-16)	4.4
Combo Equity Line	4.35	16.53	11.96	15.6	0.12	-0.32	13.5	-41.6% (2018-01-26..2020-05-16)	5.6
S&P 500 Materials TR	8.7	21.95	15.09		0.29			-60.6% (2008-05-16..2009-03-07)	

Figure 5) Capital-Weighted Volumes, Industrial Sector

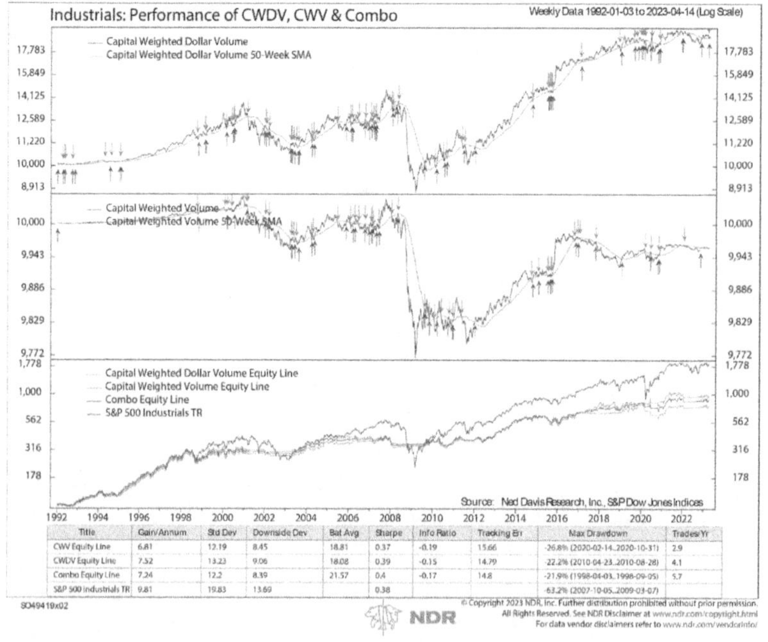

Title	Gain/Annum	Std Dev	Downside Dev	Bat Avg	Sharpe	Info Ratio	Tracking Err	Max Drawdown	Trades/Yr
CWV Equity Line	6.81	12.19	8.45	18.81	0.37	-0.19	15.66	-26.8% (2020-02-14..2020-10-31)	2.9
CWDV Equity Line	7.52	13.23	9.06	18.08	0.39	-0.15	14.79	-22.2% (2010-04-23..2010-08-28)	4.1
Combo Equity Line	7.24	12.2	8.39	21.57	0.4	-0.17	14.8	-21.9% (1998-04-03..1998-09-05)	5.7
S&P 500 Industrials TR	9.81	19.83	13.69		0.38			-63.2% (2007-10-05..2009-03-07)	

Figure 6) Capital-Weighted Volumes, Consumer Discretionary Sector

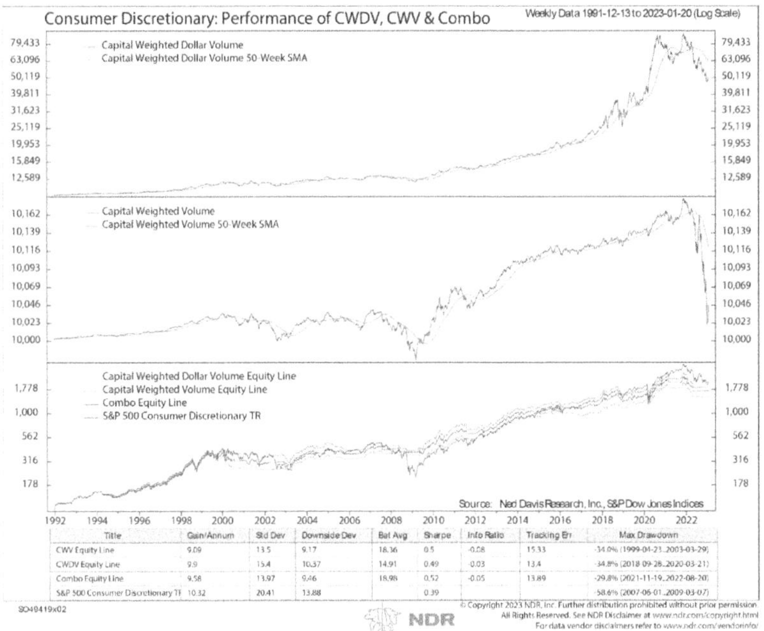

Title	Gain/Annum	Std Dev	Downside Dev	Bat Avg	Sharpe	Info Ratio	Tracking Err	Max Drawdown
CWV Equity Line	9.09	13.5	9.17	18.36	0.5	-0.08	15.33	-34.0% (1999-04-23..2003-03-29)
CWDV Equity Line	9.9	15.4	10.37	14.91	0.49	-0.03	13.4	-34.8% (2018-09-28..2020-03-21)
Combo Equity Line	9.58	13.97	9.46	18.98	0.52	-0.05	13.89	-29.8% (2021-11-19..2022-08-20)
S&P 500 Consumer Discretionary TF	10.32	20.41	13.88		0.39			-58.6% (2007-06-01..2009-03-07)

Figure 7) Capital-Weighted Volumes, Consumer Staples Sector

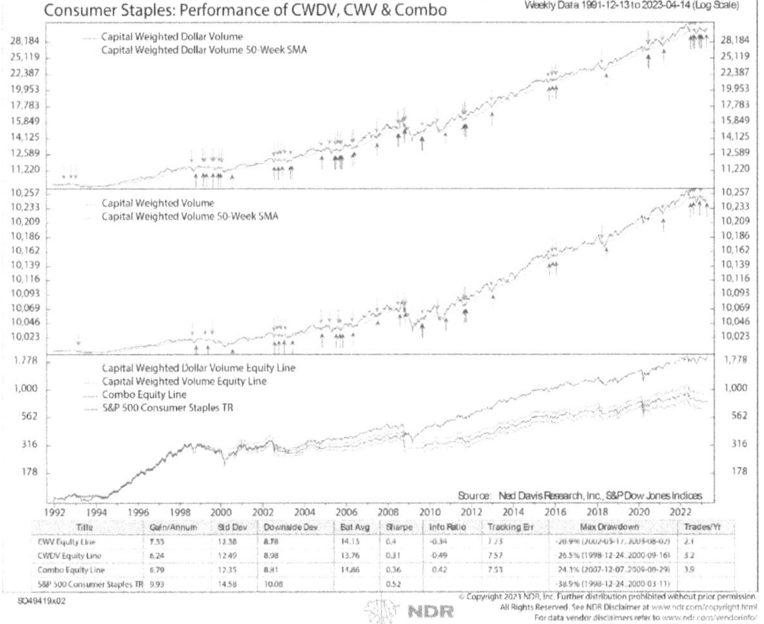

Title	Gain/Annum	Std Dev	Downside Dev	Bat Avg	Sharpe	Info Ratio	Tracking Err	Max Drawdown	Trades/Yr
CWV Equity Line	7.53	12.38	8.78	14.13	0.4	-0.34	7.73	-28.9% (2002-05-17..2003-08-02)	2.1
CWDV Equity Line	6.24	12.49	8.98	13.76	0.31	-0.49	7.57	-26.5% (1998-12-24..2000-09-16)	3.2
Combo Equity Line	6.79	12.35	8.81	14.86	0.36	0.42	7.53	-24.1% (2007-12-07..2009-03-29)	3.9
S&P 500 Consumer Staples TR	9.93	14.58	10.08		0.52			-38.9% (1998-12-24..2000-03-11)	

Figure 8) Capital-Weighted Volumes, Health Care Sector

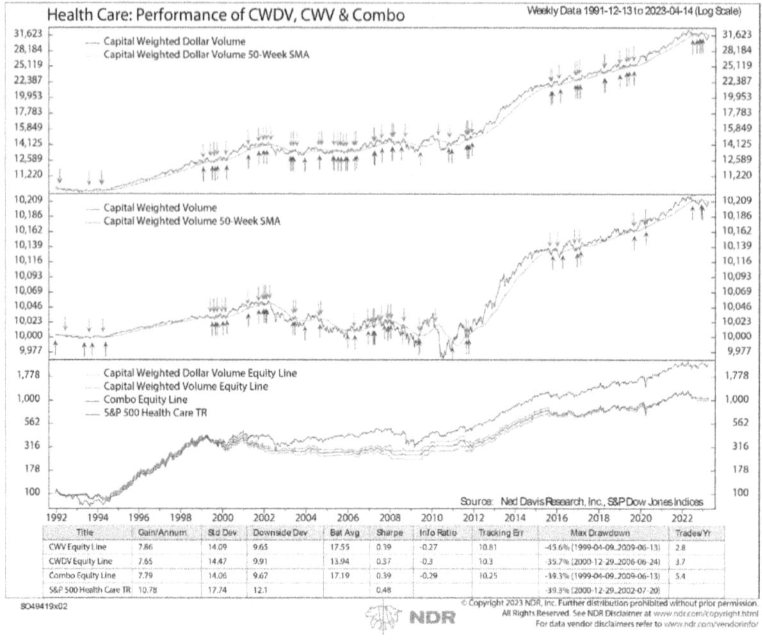

Title	Gain/Annum	Std Dev	Downside Dev	Bat Avg	Sharpe	Info Ratio	Tracking Err	Max Drawdown	Trades/Yr
CWV Equity Line	7.86	14.09	9.65	17.55	0.39	-0.27	10.81	-45.6% (1999-04-09..2009-06-13)	2.8
CWDV Equity Line	7.65	14.47	9.91	13.94	0.37	-0.3	10.3	-35.7% (2000-12-29..2006-06-24)	3.7
Combo Equity Line	7.79	14.06	9.67	17.19	0.39	-0.29	10.25	-39.3% (1999-04-09..2009-06-13)	5.4
S&P 500 Health Care TR	10.78	17.74	12.1		0.48			-39.3% (2000-12-29..2002-07-20)	

Figure 9) Capital-Weighted Volumes, Financial Sector

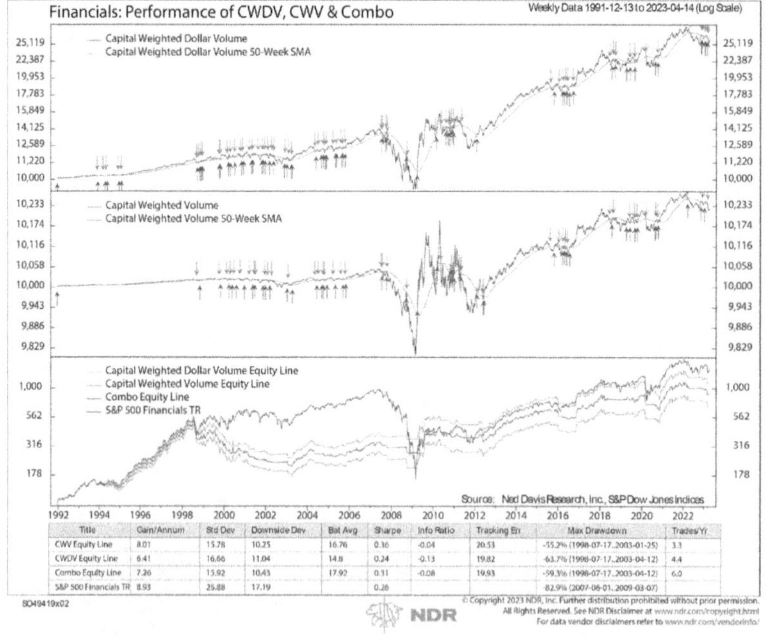

Title	Gain/Annum	Std Dev	Downside Dev	Bat Avg	Sharpe	Info Ratio	Tracking Err	Max Drawdown	Trades/Yr
CWV Equity Line	8.01	15.78	10.25	16.76	0.36	-0.04	20.53	-55.2% (1998-07-17..2003-01-25)	3.3
CWDV Equity Line	6.41	16.66	11.04	14.8	0.24	-0.13	19.82	-63.7% (1998-07-17..2003-04-12)	4.4
Combo Equity Line	7.26	15.92	10.43	17.92	0.31	-0.08	19.93	-59.3% (1998-07-17..2003-04-12)	6.0
S&P 500 Financials TR	8.93	25.88	17.19		0.26			-82.9% (2007-06-01..2009-03-07)	

Figure 10) Capital-Weighted Volumes, Information Technology Sector

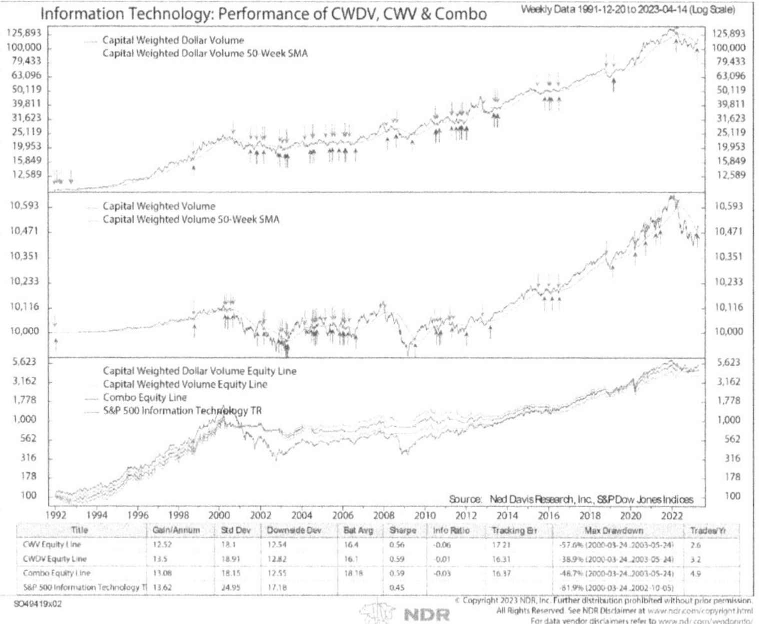

Title	Gain/Annum	Std Dev	Downside Dev	Bat Avg	Sharpe	Info Ratio	Tracking Err	Max Drawdown	Trades/Yr
CWV Equity Line	12.52	18.1	12.54	16.4	0.56	-0.06	17.21	-57.6% (2000-03-24..2003-05-24)	2.6
CWDV Equity Line	13.5	18.91	12.82	16.1	0.59	-0.01	16.31	-38.9% (2000-03-24..2003-05-24)	3.2
Combo Equity Line	13.08	18.15	12.55	18.18	0.59	-0.03	16.37	-46.7% (2000-03-24..2003-05-24)	4.9
S&P 500 Information Technology T	13.62	24.95	17.18		0.45			-81.9% (2000-03-24..2002-10-05)	

Figure 11) Capital-Weighted Volumes, Communications Sector

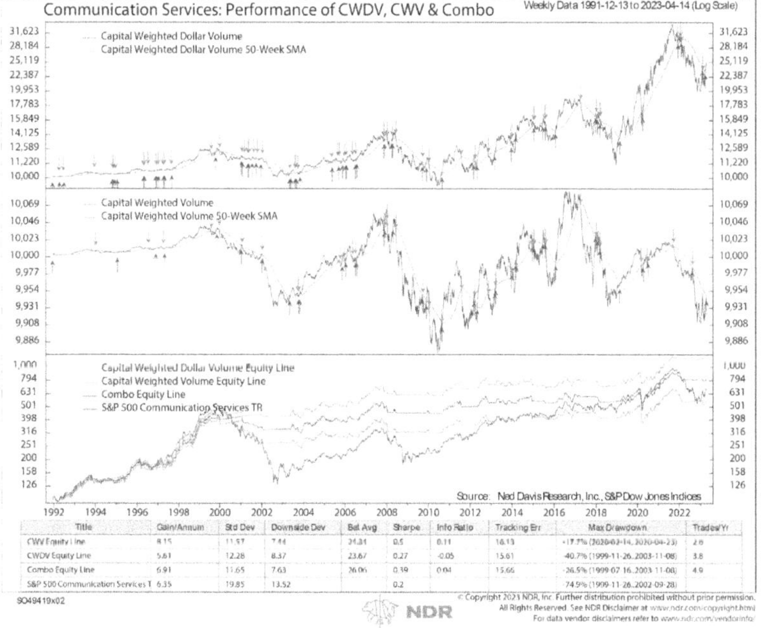

Title	Gain/Annum	Std Dev	Downside Dev	Bat Avg	Sharpe	Info Ratio	Tracking Err	Max Drawdown	Trades/Yr
CWV Equity Line	8.15	11.57	7.44	24.31	0.5	0.11	16.13	-17.7% (2020-02-14..2020-04-23)	2.6
CWDV Equity Line	5.61	12.28	8.37	23.67	0.27	-0.05	15.61	-40.7% (1999-11-26..2003-11-08)	3.8
Combo Equity Line	6.91	11.65	7.63	26.06	0.39	0.04	15.66	-26.5% (1999-07-16..2003-11-08)	4.9
S&P 500 Communication Services T	6.35	19.85	13.52		0.2			-74.9% (1999-11-26..2002-09-28)	

Figure 12) Capital-Weighted Volumes, Utilities Sector

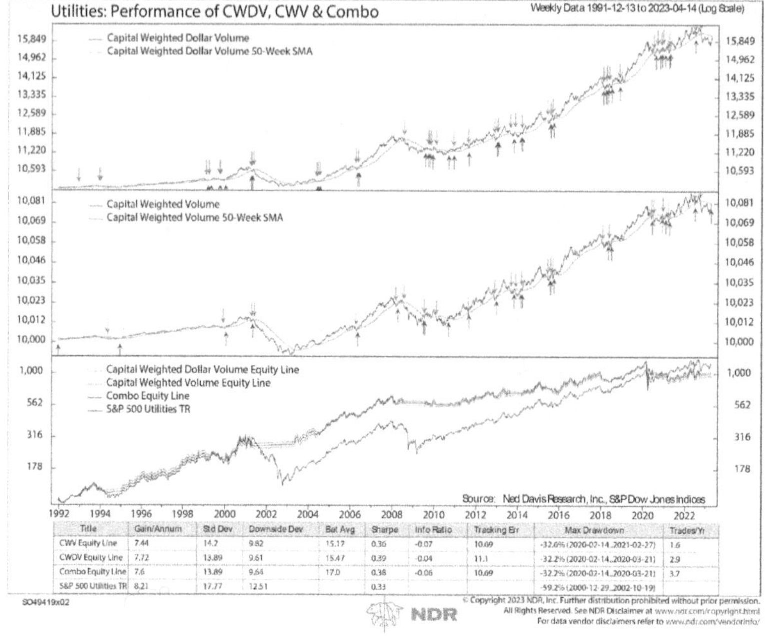

Title	Gain/Annum	Std Dev	Downside Dev	Bat Avg	Sharpe	Info Ratio	Tracking Err	Max Drawdown	Trades/Yr
CWV Equity Line	7.44	14.2	9.82	15.17	0.36	-0.07	10.69	-32.6% (2020-02-14..2021-02-27)	1.6
CWDV Equity Line	7.72	13.89	9.61	15.47	0.39	-0.04	11.1	-32.2% (2020-02-14..2020-03-21)	2.9
Combo Equity Line	7.6	13.89	9.64	17.0	0.38	-0.06	10.69	-32.2% (2020-02-14..2020-03-21)	3.7
S&P 500 Utilities TR	8.21	17.77	12.51		0.33			-59.2% (2000-12-29..2002-10-19)	

Figure 13) Capital-Weighted Volumes, Real Estate Sector

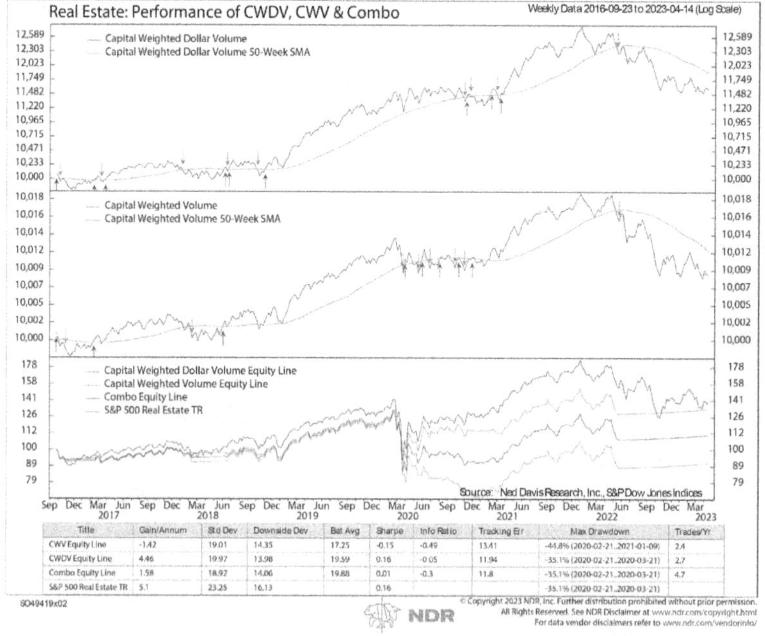

Title	Gain/Annum	Std Dev	Downside Dev	Bat Avg	Sharpe	Info Ratio	Tracking Err	Max Drawdown	Trades/Yr
CWV Equity Line	-1.42	19.01	14.35	17.25	-0.15	-0.49	13.41	-44.8% (2020-02-21..2021-01-09)	2.4
CWDV Equity Line	4.46	19.97	13.98	19.59	0.16	-0.05	11.94	-35.1% (2020-02-21..2020-03-21)	2.7
Combo Equity Line	1.58	18.92	14.06	19.88	0.01	-0.3	11.8	-35.1% (2020-02-21..2020-03-21)	4.7
S&P 500 Real Estate TR	5.1	23.25	16.13		0.16			-35.1% (2020-02-21..2020-03-21)	

SECTOR ANALYSIS SPECIAL TEAMS

Volume Factor special teams swiftly transitions defense back to offense. Combining Capital-Weighted Volume and Dollar Volume with the SPY ETF's VPCI V bottoms identifies excellent reentry points. The SPY ETF boasts substantial trading volume, and the S&P 500 offers greater diversification compared to narrower sectors. As a result, applying the same settings to VPCI V Bottoms has yielded mixed results, varying depending on the sector. However, Dr. Matthew Lutey has proposed an intriguing theory: strong shifting the Sigma or Standard Deviations up on the VPCI Bollinger Band to pinpoint exceedingly deep capitulation points may aid in identifying profound oversold volume analysis buy opportunities within ETF sectors.

According to Dr. Lutey, a Sigma of 25 offers exceptionally high returns with low risk. It appears that as you increase the Sigma, improved returns are achieved and reduced risk but at the cost of fewer signals.

		Ret			Risk		25	Stdev			
	30	60	90	30	60	90	Ret	Risk	BH	Risk	#Vbot
XLB	8.63%	12.27%	21.85%	1.11%	0.21%	5.76%	0.13%	2.31%	0.18%	2.71%	2
XLY	43.84%	62.36%	86.99%	0.00%	0.00%	0.00%	0.00%	0.26%	2.64%	0.00%	1
XLP	17.60%	29.21%	39.31%	0.00%	0.00%	0.00%	5.02%	0.00%	0.16%	1.92%	1
XLK	42.25%	66.63%	94.75%	0.00%	0.00%	0.00%	4.77%	0.00%	0.32%	2.55%	1
XLC	37.66%	71.38%	64.14%	0.00%	0.00%	0.00%	3.95%	0.00%	0.14%	3.01%	1
XLE	-6.22%	13.58%	28.91%	6.13%	49.73%	51.98%	-0.84%	0.96%	0.09%	3.79%	2
XLRE	5.95%	24.81%	34.05%	0.38%	3.08%	4.62%	0.47%	3.25%	0.11%	3.16%	2
XLU	14.20%	20.83%	31.67%	9.63%	5.43%	6.54%	7.33%	10.13%	0.16%	2.50%	2
XLI	44.37%	86.97%	87.81%	0.00%	0.00%	0.00%	12.21%	0.00%	0.21%	2.65%	1
XLF	27.09%	95.88%	98.83%	0.00%	0.00%	0.00%	19.04%	0.00%	0.23%	2.92%	1
XLV	14.89%	21.97%	42.88%	11.77%	18.72%	19.48%	5.93%	3.35%	0.26%	2.27%	2
return	42.04%									#Vbot	1.454545
risk	5.90%										

While utilizing a high Sigma led to a reduction in the number of signals, the signals generated proved to be extremely dependable in forecasting pivotal turning points, resulting in outstanding returns. In summary, the high Sigma strategy yielded an impressive 42.04% return over a 90-day period following the triggering of the deeper VPCI V bottom signal, all while maintaining a Standard Deviation of only 5.9%. With the exception of the energy sector (XLE) over 30 days, all other sectors demonstrated highly favorable outcomes over 30, 60, and 90-day periods when using VPCI V-Bottoms.

An important distinction to note is that our volume analysis worked better in the more cyclical sectors. A profitable strategy could be to position a portfolio in the cyclical growth sectors during bull markets and to rotate defensively to noncyclical sectors in bear markets. For these reasons, in our sector model, we only consider sectors with both liquidity (Capital-Weighted Volume) and capital flows (Capital-Weighted Dollar Volume). In other words, only sectors experiencing both Capital-Weighted Volume and Capital-Weighted Dollar Volume uptrends are eligible for investment in our Volume Factor Sector Model. Once the list of 11 sectors is reduced to only the passing sectors, it is desirable to be in those sectors displaying the strongest momentum in terms of capital flows. To identify and rank these remaining bullish sectors, I developed a unique indicator tailored to sectors and indexes called Capital-Weighted Money Flow (CW-MF).

The problem with the traditional Money Flow Indicator is that it assumes all volume is either upside or downside based on price changes. However, we know through our Capital-Weighted Volume studies that this is often not true. For example, it is not uncommon for the S&P 500 to be up and capital flows to be negative. In the same vein, the S&P 500 Index could be down while capital flows are positive. These divergences are often important signals regarding the future direction of the markets. With stocks, we have no true way of distinguishing between positive and negative capital flows. However, by employing Capital-Weighted Volume and Capital-Weighted Dollar Volume within indexes, we can delineate between actual upside and downside volume. The CW-MF indicator incorporates this important distinction in calculating the Money Flow Indicator (See Figure 14).

Figure 14) S&P 500 Capital-Weighted Money Flow

Source: https://www.optuma.com/trial/cname=VOLUMEANALYSIS

Capital-Weighted Money Flow =

Step 1: = CW$ Volume.

Step 2: Then multiply the CW$ Volume by the CW$ Upside Volume. This produces the CW Money Flow Indicator.

When CW$ Volume > previous period, CW Money Flow = CW$ x Upside CW Volume (positive money flow)

When CW$ Volume < previous period, CW Money Flow = CW$ Volume * Downside CW Volume (negative money flow)

Step 3: Now let us calculate the Positive and Negative Money Flow.

For a trailing time window (usually 14 days):

- Add the money flows where the CW$ Volume is greater than the previous day's CW$ Volume value. This is the Positive Money Flow.
- Add the money flows where the CW$ Volume is lower than the previous day's CW$ Volume value. This is the Negative Money Flow.

Step 4: The CW$ Volume Money Ratio is simply the Positive Money Flow divided by the Negative Money Flow.

Step 5: The CW$ Volume Money Flow is then simply calculated with the following formula.

CW Money Flow = 100 – 100 / (1 + Money Ratio)

In essence, Capital-Weighted Money Flow is Money Flow using Capital-Weighted Dollar Volume inflows and outflows in lieu of volume. Unlike Money Flow, Capital-Weighted Money Flow takes the guesswork out of the presumption that volume is positive or negative. With Capital-Weighted Volume, we not only know if the volume is positive or negative, but also the exact amount of capital flowing in and out of the index.

With Capital-Weighted Money Flow, we now have a brand-new tool to rank sectors and indexes according to liquidity and capital flows. Our Volume Factor Sector system first screens out those sectors that do not pass our initial screen of both positive trends in Capital-Weighted Volume and Capital-Weighted Dollar Volume. After identifying the passing sectors, we only keep the top five sectors according to the Capital-Weighted Money Flow (CW-MF) analysis.

Should more than five ETF sectors pass the initial screen, we then rank the top five according to CW-MF. When a held sector's Capital-Weighted Dollar Volume or Capital-Weighted Volume falls below the trend, then the top five passing sectors are reranked according to CW-MF investing in the top five passing sectors. When fewer than five sectors pass the CW$/ CW trend test, then the investment proceeds into the remaining passing sectors equally. The maximum position size is limited to 35% per Select Sector ETF. If fewer than three sectors pass the CW /CW$ trend, then the excess cash is invested in T-bills.

FREE CASH FLOW / ENTERPRISE VALUE — THE ICING ON CAKE

Now, that we know which sectors our in bull market via Capital-Weighted Volume and Dollar Volume, which sectors have capital flow momentum through Capital Weighted Money Flow, and how to identify capitulation points through extra deep VPCI V bottoms, we will return to the fundamental factor of Free Cash Flow divided by Enterprise Value to complete our sector model.

We initiate our free cash flow model design by calculating the median FCF/EV for S&P 500 sectors, excluding financials. Financials are excluded due to variations in the definition of Free Cash Flow, which is not consistently represented in the same manner within financials, especially within the banking industry. Moreover, certain sectors exhibit higher FCF/EV ratios, such as Technology and Healthcare, while others show lower FCF/EV, like Utilities. Our ranking involves selecting the top 3 sectors to form an index utilizing the corresponding Select SPDR Sector ETFs.

The referenced study on FCF/EV Top 3 comprises two sections. The first section presents two graphs. One graph illustrates an equal-weighted index, rebalanced monthly, for the top 3 sectors with the highest median FCF/EV (depicted by the blue line). In contrast, it also displays an index for the bottom 3 sectors with the lowest median FCF/EV (depicted by the red line). The "middle" sectors are represented by the black line. The chart also includes two benchmark indices for reference: an equal-weighted index of all sectors (excluding Financials) in green and the S&P 500 Index in orange. The second section plots the sector selection over time.

In general, these charts reveal that the top sectors consistently outperform the middle and bottom sectors. Furthermore, the top sectors exhibit superior performance compared to both the S&P 500 Index and an equal-weighted index of all sectors (excluding Financials). To further evaluate the effectiveness of the switching mechanism, we introduced an equal-weighted index of the top-performing sectors, namely Technology, Healthcare, and Consumer Discretionary (illustrated by the purple line in the Top 3 chart). This additional analysis reinforces the value of the model's switching mechanism, as the FCF/EV top 3 sectors continue to outperform the index of top performers.

In conclusion, the Volume Factor Sector Model stands out as a unique and effective approach due to its combination of a risk overlay and sector selection. By extending its application from the broad market to narrow sector indexes, we unlock a wealth of opportunities. Investing in market sectors offers several advantages, including diversification, targeted exposure to growth areas, capitalizing on sector trends, strategic allocation, and active management opportunities. This chapter has showcased the impressive potential of this model, particularly when applied to the more cyclical sectors. Through a combination of Capi-

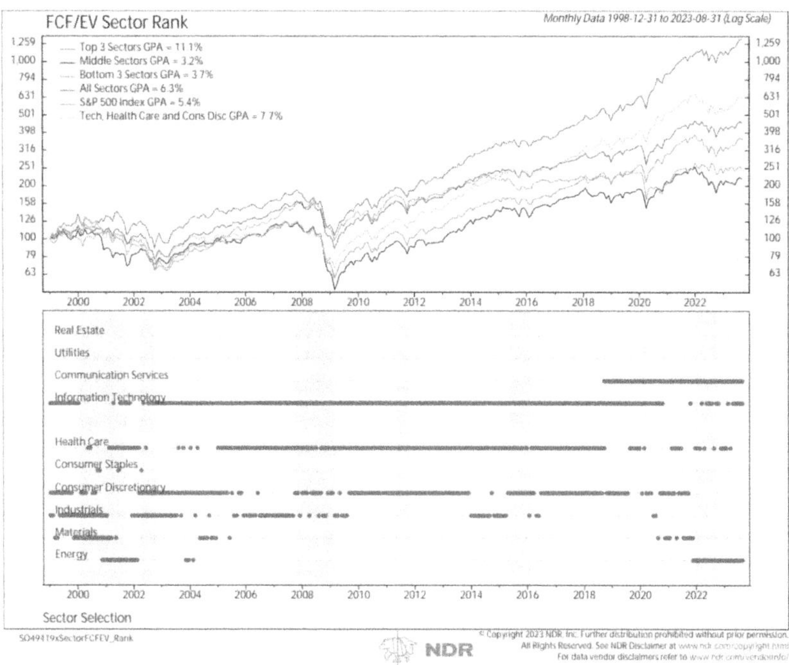

tal-Weighted Volume, Capital-Weighted Dollar Volume, and Free Cash Flow to Enterprise Value analysis, we have identified a robust framework for sector selection and investment. Third-party verification and academic studies further support the effectiveness of this methodology. By incorporating Capital Weighted Money Flow analysis and applying a dynamic sector allocation model, investors can potentially enhance returns and reduce risks, ultimately providing a valuable tool for financial advisors, analysts, and sector-focused investors.

CHAPTER 8:

THE DIVIDEND TREE

"Blessed is the man who trusts in the Lord, whose trust is the Lord. He is like a tree planted by the water that sends its roots out by the stream, and does not fear when the heat comes, for its leaves remain green, and is not anxious in the year of drought, for it does not cease to bear fruit"

– Jeremiah 17:7-8[1]

Some of the data presented in this chapter is hypothetical and back-tested data. This data is not based on any advisory client assets. Past performance of a model is not a guarantee of future results. Actual performance may vary significantly from the hypothetical results shown. Please see the section titled 'Important Information Regarding Hypothetical, Back-Tested Performance' for a full description of this data and the limitations associated with it.

The Volume Factor dividend growth model is a tactically constructed multifactor growth of income investment strategy covering the following five accepted factors.

The Size Factor: The Volume Factor dividend growth model's strategy is designed to select dividend stocks of all sizes, allowing the model to potentially hold stocks as large as mega-caps or as tiny as micro-caps.

The Dividend Factor: All stocks in our Volume Factor dividend growth model must not only pay dividends but must also have grown their dividend over three or five years.

The Quality Factor: The Volume Factor dividend growth model employs the quality factor via Free Cash Flow to filter the dividend stock universe down to just high-quality candidates.

The Momentum and Volume Factors: After being screened out by the quality and dividend factors, the stocks are then ranked by the Volume Factor for momentum and factor attributes.

The Volatility Factor: After the Volume Factor dividend growth model has been constructed, a customizable Volume Factor Risk Model is overlaid to lower drawdowns and volatility during unfavorable market climates.

Thus, five known factor attributes are covered in the Volume Factor dividend growth model: size, dividend, quality, momentum, and low volatility. Additionally, the unknown factor, volume, the factor that truly rules them all, is applied through both the security selection process and the risk overlay.

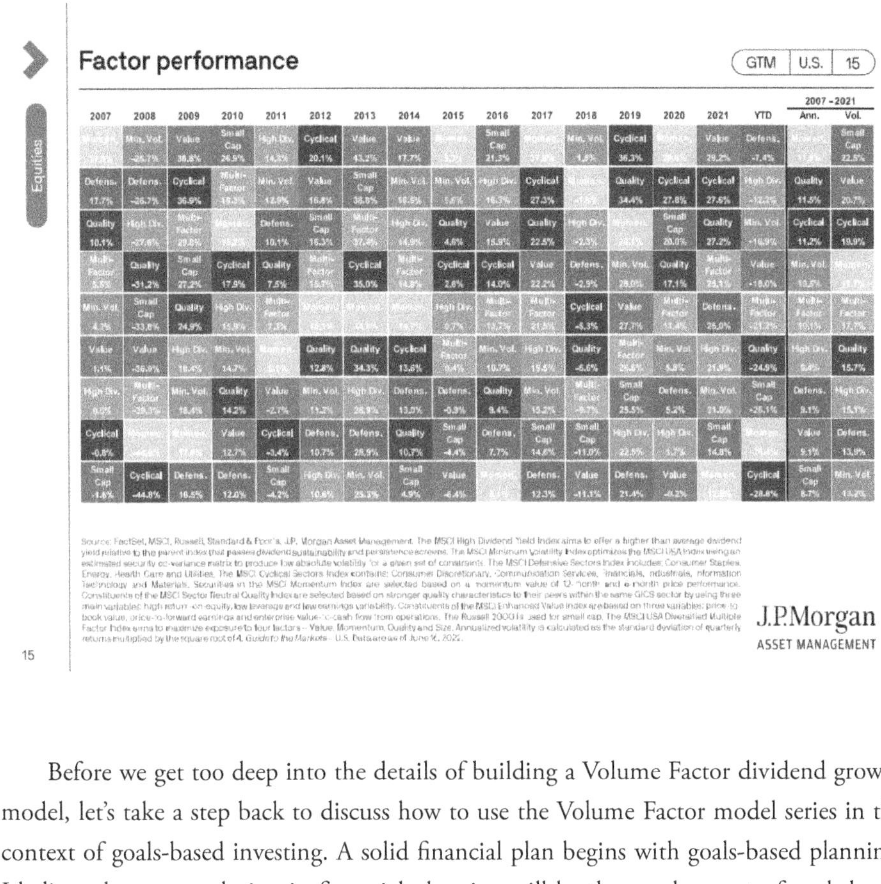

Equities

Factor performance

GTM | U.S. | 15

2007	2008	2009	2010	2011	2012	2013	2014	2015	2016	2017	2018	2019	2020	2021	YTD	2007 - 2021 Ann.	2007 - 2021 Vol.
[illegible]	Min. Vol. -25.7%	Value 38.8%	Small Cap 26.9%	High Div. 14.3%	Cyclical 20.1%	Value 43.2%	Value 17.7%	[illegible]	Small Cap 21.3%	[illegible]	Min. Vol. 1.5%	Cyclical 36.3%	[illegible]	Value 29.2%	Defens. -7.4%	[illegible]	Small Cap 22.5%
Defens. 17.7%	Defens. -26.7%	Cyclical 36.9%	Multi-Factor 18.3%	Min. Vol. 12.9%	Value 16.8%	Small Cap 38.8%	Min. Vol. 16.5%	Min. Vol. 5.6%	High Div. 16.3%	Cyclical 27.3%	[illegible]	Quality 34.4%	Cyclical 27.8%	Cyclical 27.5%	High Div. -12.2%	Quality 11.5%	Value 20.7%
Quality 10.1%	High Div. -27.6%	Multi-Factor 29.8%	[illegible]	Defens. 10.1%	Small Cap 16.3%	Multi-Factor 37.4%	High Div. 14.9%	Quality 4.6%	Value 15.9%	Quality 22.5%	High Div. -2.3%	[illegible]	Small Cap 20.0%	Quality 27.2%	Min. Vol. -16.9%	Cyclical 11.2%	Cyclical 19.9%
Multi-Factor 3.6%	Quality -31.2%	Small Cap 27.2%	Cyclical 17.9%	Quality 7.5%	Multi-Factor 15.7%	Cyclical 35.0%	Multi-Factor 14.2%	Cyclical 2.6%	Cyclical 14.0%	Value 22.2%	Defens. -2.9%	Min. Vol. 28.0%	Quality 17.1%	Multi-Factor 25.1%	Value -18.0%	Min. Vol. 10.5%	[illegible]
Min. Vol. 4.2%	Small Cap -33.8%	Quality 24.9%	High Div. 15.8%	Multi-Factor 7.3%	[illegible]	[illegible]	[illegible]	High Div. 0.7%	Multi-Factor 13.2%	Multi-Factor 21.5%	Cyclical -8.3%	Value 27.7%	Multi-Factor 11.4%	Defens. 25.0%	Multi-Factor -21.2%	Multi-Factor 10.1%	Multi-Factor 17.7%
Value 1.1%	Value -36.9%	High Div. 18.4%	Min. Vol. 14.7%	[illegible]	Quality 12.8%	Quality 34.3%	Cyclical 13.6%	Multi-Factor 0.4%	Min. Vol. 10.7%	High Div. 19.5%	Quality -6.6%	Multi-Factor 25.6%	Min. Vol. 5.8%	High Div. 21.9%	Quality -24.9%	High Div. 9.4%	Quality 15.7%
High Div. 0.6%	Multi-Factor -39.3%	Min. Vol. 18.4%	Quality 14.2%	Value -2.7%	Min. Vol. 11.2%	High Div. 26.9%	Defens. 13.0%	Defens. -0.9%	Quality 9.4%	Min. Vol. 15.2%	Multi-Factor -9.7%	Small Cap 25.5%	Defens. 5.2%	Min. Vol. 21.0%	Small Cap -25.1%	Defens. 9.1%	High Div. 15.1%
Cyclical -0.8%	[illegible]	[illegible]	Value 12.7%	Cyclical -3.4%	Defens. 10.7%	Defens. 28.9%	Quality 10.7%	Small Cap -4.4%	Defens. 7.7%	Small Cap 14.6%	Small Cap -11.0%	High Div. 22.5%	High Div. 1.7%	Small Cap 14.8%	[illegible]	Value 9.1%	Defens. 13.9%
Small Cap -1.6%	Cyclical -44.8%	Defens. 16.5%	Defens. 12.0%	Small Cap -4.2%	High Div. 10.6%	Min. Vol. 25.3%	Small Cap 4.9%	Value -6.4%	[illegible]	Defens. 12.3%	Value -11.1%	Defens. 21.4%	Value -0.2%	[illegible]	Cyclical -28.8%	Small Cap 8.7%	Min. Vol. 13.2%

Source: FactSet, MSCI, Russell, Standard & Poor's, J.P. Morgan Asset Management. The MSCI High Dividend Yield Index aims to offer a higher than average dividend yield relative to the parent index that passes dividend sustainability and persistence screens. The MSCI Minimum Volatility Index optimizes the MSCI USA Index using an estimated security co-variance matrix to produce low absolute volatility for a given set of constraints. The MSCI Defensive Sectors Index includes: Consumer Staples, Energy, Health Care and Utilities. The MSCI Cyclical Sectors Index contains: Consumer Discretionary, Communication Services, Financials, Industrials, Information Technology and Materials. Securities in the MSCI Momentum Index are selected based on a momentum value of 12-month and 6-month price performance. Constituents of the MSCI Sector Neutral Quality Index are selected based on stronger quality characteristics to their peers within the same GICS sector by using three main variables: high return-on-equity, low leverage and low earnings variability. Constituents of the MSCI Enhanced Value Index are based on three variables: price-to-book value, price-to-forward earnings and enterprise value-to-cash flow from operations. The Russell 2000 is used for small cap. The MSCI USA Diversified Multiple Factor Index aims to maximize exposure to four factors – Value, Momentum, Quality and Size. Annualized volatility is calculated as the standard deviation of quarterly returns multiplied by the square root of 4. *Guide to the Markets* – U.S. Data are as of June 30, 2022.

J.P.Morgan
ASSET MANAGEMENT

15

Before we get too deep into the details of building a Volume Factor dividend growth model, let's take a step back to discuss how to use the Volume Factor model series in the context of goals-based investing. A solid financial plan begins with goals-based planning. I believe the next evolution in financial planning will be the employment of goals-based investment strategies to achieve goals-based financial plans. Goals-based investing strives for successful financial outcomes. Both investors and their advisors focus too intently on strategy performance. Outcomes are what matter, not investment returns. Goals-based investing focuses on raising the probability of realizing desired financial outcomes over short-term returns.

Today, as in past generations, most personal wealth is concentrated into two categories. The first and largest category is retirees, age 67 and above. The second largest concentration of wealth is the 50 to 67 age demographic, typically those rapidly approaching retirement. I believe there are two strategic investment methodologies appropriate for these investors, who are or will soon be making withdrawals to meet their daily living expenses. The first viable method of withdrawal is the endowment method. This is a planned variable distribution based on the value of the investments. The key to success in employing the endowment method of withdrawal is low volatility and low drawdowns. Preserving the asset base positions investors for success in the face of bear markets and the sequence of returns risk. The Volume Factor goals-based investment options designed for the endowment method of withdrawal are the Bull-Run and Bear-Hide models.

The second viable method of withdrawal is the income methodology. Investors apply the income methodology to build strategies providing future income streams. As long as investors' income stream is greater than their withdrawal rate, they will not run out of money. This concept is akin to the methodology espoused by Warren Buffet: "The only way to build wealth is to earn more than you spend." Similarly, employing the income withdrawal methodology, investors shoot to yield as much or more than they withdraw.

Two Volume Factor models for the income method of goals-based investing are Volume Factor dividend growth for yield growth and the Target % Series for high yield and dividend growth. In this chapter, we will introduce the Volume Factor dividend growth models. In the next chapter, we will cover the Target % series.

The Volume Factor dividend growth model's investment objective is dividend growth. The model is appropriate for the following investors:

1. Those who currently need a modest withdrawal rate, desire to grow their income significantly above inflation, and may wish to pass on their wealth to the next generation.
2. Those with wealth or savings foresight to lay the groundwork in preparation for a future income stream.

The Volume Factor dividend growth models are designed investment models for individuals with a growth of income objective. The Volume Factor dividend growth models are true "quantamental strategies." Quantamental investing fuses fundamental and technical analysis via a quantitative process. The goals of a Volume Factor dividend growth model are three-fold, seeking to provide the following:

1. Growth of income.
2. Growth of the capital base.
3. Mitigation of risk by preserving the capital base.

THE ORIGINS OF THE DIVIDEND GROWTH MODEL

To understand the concept of the Volume Factor dividend growth model, allow me to take you back to its origins. My father-in-law was a farmer. Every year he planted and then harvested his crop. His revenue was derived from the crop yield, multiplied by the price of the commodities, usually a mix of beans and corn. Unstable changes in crop yield and varying commodity prices led to a volatile income stream. To diversify his income stream, he planted a small apple orchard. As the trees grew, they provided more apples, creating more and more income each year. If a tree became unhealthy, he would cut it down and sell the wood, which was valuable for smoking. He would then plant another tree to replace the felled one.

Volatile crop income led to some lean years. With this in mind, I asked investors this question. How many good, strong, healthy, fruit-producing trees did my father-in-law cut down in his lifetime to make up for those lean years? The answer is usually none. So, the follow-up question is why? The obvious answer is that if he cut down the tree, there would not be apples the next year, or in any of the ensuing years. Despite this, most financial planners and investment advisors never shift from planting hardwood (growth strategies) as opposed to fruit trees (income strategies) in the distribution or preretirement phase. As a result, most investors in the distribution phase systematically cut down their portfolios to meet their spending needs.

THE FRUIT: DIVIDENDS = THE FRUIT OF THE VOLUME FACTOR DIVIDEND GROWTH MODEL

Dividend growth represents the same tree and apples analogy, replaced with stocks and dividends. Imagine in your mind's eyes, picture, if you will, your own dividend tree. On the top of the dividend tree is its fruit, the dividends. This is the first attribute of the Volume Factor dividend growth models.

THE SHOOTS = DIVIDEND GROWTH

Connected to the trunk are healthy, growing, fruit-bearing branches. These growing branches lead us to the second quality of our Volume Factor dividend growth model. All of the stocks in a Volume Factor dividend growth model must raise their dividends, in this way, like the healthy apple tree that grows more and bigger branches, the branches or stocks must also show continued, above-the-mean dividend growth.

THE ROOTS = FREE CASH FLOW

> "If the roots of a tree are holy, then the tree's branches are holy too"
>
> – Romans 11:16 New Century Version

The next part of the tree is the most critical piece, yet it is the component not visualized when imagining your dividend tree in your mind's eye. The root system is the most vital part of the tree, enabling it to grow and produce fruit. The vital root of our Volume Factor dividend growth models is Free Cash Flow. If the stock has abundantly strong and growing Free Cash Flow, it can pay and continue to rapidly grow its dividend. Notice that we do not suggest using earnings. Earnings can be easily manipulated on an income statement. Free Cash Flow is how much money came in versus how it came out. And in most industries, Free Cash Flow data is difficult to fudge.

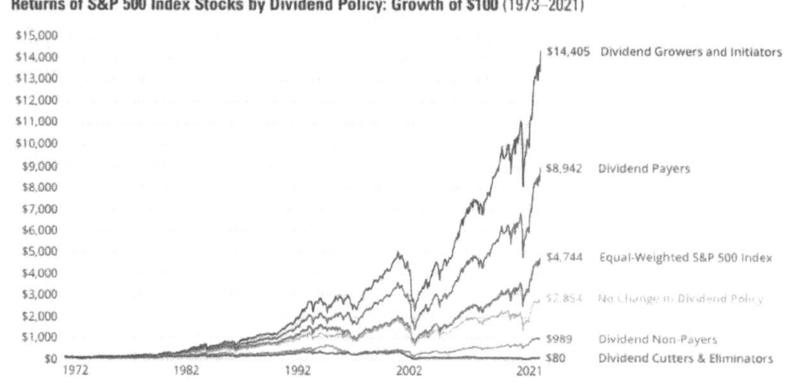

Past performance does not guarantee future results. Indices are unmanaged and not available for direct investment. For illustrative purposes only. Data Sources: Ned Davis Research and Hartford Funds, 2/21.

Although the goal of the Volume Factor dividend growth models is the growth of yield, it should not necessarily be at the expense of long-term performance. You'll recall that our first attribute of the Volume Factor dividend growth models is dividends. Notice that over time, dividend payers have outperformed the S&P 500 Equal Weight Index. One hundred dollars invested in 1972 grew to $4,744 by 2021 in the S&P 500 Equal Weight Index. In contrast, stocks without dividends only grew to $989, while the dividend-paying stocks grew to $8,942.

The second trait of our Volume Factor Volume Factor dividend growth is dividend growth. Notice that dividend growers historically have outperformed even dividend payers. Following the same illustration above, stocks that raised their dividends grew to $14,405 compared to the dividend payers' growth of $8,942. In contrast, look at the dividend cutters and eliminators. A $100 investment in dividend cutters in 1972 actually lost money. Invest in the inverse of the cutter, the dividend growers. That's a solid bet.

Why are dividend growers generally a worthwhile investment? Imagine being the CEO or CFO of a publicly traded company that has consistently raised its dividend year in and year out. As the CEO, how would you manage this company? As CEO, you had better meet your investors' expectations, or you will lose your job. With this in mind, you will most likely take a conservative approach when considering high-risk projects with low probabilities of achieving returns on investment. Rather, as the CEO, you would be calculated and strategic, knowing that you must consistently exceed your bottom line to meet your shareholders' expectations. In this way, stocks that consistently grow dividends tend to have solid management teams ultra-focused on consistency.

The dividends in our Volume Factor dividend growth models bear the fruit our investors need to live on. Long term, the aim of growing branches is to provide a rising dividend yield consistently exceeding the cost of living—in other words, inflation. Thus, another goal of our Volume Factor dividend growth models is to produce yield growth exceeding the inflation rate. Over the long term, a healthy dividend growth target is two or three times that of inflation.

In the orchard, the fruit has all of the luster. Yet, the most essential quality of a healthy tree is not found in what is visible, but in what lies underneath. Although the fruit of the tree is what comes to mind when envisioning the Volume Factor dividend growth model, it is the root system that causes the visible part of the tree to flourish or die. A tree without healthy roots will one day cease to produce (Jeremiah 17:7).

A strong, vibrant, growing tree almost always possesses a robust, healthy root system. The root system is our third attribute or subfactor of the Volume Factor dividend growth model, and it takes the form of Free Cash Flow. Specifically, we use the quality subfactor Free Cash Flow (FCF)/Enterprise Value (EV). Not only does Free Cash Flow provide the necessary financial nutrients to maintain and grow the dividend payout, but it also provides the alpha (performance above benchmark) to grow our model basis. Identified as the quality factor in Figure 3 below, FCF/EV has been shown to be the strongest of subfactors according to Bank of America (BAC) research.

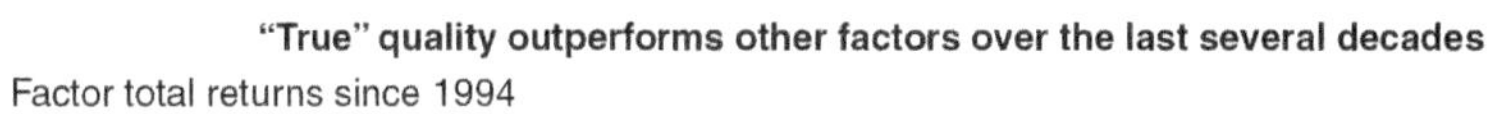

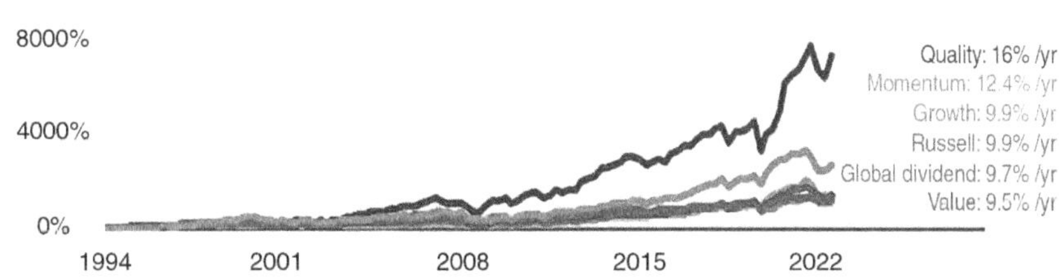

Source: BofA Research Investment Committee, Bloomberg, Global Financial Data; Quality COWZTR Index; Value = RU10VATR Index; Growth = RU10GRTR Index, Russell 1000 = RUITR Index; Dividend = M1WDHDVD Index; Momentum = M1USMMT Index

BofA GLOBAL RESEARCH

Referencing Figure 4, the subfactor of FCF/EV outperforms the most substantial factor, momentum, 16.3% to 12.4%. This is followed by a more broadly defined quality factor returning 11.3%. In contrast, the growth, and large-cap options (Russell 1000) both returned 9.9%. Growth returned only 9.7% in this study, and value registered a 9.5% annualized return.

Not only did the Volume Factor dividend growth model's root system of FCF/EV produce the strongest returns, but also the highest risk-adjusted rate of returns as defined by the Sortino ratio at 1.4, versus the quality factor at 1.0, followed by the momentum factor at 0.9 (see Figure 4). The Sortino ratio is my favorite metric in building a strategy forged to stand the tests of time and volatility. The Sortino ratio is calculated just like the Sharpe ratio, except it excludes upside volatility. Thus, a strategy with strong upside or downside volatility is penalized under the Sharpe ratio. Conversely, the Sortino ratio ignores upside volatility. This is key, because upside volatility does not harm but, rather, compounds the probability of successful financial plans. Because the Sortino ratio does not penalize upside volatility like the Sharpe ratio, the Sortino ratio is my go-to stat in financial plan modeling.

FCF/EV has been the superior factor, outperforming MSCI quality by >6% per year

Performance stats for different factors since 1994, quarterly data

	Quality (FCF/EV)	Momentum	Quality (MSCI Index)	Russell 1000	Growth	Global Dividend	Value
Annualized Return	16.3%	12.4%	11.3%	10.0%	9.9%	9.7%	9.5%
Annualized Downside Vol.	9.9%	10.7%	8.5%	9.9%	11.3%	9.4%	10.1%
Sortino Ratio	1.4	0.9	1	0.7	0.6	0.8	0.7
Max Drawdown	-28.0%	-23.9%	-18.4%	-22.5%	-22.8%	-22.4%	-26.7%
Hit Ratio	2.8	2.3	2	2.5	2.4	2.1	2.4

Source: BofA ETF Research, Bloomberg, Global Financial Data; Quality (FCF/EV) = COWZTR Index; Value = RU10VATR Index; Growth = RU10GRTR Index, Russell 1000 = RUITR Index; Dividend = R1DSEWRT Index Index; Momentum = M1USMMT Index; MSCI Quality = M1USQT Index; Quality (MSCI) = M1USQU Index

In choosing the attributes that best define a healthy tree or root system, many options could be considered. Figure 5 below shows the historical performance of a host of quality factor ETFs from 1999 to 2022. Notice that the COWZ (Pacer US Cows 100 ETF), which, like our Volume Factor dividend growth model, employs Free Cash Flow/Enterprise Value (FCF/EV), has produced the strongest historical returns by far. COWZ's FCF/EV yielded a 2,437% cumulative total return/15% annualized. That compares to the next closest risk-adjusted return of SPHQ (Invesco S&P 500 Quality), employing a high return on equity (ROE) with low accruals and leverage. SPHQ yielded a 701% cumulative return/9.4% annualized relative to the S&P 500 Index of only 305% cumulative/6.2% annualized return. Thus, our FCF attribute not only makes sense from the perspective of creating the cash flow needed to meet our dividend payout demands, but it has also shown the strongest returns.

Although we know Volume is the "One Factor that Rules Them All", researchers from Bank of America/Merrill Lynch refer to FCF/EV as the "One Factor to Rule Them All." Per Bank of America's report, *Quality is Job One,* "One quality metric to rule them all, Free Cash Flow yield (Free Cash Flow divided by enterprise value), might be the best measure of the quality of a company. Free Cash Flow measures the amount of cash a company generates after operating expenses and capex. The total enterprise value of a company is the equity market cap plus total debt minus cash. FCF/EV captures how efficiently a company employs the capital it raises. Free Cash Flow yield also combines many of the best criteria that other quality studies have used."

Index	ETF	Quality Type	Absolute	Annualized	Sortino	Downside Vol	Max Drawdown
SPXT	S&P 500		305%	6%	0.37	11.60%	-54.70%
COWZTR	COWZ	Free Cash Flow Yield	2437%	15.00%	1.02	12.90%	-54.70%
NTUQLVTR	QLV	Low beta and quality: - Management Expertise - Profitability - Cash Flow Generation	577%	8.60%	0.7	9.60%	-41.30%
SPXQUT	SPHQ	- High ROE - Low Accruals Ratio (Earnings Qual) - Low Leverage	701%	9.40%	0.7	10.70%	-46.70%
JQUATR	JQUA	- Profitability - Earnings Quality - Solvency	615%	8.90%	0.65	10.80%	-46.50%
NTUQVMTR	QLC	Value, Momentum, & Quality; Quantity = .Management Expertise - Profitability - Cash Flow Generation	515%	8.20%	0.55	11.40%	-51.10%
FIDUSQLT	FQUAL	- FCF Margin - ROIC - FCF Stability	406%	7.30%	0.48	11.10%	-50.00%
M2USSNQ	QUAL	- High ROE - Stable EPS Growth - Low Leverage	333%	6.60%	0.41	11.20%	-46.60%
M2USQMAR	QUS* (Start date is Dec '14)	Equal-Weighter Combination of MSCI USA Value Weighted, MSCI USA Min Vol, & MSCI USA Quality	119%	10.20%	0.76	10.90%	-31.30%
VTUSQM	JOET* (Start date is May '08)	Positive Momentum, Equal Weighted, Quality Screens: Quality = ROE, Debt to Equity, 3y Annualized Sales Growth	354%	10.80%	0.7	12.70%	-50.60%

Source: Research Investment Committee, Bloomberg, Fund Sponsors

Per Bank of America/Merrill Lynch, *"One to Rule Them All: FCF/EV,"* Free Cash Flow is the cash available after operating expenses, dividends, and capital expenditures. This equation is expressed through three key quality indicators:

- Accounting quality: FCF is difficult to manipulate.
- Stability: High cash-generating companies can turn to cash coffers in a downturn.
- Profitability: Higher cash balances often reflect profitability.

In contrast, enterprise value is a company's value inclusive of net debt, also expressed through three quality indicators:

- Capital Structure
- Leverage
- Solvency

Therefore, excessive amounts of debt increase enterprise value and lower earnings yield. Given such a track, one might naturally assume FCF/EV would be the most popular subfactor employed in institutional research. Not so. In application, FCF/EV is one of the least employed subfactors, with only a 25% adoption rate.

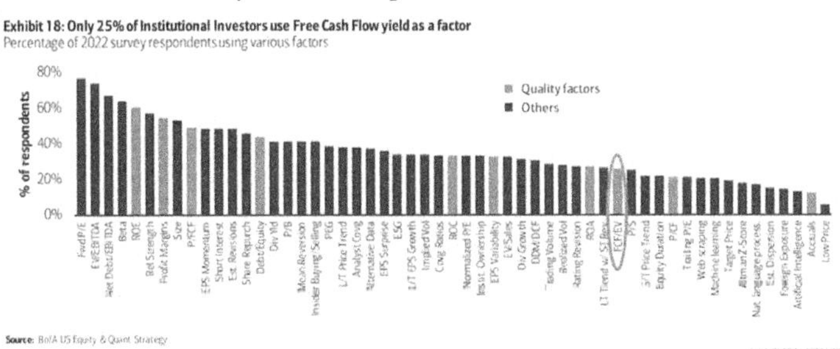

Moreover, per Bank of America, FCF/EV is also a naturally nimble metric. Sectors that naturally develop higher FCF/EV ratios tend to outperform.

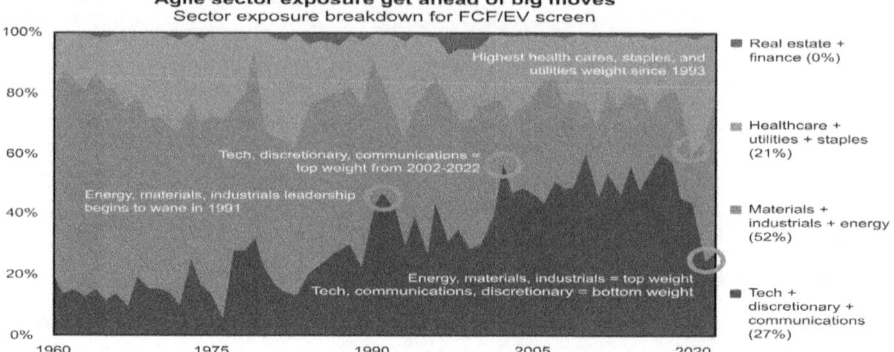

Source: BofA Research Investment Committee, Global Financial Data, Bloomberg, Factset, Pacer ETF. Note: Full sample is all US stocks in Russell 1000, by year, since 1984. This performance is backtested and does not represent the actual performance of any account or fund. Back - tested performance depicts the theoritical (not actual) performance of a particular strategy over the time period indicated. No representation is being made that any actual portfolio is likely to have achieved returns similar to those shown herein. See appendix avfor more details.

BofA GLOBAL RESEARCH

According to Bank of America Global Research, "Agility Free cash flow yield is a nimbler measure; it rotated to tech and then to energy at opportune moments over the past several decades (Figure 7). Our preferred FCF yield screen was overweight 'new economy' sectors (tech, discretionary, communication services for the first two decades of the 21st century after large 'old economy' (energy, materials, industrials) tilts for much of the 20th century. Today (January 2023), our preferred measure is 52% old economy, which has insulated it from much of the recent market tumult (Figure 7). This sector shift has been recent, so the FCF yield screen did not miss the tech rally that marked 2020. The S&P 500, by contrast, tends to lag these market shifts. Index exposure is still heavily skewed toward new economy sectors, leaving it vulnerable to leadership changes."

However, notice in Figure 5 that FCF/EV did not assist with downside protection of the model. FCF/EV maximum drawdown equaled the S&P 500 Index at 54.7%, well above the other quality metric factors. However, this weakness is not to be fretted over, as we will soon address this drawback when discussing crop insurance through Volume Factor dividend growth model's Risk Overlay.

VOLUME FACTOR DIVIDEND GROWTH MODEL CONSTRUCTION

For these reasons, I recommend Volume Factor dividend growth models only picked from the top-ranked stocks as ranked by Free Cash Flow/Enterprise Value. Why Free Cash Flow and not earnings? Earnings can be manipulated, but Free Cash Flow represents how much money is being generated from operations from the starting point versus the ending point, after expenses. Notice the even, symmetrical distribution between the deciles of large-cap stocks with high Free Cash Flow yields compared to those with low Free Cash Flow yields.

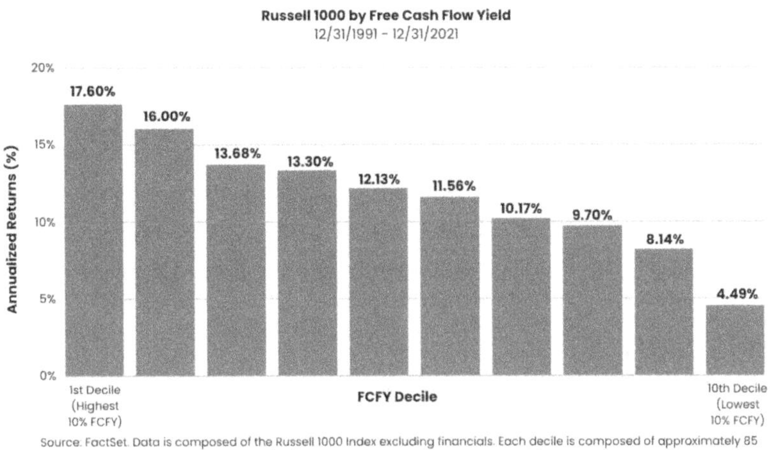

Our dividend growth models do not have to be just a large-cap strategy but could also be an all-cap strategy incorporating the size factor. The S&P 600 constitutes small-cap stocks.

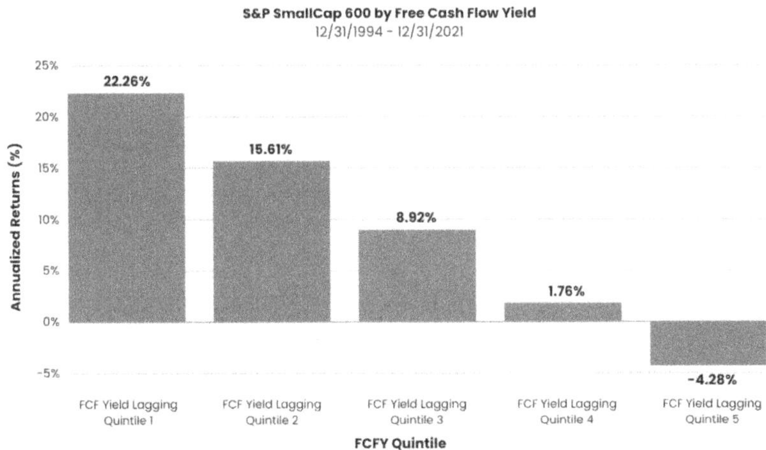

VOLUME FACTOR DIVIDEND GROWTH OFFENSE

Now that we have filtered candidates by the attributes of dividends and fundamentals down to just quality stocks, next, we will identify those poised for current price appreciation. To accomplish this, we have already introduced a uniquely effective quantitative screening process, the Volume Factor ranking system. Applying the Volume Factor various aspects of the ranking model to Volume Factor dividend growth model's quality/dividend growth filter, we identify the stocks garnering the strongest and most momentous capital flows. In this way, when value is in favor, the model may rotate toward value stocks, and when growth is in favor, the model can be positioned in growth stocks. Furthermore, when large caps are performing well, the model may tilt to large caps or mid and small caps—that is, whichever sizes, styles, sectors, or industries are in vogue. The goal of the Volume Factor dividend growth models is to be in the highest quality dividend stocks currently working, keeping the model's style and factor relevant for whichever style may be in favor. In this way, we reconstitute our Volume Factor dividend growth orchard from the quality dividend stocks most poised for appreciation according to our Volume Factor analysis.

CROP INSURANCE

The final component of strong investment stewardship is protecting our Volume Factor dividend growth orchard. Typically, farmers purchase crop insurance to protect against catastrophes. Likewise, we employ our own "crop insurance," that is, the Volume Factor Risk Overlay, to preserve our orchard's capital base against bear market catastrophes. Because the combination of quality and dividend historically has provided strong downside protection, the Volume Factor Risk Overlay does not necessarily need to be applied across the entire model. Notice in Figure 11 that dividend growers have fallen less in down months. During

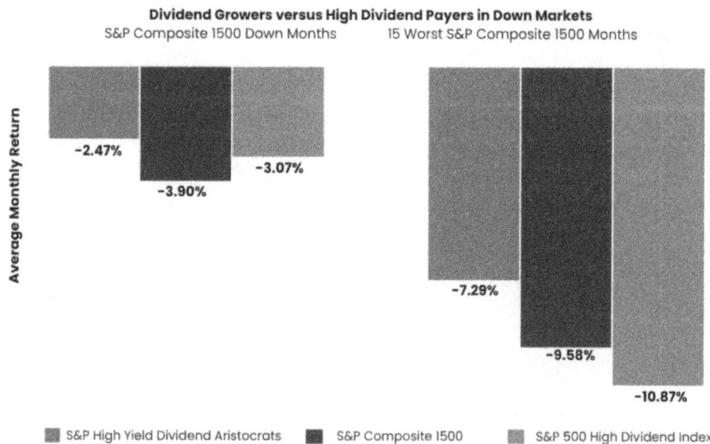

Source: S&P Dow Jones Indices LLC. Data from Dec. 31, 1999 to April 30, 2021. Index performance based on total return in USD. Past performance is no guarantee of future results. Chart is provided for illustrated purposes and reflects hypothetical historic performance. Please see the Performance Disclosure at the end of this book for more information regarding the inherent limitations associated with back-tested performance.

down months over the previous two decades, dividend growers fell less than 2.5% during down months compared to the S&P 1500 Index, which fell by 3.9%. During the 15 worst months, dividend growers declined an average of 7.29% versus the index average of 9.58%.

Additionally, according to Manning and Napier, combining Free Cash Flow with dividend yield lowered drawdown, especially during the lost decade. Over the brutal declines of 2000-2009, stocks in the top quartile of Free Cash Flow and dividends only declined 10.7% compared to the Russell 1000, which was down 26.5% over the same period. Moreover, these stocks participated in 77.57% of the downside compared to the index participating in nearly 110% of the downside.

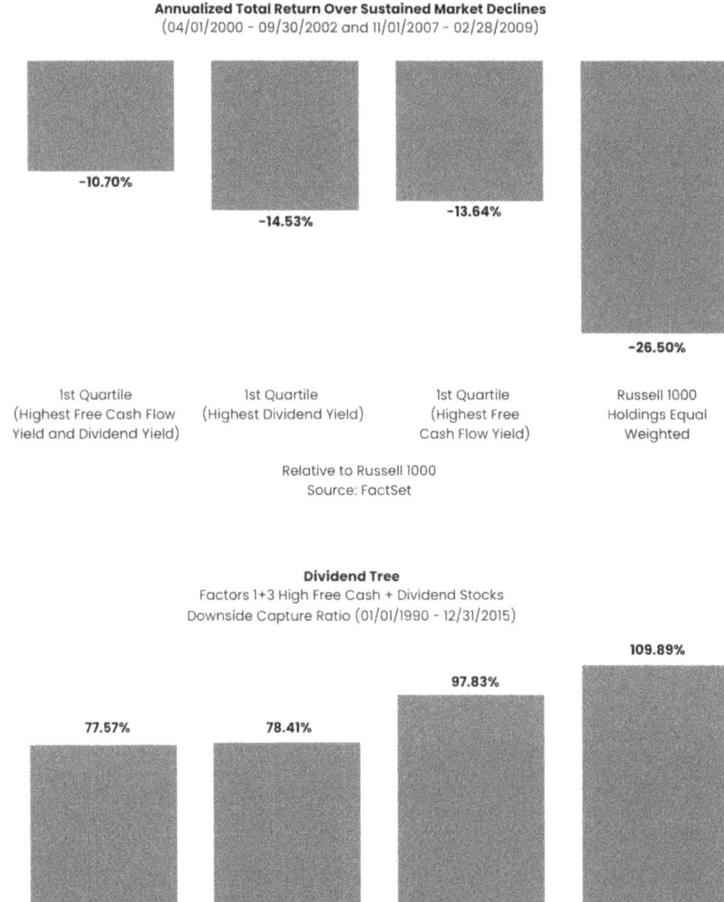

Although we have strong confidence that our Volume Factor dividend growth models yields strong results for those investors with the objectives of preretirement, retirement, and estate growth long term, our Volume Factor Risk Overlay provides intermediate protection from severe bear market famines.

The unique defensive attributes of the Volume Factor dividend growth stocks may better weather brutal bear market storms. Due to the sturdy characteristics of the Volume Factor dividend growth model's underlying investments, the Volume Factor dividend growth model's Risk Overlay may be designed to maintain a long-term equity investment bias except in the most drastic bear market investment environments. This means the Volume Factor dividend growth should be designed to maintain a greater equity weight than our other Volume Factor models, such as the Bull-Run, Bear-Hide model.

DIVIDEND GROWTH'S SPECIAL TEAMS

Inserting VPCI V bottoms into the Volume Factor dividend growth model's Risk Overlay rules affords the model opportunistic reentries. Like the Bull-Run, Bear-Hide models, the Volume Factor dividend growth may combine both VPCI V and W Bottoms to its Risk Overlay. This allows the model to capture both types of bottoming formations. Applying just a 50% Volume Factor Risk Overlay with VPCI Bottoms participated in a whopping 97% of the upside and only 84% of the downside. The rationale behind the higher equity exposure is due to the composition of the underlying investments. Bull-Run, Bear-Hide can move into any style of investment. However, because of the Volume Factor dividend growth model's quality constraints of Free Cash Flow and dividend growth, the components are expected to hold up better in many downside market environments. As an example, during the lost decade, FCF/EV exhibited roughly half the drawdown of the market averages. Adding a dividend component cuts losses down even further.

Preserving the capital base not only leads to more stable investor mindsets but also creates a framework to protect and grow the dividend yield. Keeping drawdowns low preserves, the dividend yield in bear markets and allows it to compound faster from a larger base when the market eventually recovers.

Take, for example, Costco. In 2011, Costco's dividend yield was 1.2%. By 2022, Costco's dividend yield was only 0.7%. However, in 2011, the **annual** dividend was 96 cents. Now the **quarterly** dividend is 90 cents, or $3.60 a year. So even though the yield is lower, the dividend received is almost four times that of 2011. The yield is lower because the stock price, or base, is higher. In this way, preserving the model's base allows us to replant the dividend orchard from lower levels.

This concept is similar to taxes. Nearly every time the federal government lowers the income tax rate, it increases revenue. That is because the base grows. After the tax cut, the economy improves, producing higher incomes or profits to be taxed, even though the tax rate is lower. The same holds true with dividends. Price appreciation leads to a lower dividend yield, but so long as the dividend grows, so does the yield to cost. This leads to more dividends received by shareholders. Allow me to provide you with an illustration of how this might work. Below is a hardwood vs. fruit trees analogy in the distribution phase.

Hardwoods				Versus
Year	SPX	Withdrawl	Market Value	
1999/2000		$0.00	$1,000,000.00	
2000	-10.00%	$50,000.00	$850,000.00	
2001	-13.00%	$50,000.00	$689,500.00	
2002	-23.00%	$50,000.00	$480,915.00	
2003	26.00%	$50,000.00	$555,952.90	
2004	9.00%	$50,000.00	$555,988.66	
2005	3.00%	$50,000.00	$522,668.32	
2006	15.00%	$50,000.00	$551,068.57	
2007	5.00%	$50,000.00	$528,622.00	
2008	-37.00%	$50,000.00	$283,031.86	
2009	26.00%	$50,000.00	$306,620.14	
2010	15.00%	$50,000.00	$302,613.16	
2011	2.00%	$50,000.00	$258,665.43	
2012	15.00%	$50,000.00	$247,465.24	
2013	32.00%	$50,000.00	$276,654.12	
2014	14.00%	$50,000.00	$265,385.69	
2015	1.00%	$50,000.00	$219,101.09	
2016	12.00%	$50,000.00	$172,168.51	
2017	22.00%	$50,000.00	$149,045.58	
2018	-5.00%	$50,000.00	$91,593.30	
2019	32.00%	$50,000.00	$70,445.19	
2020	18.00%	$50,000.00	$33,407.10	
Total Income		$1,050,000.00		

Fruit Trees			
Year	Divident Achievers + FCF	$1,000,000.00	Yield to Cost 2.25%
2000	9.00%	$24,525.00	2.45%
2001	8.00%	$26,487.00	2.65%
2002	7.00%	$28,341.09	2.83%
2003	11.00%	$31,458.61	3.15%
2004	14.00%	$35,862.82	3.59%
2005	11.00%	$39,807.72	3.98%
2006	16.00%	$46,176.96	4.62%
2007	16.00%	$53,565.27	5.36%
2008	11.00%	$59,475.45	5.95%
2009	2.00%	$60,646.60	6.06%
2010	10.00%	$66,711.26	6.67%
2011	12.00%	$74,716.62	7.47%
2012	11.00%	$82,935.44	8.29%
2013	13.00%	$93,717.05	9.37%
2014	11.00%	$104,025.93	10.40%
2015	9.00%	$113,388.26	11.34%
2016	8.00%	$122,459.32	12.25%
2017	8.00%	$132,256.07	13.23%
2018	11.00%	$146,804.23	14.68%
2019	8.00%	$158,842.18	15.88%
2020	3.00%	$164,242.82	16.42%
Total Income		$1,666,427.72	

*Divident Achievers + FCF Source: Wells Fargo Advisors DSIP and Factset

CONSUME THE FRUIT NOT THE TREE

"Wealth is like an orchard. You have to share the fruits, not the trees"

– Carols Slim Helu

In the hardwoods illustration Figure 21, the client purchased the S&P 500 in 2000, taking 5% from their original cost base of $1 million. This equates to $50,000 per year. After three consecutive years of down markets, by 2003, their strategy value dropped from $1 million to $556,000. Thus, the strategy is cut nearly in half in three short years. At $556,000, the withdrawal rate is no longer 5%, but 9% annualized.

In contrast, the client investing in dividend growth stocks with high Free Cash Flow only withdraws the dividends paid, or the fruit born. In 2000, the fruit tree dividend growth investor began withdrawals yielding only 2.25%, or $22,500 annually. However, by 2003, the yield to cost had grown to 3.15%, or $31,500. Most importantly, the fruit tree investor has not sold any stocks for income in decline. By 2008, the yield to cost grows to 5.95%, or $59,500, exceeding the original 5%.

Meanwhile, with a 37% drop in the S&P 500 in 2008, the hardwood investor only has $283,000 left, equating to a 17.5% annualized withdrawal rate. By the end of 2020, the hardwood investor is down to his very last withdrawal before being depleted. Meanwhile, over the two decades, the fruit tree investor's dividend yield has grown from $22,500 to $164,000. That is a 16.4% yield to cost! Moreover, the fruit tree investor has not cut down any stocks without replacing them.

Now think about what it would be like to be the financial advisor of the hardwood investor facing the destruction of wealth, the financial plan, the client-advisor relationship, and their investment fees. In comparison, the experience of the advisor employing the fruit tree approach is the creation of more and more wealth for their client and the growth of their own asset-based revenue. After such an experience, the fruit tree advisor may now shift their focus to passing the wealth creation on to the next generation. The end game is investor outcomes. In this way, the Volume Factor dividend growth models are designed to meet client objectives in the growth and distribution phases.

"The Volume Factor is the missing puzzle piece
to tactical strategies driving successful investment outcomes."

VOLUME FACTOR'S GROWTH OF INCOME TRAITS SUMMARY

In the Volume Factor growth on income models, first, all of the stocks must pay dividends. Second, the stocks must all bear more fruit; all of the stocks must be dividend growers, growing new fruit-bearing branches every year. Third, the companies must be in a financial position to pay and increase their dividends, not by strong earnings, because earnings can be manipulated, but, rather, by Free Cash Flow. Free Cash Flow is how much you started with versus how much you ended up with. In this way, our Volume Factor dividend growth model has a deep, strong root system, allowing companies to pay their dividend and be in a financial position to increase their dividend yield.

How to pick em', I am not the smartest person in the world, nor am I the best capitalized, nor can I afford the best resources, but what I can do, perhaps better than anyone else on this planet, is track where the money or capital flows are going; that is my unique superpower. Of the stocks that meet the fundamental and dividend criteria, we invest in those top-ranked by our Volume Factor ranking algorithms which determine where capital is currently being positioned. Thus, according to our Volume Factor analysis, we are building an orchard of stocks ripe for the picking.

With the Volume Factor income models, we live off the fruit of the trees, avoiding the need to cut them down for income distribution needs. This is important in retirement income planning but even more critical for CRUTs and charities utilizing spending policies. I have experienced this not because I am a tax or legal expert, but because I specialize in accomplishing desired investment outcomes. The charity wants the principal to grow so they have significant assets to advance their mission. The grantor wants a high- and growing-income stream. The Volume Factor income models are designed to be highly effective in accomplishing these dual mandates of growth and income for charitable trusts, endowments, retirees, and their financial advisors.

In the end, it is a math game, and math always wins. These Volume Factor growth of income models may help you preserve your assets for yourself and your estate while also giving them away to the causes you value.

[1] *Holy Bible: English Standard Version*. Crossway Bibles, 2001.

CHAPTER 9:

VOLUME FACTOR DIRECT INDEXING

"A successful outcome is like completing a puzzle;
you need the missing piece to achieve it."

Some of the data presented in this chapter is hypothetical and back-tested data. This data is not based on any advisory client assets. Past performance of a model is not a guarantee of future results. Actual performance may vary significantly from the hypothetical results shown. Please see the section titled 'Important Information Regarding Hypothetical, Back-Tested Performance' for a full description of this data and the limitations associated with it.

Volume Factor Models for After-Tax Alpha Generation Direct Indexing

Both the Volume Factor Ranking System and the Volume Factor Risk Overlay create an enormous amount of turnover. For those investing in non-qualified accounts, this activity creates significant issues in the tax management of a portfolio. Note that this is not an issue with IRAs or other retirement plans, because these ERISA accounts grow on a tax-deferred basis (tax free if a Roth IRA/Roth 401k). High turnover also is not an issue with charitable foundations or endowments, as these organizations do not pay taxes. The turnover in a Volume Factor model may exceed 400% per year, making the tax consequences of capital gains in these taxable accounts quite significant outside an ETF structure.

Yet with taxes, it is not what you make, but what you are able to keep. With this thought in mind, there is a tax management investment strategy known as ***Direct Indexing***, which may flip this excessive tax problem into a very favorable tax-efficient solution. Direct Indexing is a type of professional tax management investment strategy within a separately managed (SMA) portfolio directly owned by the investor, as opposed to a mutual fund or exchange-traded fund (ETF). Below are five key aspects and potential benefits of Direct Indexing for investors.

1. Customization: With Direct Indexing, investors can tailor their portfolios to match their specific investment preferences, such as environmental, social, and governance (ESG) criteria, sector allocations, factor investing, or tax considerations. Direct Indexing offers greater control and flexibility compared to traditional fund investments.

2. Tax Efficiency: Direct Indexing allows for greater tax control and optimization. Investors can strategically manage tax losses and gains by selectively harvesting losses for tax benefits, offsetting gains, or implementing tax-efficient investment strategies.

3. Fee Savings: Direct Indexing can potentially lower investment expenses, especially for larger portfolios. In bypassing fund fees and associated expenses, investors may achieve cost savings, although there are costs associated with implementing and managing the strategy.

4. Enhanced Returns: Through Direct Indexing, investors can potentially generate enhanced returns by utilizing techniques such as factor investing, which aims to capture specific risk premia associated with factors such as value, growth, quality, and momentum.

5. Exclusionary or Inclusionary Strategies: Direct Indexing can be employed to exclude or include specific companies or sectors based on investor preferences and values. For example, an investor may choose to exclude tobacco or "sin" stocks from their portfolio.

Almost all Direct Indexing strategies replicate an index in the buildout of a Direct Index portfolio. The advantage of this approach is that the index's performance can often be easily replicated. A broad index contains multiple securities with high correlations. For example, the portfolio may have positions in both AT&T and Verizon, securities which typically have a 99% correlation. At the end of the year, AT&T is down 12% and Verizon is down 9%. To harvest the tax loss, the portfolio of the Direct Index may sell AT&T and purchase Verizon. In effect, the portfolio should perform relatively the same as if both securities had been retained. However, by selling AT&T, the investor harvests losses useful to offset gains.

The Volume Factor Tax Harvesting model works the same way as traditional Direct Indexing, but on steroids. Keep in mind that our Volume Factor models are not passive but, rather, tactically active strategies. The hyperactivity of frequent changes to the holdings and weightings affords significantly more opportunities to harvest losses. At the end of each quarter, the Volume Factor modelss are reranked according to their Volume Factor rankings. Each quarter, some securities are sold, while in other portfolios, position sizes are reduced. The proceeds from these sales are then used to purchase the highest newly ranking securities not already in the portfolio.

The tax twist on the Volume Factor Direct Indexing model sells only those stocks with losses while retaining stocks in the model with gains. The Direct Indexing Overlay encourages the rapid harvesting of losses. This is because the Volume Factor Index is not a static index. Rather, the Volume Factors are tactical indexes, reallocated into completely new portfolios, potentially with all new securities and weightings each quarter. Thus, many, if not most, positions are not retained. New issues are then added to the index, creating an opportunity to frequently harvest losses. Next, we will examine a few examples of possible Volume Factor Index modelss.

This Figure 1 sample Volume Factor model invests in the top 5% of ranked stocks within the Russell 1000 according to their Volume Price Momentum Confirmation Indicator (VPMCI) ranking. In effect, each quarter, the Russell 1000 is reranked to identify and invest in the top 20 stocks according to the VPMCI. In the Direct Indexing VPMCI model, after the securities are reranked, only the securities which did not produce a profit are sold. This approach allows us to keep the winners and sell the losers.

Figure 1: VPMCI Russell 1000 from 01/01/2000 to 05/13/2022

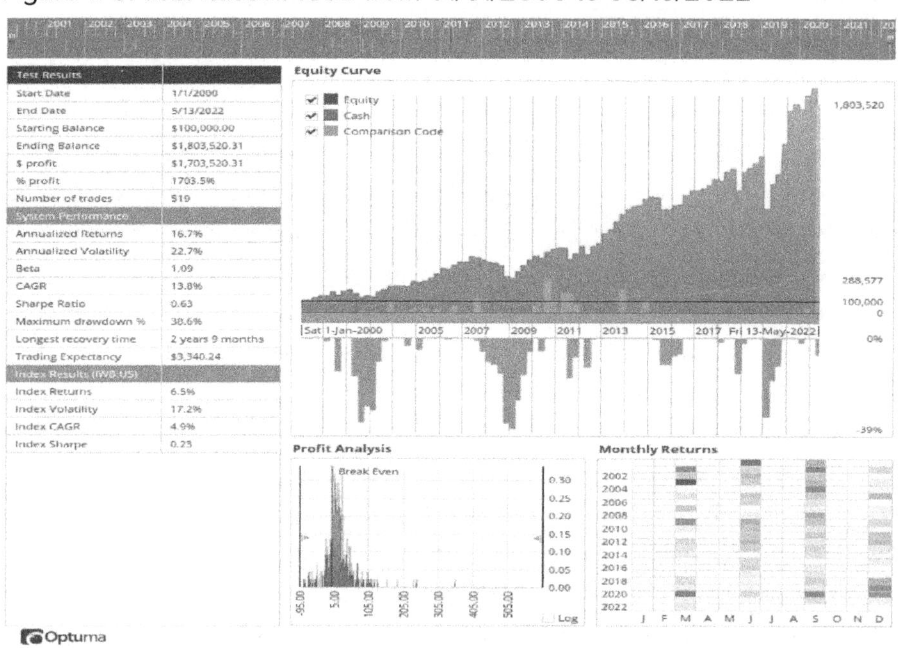

Referencing Figure 1, testing from 01/01/2000 to 05/13/2022, the VPMCI model yielded 15% returns with a Sharpe ratio of 0.60 compared to the S&P 500 yielding 6% with a 0.21 Sharpe ratio over the same period. The yellow bands in the Figure show the percentage of cash in the model when fewer than 20 stocks meet the 0.5% criteria.

Utilizing the same model of a VPMCI greater than 0.5 with securities in the Russell 2000 Index provides a larger pool of stocks from which to select. In this illustration, the Russell 2000 components were tested using a smaller position size of 2.5%. Thus, we show an investment in the top 40 VPMCI stocks from 2000. This model produces a 15.9% return compared to the IWM ETF (Russell 2000 Index ETF) return of only 8.4%.

Figure 2: VPMCI Russell 2000 from 01/01/2000 to 05/13/2022

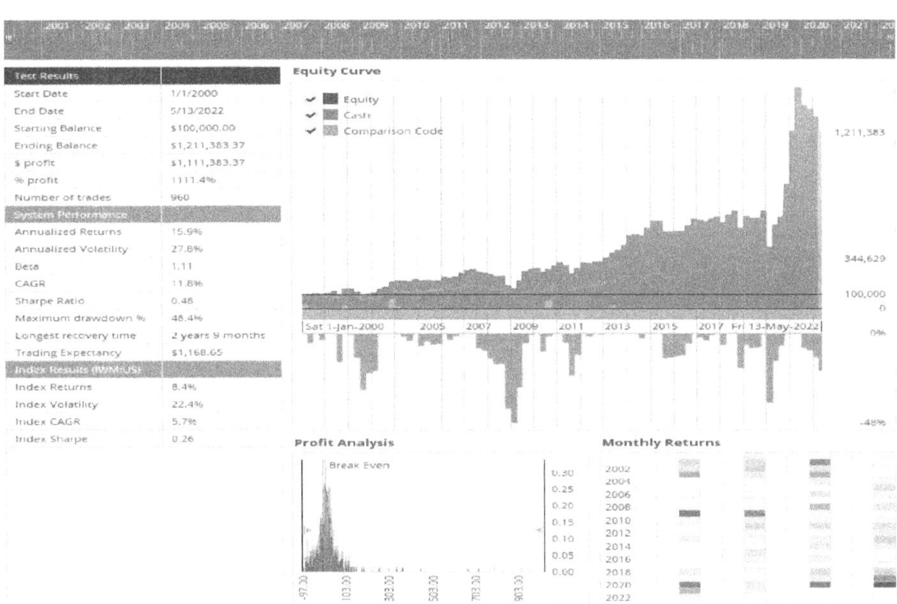

Employing the Volume Direct Indexing model may also afford a potential performance advantage by providing an opportunity to achieve "tail" returns. In momentum investing, it is common for a few outliers to become incredibly large drivers of a portfolio's returns. These outliers are often referred to as the "tail," because their returns reside outside the normal distribution of the bell curve. Retaining tail stocks often accounts for most of the returns in most momentum-based and other strategies. For example, one amazing acquisition, Geico by Berkshire Hathaway, is strongly attributed to Berkshire's esteemed historical returns. Geico is a tail stock for Berkshire Hathaway.

Yet, under the Volume Factor ranking system, all stocks are subject to sale if they do not consistently rank in the very upper decile. Thus, when a stock falls out of the upper echelon decile, it gets sold, even though it may still rank very favorably. In this way, tail stocks are generally not the drivers of the Volume Factor's alpha. Retaining the winners via the Direct Indexing methodology allows for the possibility of tail outliers to become performance drivers.

A Direct Indexing model can be employed using the Dividend Tree's ranking system alone. One can also apply the Dividend Factor's additional factors of free cash flow and dividend growth. In this way, the Volume Factor identifies the catalyst that determines when to purchase a "forever" quality stock that could become a "tail" stock. Adding these supplemental quality factors into the Direct Indexing model may create a strong fundamental model appropriate for holding over the long term. Additionally, the Volume Factor Risk Overlay can also be applied to a Direct Indexing model. However, one would need to weigh the *importance of risk mitigation versus tax management.*

A major drawback exists in the Volume Factor Direct Indexing model. Over time, by constantly selling the losers while retaining the winners, the model may eventually run out of losers to sell. At such a time, the model is essentially tax-stuck into a basket of Volume Factor winners. A model to overcome this drawback is to use realized losses to offset the unrealized gains, raising capital for investment in current Volume Factor stocks. This strategy can be employed at the end of every year, or whenever deemed appropriate. Many Direct Indexing firms utilize software programs designed to execute these types of strategies.

To conclude, the exploration of Volume Factor Direct Indexing reveals a nuanced landscape where the pursuit of after-tax alpha generation is both challenging and rewarding. The analogy of completing a puzzle aptly captures the intricate nature of this investment model—each piece, whether it be the Volume Factor Ranking System, the Volume Factor Risk Overlay, or the tax-efficient Direct Indexing, plays a crucial role in assembling the overall picture.

The recognition of the significant turnover generated by Volume Factor models in taxable accounts serves as a catalyst for the development and implementation of Direct Indexing as a tax management investment model. Direct Indexing's ability to tailor portfolios to specific investor preferences and strategically manage tax implications brings forth a compelling proposition.

The Volume Factor Tax Harvesting model, operating as a turbocharged version of traditional Direct Indexing, amplifies the potential for tax-efficient gains. The dynamic nature of the Volume Factor Index, with its frequent changes and tactical reallocations, provides abundant opportunities for tax loss harvesting.

In navigating the intricacies of Volume Factor Direct Indexing, investors must carefully weigh the trade-offs between risk mitigation and tax management. The models's success lies not only in assembling the puzzle pieces but also in adapting and evolving the approach to address challenges and seize opportunities in the ever-changing landscape of the financial markets. As the puzzle of after-tax alpha generation continues to evolve, Volume Factor Direct Indexing stands as a dynamic and innovative piece in the larger investment mosaic.

CHAPTER 10:

YIELD MATTERS

"Success is like completing a puzzle; you need every missing piece to achieve it."

Some of the data presented in this chapter is hypothetical and back-tested data. This data is not based on any advisory client assets. Past performance of a model is not a guarantee of future results. Actual performance may vary significantly from the hypothetical results shown. Please see the section titled 'Important Information Regarding Hypothetical, Back-Tested Performance' for a full description of this data and the limitations associated with it.

Once upon a time in our upscale community, a well-to-do and influential fellow shared with me this little tale that had me questioning the cosmic comedy of wealth management. So, picture this: an old friend offloaded his business in 1980, raking in a cool million. Curious about his fiscal stewardship, I inquired about the fate of the million-dollar moolah.

To my sheer amazement, he nonchalantly revealed that the check proceeds were still chillin' cold in his wallet. Being the financial sage I am, I could not resist schooling him on the art of compounded returns. "Mate, you're toting around a million bucks in your wallet? Put that cash to work! T-bills, earning 14% returns await you, my dear boy!"

Fast forward a few months, and I found myself face-to-face with this financial maestro once again. Being the ever the concerned financial fairy godparent, I probed about the status of the proceeds. Lo and behold, it was still riding shotgun in his wallet!! "You could be pulling in 17% with T-bills," I advised, but it was like giving investing advice to a brick wall.

After that encounter, I could not help but suspect that I'd stumbled upon a bona fide contender for the "Stupidest Investor on the Planet" award. I discreetly distanced myself, thinking, "Good luck with that million-dollar wallet accessory, pal." I guess some folks are just born to dance to the beat of their own financial drum – even if it is out of tune!

Fast forward through the sands of time, and our paths crossed anew. With pleasantries exchanged, I couldn't resist revisiting the million-dollar question, half-expecting the check to have become a relic in his wallet museum. His response? "Oh, I bought a CD." Cue my internal facepalm, as CD rates were less than 1%. Meanwhile, I had been riding the waves of a bull market for decades. Utter disbelief washed over me. So, I decided to grace my old friend with a grand finale lecture on the joys of long-term investing.

So, in a final last-ditch effort to save him from his financial foibles, I inquired about the terms of the CD he was trapped in. But then the punchline hit me, – "I snagged a 30-year CD yielding 16% right after our last chat."

The point of this story is that yield is important. However, unless you are the old friend of the story, "the stupidest investor on the planet," you probably require a greater return than what riskless investments presently provide. Unfortunately for even the most brilliant fixed-income investors, since 1982, yields have steadily declined. A traditional CD investor who purchased a 1 or even 5-year CD saw their income drop over 90% over the course of the last three decades. As I presently write, riskless rates are so low that high-quality bonds are primarily utilized as an equity hedge as opposed to a viable vehicle for income replacement.

Meanwhile, the cost of living has steadily risen. Thus, today many income investors have gravitated over to stocks as "There Is No Alternative"(TINA) with low bond yields. Yet many of these same investors who jumped the fixed income ship, did so just in time to endure the pain of market volatility brought about in the lost decade/ great recession. Only then to be followed by the post-pandemic inflationary market.

I do not believe in this fixed income solely for hedging purposes approach. Bonds pay interest while incurring credit and duration risk. When I invest in bonds, I look for the bonds with the highest yields with the least amount of risk. Often our Volume Factor Bond models agree with this approach. For instance, in the bond crash of 2022, our algorithmic Volume Factor Bond models were primarily positioned in T-Bills and other high-quality low-duration instruments. At the time the yields paid by T-bills were among the highest while taking on the least amount of risk.

Please make no mistake about it; retirement is all about income. Yet, CDs and government bonds have not kept up with inflation. Despite these circumstances, upon entering retirement, most retirees and financial advisors still fail to shift away from their total return strategies that worked so well in the accumulation phase. Yet, your retirement is about replacing your income, not portfolio growth. A retirement income plan is what this Volume Evangelist prescribes for most retirees.

Retirement Requires Income Replacement Above Growth

Advisors will often change their client's allocations in retirement to be more conservative. This should help with volatility, which is very important, but in isolation, fails to meet the real goal – income replacement. In contrast, our Volume Factor models are all about achieving specific goals to attain a successful financial outcome. So, let's start with this example illustrating the importance of income or dividend yield to meet the goal of income replacement.

Currently, a widespread misconception prevails among investors and even financial advisors, asserting that the optimal investment strategy is invariably the one yielding the highest total return. This assumption holds true if the capital base is not drawn out. However, when transitioning into the distribution phase, the effectiveness of an investment strategy hinges on a delicate balance involving cumulative return, yield, volatility, and distribution requirements. The next study illustrates this point.

In the above study conducted from 04/01/2015 to 05/01/2020, we observed how five different one-million-dollar portfolios each performed given varying distribution needs. For each distribution scenario, the portfolio with the greatest return post distribution is highlighted in blue, the portfolio with the second greatest return is highlighted in red, and the portfolio with the third highest return is highlighted in yellow. First, the benchmark index (S&P 500), produced the highest cumulative return with the lowest yield. Then we have four different income-based portfolios, 1, 2, 3, and 4. Income Portfolio #1 had the highest cumulative return and the lowest yield of the four income portfolios. Next, Income Portfolio #2 experienced the second-highest cumulative return as well as the second-lowest yield. Next, Income Portfolio 3 produced the second-lowest cumulative return and the second-highest yield. And finally, Portfolio 4 had the lowest cumulative return but the highest yield.

No Withdrawals Required

First, let us start with an investor who does not require withdrawals. Although the benchmark had the highest cumulative return, when also factoring in the annualized 4.23% yield, Income Portfolio #2 had the best overall total return of $1,607,540. Next best, the benchmark returned $1,604,482.83, compared to Income Portfolio #1 (highest income portfolio cumulative return and the lowest yield) $1,604,261.11, followed by Income Portfolio #3 $1,599,748.10 (second-lowest cumulative return, and the second-highest yield) and finally Income Portfolio #4 with an ending balance of $1,595,642.72 (the lowest cumulative return and highest yield).

	Benchmark	Highest Price Return Lowest Yield	2nd Highest Price Return & 2nd Lowest Yield	3rd Highest Price Return & 2nd Highest Yield	Lowest Price Return & Highest Yield
Cumulative Price Return During Period	45.98%	35.89%	31.40%	25.33%	13.69%
Cumulative Price Return	1	2	3	4	5
	Benchmark	Highest Price Return Lowest Yield	2nd Highest Price Return & 2nd Lowest Yield	3rd Highest Price Return & 2nd Highest Yield	Lowest Price Return & Highest Yield
Current Yield	1.86%	3.52%	4.23%	5.17%	6.94%
Rank Yield Value in Final Month	5	4	3	2	1
	Benchmark	Highest Price Return Lowest Yield	2nd Highest Price Return & 2nd Lowest Yield	3rd Highest Price Return & 2nd Highest Yield	Lowest Price Return & Highest Yield
0% Yield Target	$1,604,482.83	$1,604,261.11	$1,607,540.58	$1,599,748.10	$1,595,642.72
3% Yield Target	$1,405,486.38	$1,408,159.28	$1,411,418.93	$1,405,066.31	$1,403,103.36
4% Yield Target	$1,339,154.23	$1,342,792.01	$1,346,045.05	$1,340,172.37	$1,338,923.58
5% Yield Target	$1,272,822.08	$1,277,424.73	$1,280,671.16	$1,275,278.44	$1,274,743.79
6% Yield Target	$1,206,489.93	$1,212,057.45	$1,215,297.28	$1,210,384.51	$1,210,564.00
7% Yield Target	$1,140,157.78	$1,146,690.18	$1,149,923.40	$1,145,490.58	$1,146,384.22
8% Yield Target	$1,073,825.63	$1,081,322.90	$1,084,549.51	$1,080,596.65	$1,082,204.43
9% Yield Target	$1,007,493.48	$1,015,955.63	$1,019,175.63	$1,015,702.72	$1,018,024.64
10% Yield	$941,161.33	$950,588.35	$953,801.74	$950,808.78	$953,844.86
11% Yield	$874,829.18	$885,221.08	$888,427.86	$885,914.85	$889,665.07
12% Yield	$808,497.03	$819,853.80	$823,053.97	$821,020.92	$825,485.28
13% Yield	$742,164.88	$754,486.53	$757,680.09	$756,126.99	$761,305.50
14% Yield	$741,290.32	$753,620.91	$756,813.29	$755,260.32	$760,434.82
15% Yield	$740,415.75	$752,755.29	$755,946.48	$754,393.65	$759,564.14
Rank in Final Month					
	Benchmark	Highest Price Return Lowest Yield	2nd Highest Price Return & 2nd Lowest Yield	3rd Highest Price Return & 2nd Highest Yield	Lowest Price Return & Highest Yield
0% Yield Target	2	3	1	4	5
3% Yield Target	3	2	1	4	5
4% Yield Target	4	2	1	3	5
5% Yield Target	5	2	1	3	4
6% Yield Target	5	2	1	4	3
7% Yield Target	5	3	1	4	2
8% Yield Target	5	3	1	4	2
9% Yield Target	5	3	1	4	2
10% Yield	5	4	2	3	1

3% Portfolio Withdrawal

Next, let us consider what happens when the investor takes a 3% annual draw. Intuitively, most investors believe that the portfolios with the highest return are always the best option. Here we will reveal the fallacy of this idea and the consequences. With a three percent withdrawal rate, Income Portfolio #2 yielding 4.23%, remains the best option returning $1,411,418.93. However, Income Portfolio #1 yielding 3.52% leapfrogs the benchmark with a $1,408,159 net return versus the benchmark $1,405,486. Income Portfolios 3 & 4 remain in 4th and 5th place.

4% Portfolio Withdrawal

Now let us bump up our distribution from 3% up to 4%. Again, Income Portfolio #2 remains the best option, followed again by Portfolio #1. However, with a 4% annual withdrawal, Portfolio #3, with a 5.17% yield, overtakes the benchmark returning $1,340,172 compared to the benchmark's return of $1,272,822. Once again, income Portfolio #4 is the poorest performer.

Give me 5%

However, when the distribution rate is raised to 5%, Income Portfolio #4, with a 6.94% yield, also beats out the benchmark with $1,274,743 in comparison to the benchmark at $1,272,822. Income Portfolio #2 remains the best option, followed again by Income Portfolios 3&4. Thus, the benchmark (S&P 500) with the high cumulative return and the second-best overall rate of return, is the worst choice when taking a 5% withdrawal.

How about 6%?

Next, let us look at a 6% distribution. When the distribution requirement is boosted to 6%, the index and Income Portfolios #2 & #1 remain in the same order 1st and 2nd. However, the highest yield, Income Portfolio #4, overtakes income Portfolio #3 for third place. Similarly, with a 7% distribution, Income Portfolio #4, with the highest yield, vaults to the second-best portfolio option beating all options except the outlier, Income Portfolio #2.

Show me 10%

Finally, when the portfolio yield is elevated to 10%, our top-performing Income Portfolio #2, falls to second place with $953,801. The worst-performing total return portfolio, Income Portfolio #4 overtakes the field as the top model with $953,844. Notice that the benchmark, which had the second-best total return but the lowest yield, was the poorest-performing model every time the yield exceeded 5%. Nonetheless, most investors in the distribution phase will gravitate towards this option.

So how can the portfolio with the highest yield but least return outperform even the top strategy deep into the distribution phase? When investments are down, investors in the growth strategy must sell or cut down their hardwoods to meet living expenses. Whereas the total return income portfolios only need to sell a little capital, if any, to fulfill their distribution requirements.

For example, beginning the third quarter of 2022, the S&P 500 was down approximately 25%. If a retiree or endowment needed a 5% distribution, the portfolio manager would need to sell off 5% of the client's portfolio, already down 25%. After the 25% decline and then the 5% withdrawal, their portfolio must rally back over 42% to get back to even. However, portfolios with a 5% or greater distribution do not require the sale of capital because the yield has already been met. Thus, the high-yielding portfolios need to return 25% (or less if the distribution exceeds 5%) to return to breakeven, not 42%. It is a math game, and math always wins.

The Target % Series

The Target % model series is designed to meet the high distribution requirement objectives. For example, to meet a 5% distribution, we will use the Target 5% model which targets a 5% yield. If the investor needs 6%, we will employ the Target 6% model targeting a 6% distribution. The Target % models are a variant of the Volume Factor Growth of Income models, modified to achieve a specific yield target objective.

Like the Volume Factor Growth of Income models, the Target % series espouses similar themes, values, and model characteristics. Specifically, the Target % series invests in stocks that produce fruit (pay dividends), consistently grow more branches (increase their dividends), and possess a robust root system (strong Free Cash Flow). In fact, the ranking algorithms used Target % stocks use similar combinations of Volume Factor components adding one additional variable.

Target %'s Dividend Yield Factor

The Volume Factor ranking mechanism identifies those stocks garnering the most momentous capital flows, thus potentially ripe and poised to move. Like our growth of income models, Target % employs the same identical process. However, once the Volume Factor ranks all the filtered stocks, the Target % multiplies each stock's Volume Factor ranking score by its dividend yield. That is an extra step not taken in our dividend grow models.

For example, if ABC stock paying 1% were to clear all of Target % screens and produced a Volume Factor score of 1000. ABC's final Volume Factor Target score would also be 1000 (1000 (Volume Factor Score) *1 (ABC's dividend yield)). Now let's say XYZ stocks pays out a 10% dividend yield. Additionally, XYZ clears all the TGT % screens and has a Volume Factor score of 1000. However, XYZ's Volume Factor Target score vaults to 10,000 (1000 (Volume Factor Score) *10 (XYZ's dividend yield)). That compares to ABC's Volume Factor of only 1000, even though both had the same Volume Factor score. In this way, Target % boosts stocks with higher dividends toward the top of the list, causing higher-dividend-paying stocks to produce higher model weightings than those stocks with similar Volume Factor scores but lower dividend yields.

Target %'s Yield Booster

Unfortunately, the natural model yield from this process sometimes fails to reach our yield target. In these circumstances, Target % will add an allocation to an equity ETF's selling covered calls against their model until the yield target is met. Typically, these covered call ETFs yield between 9-12%. Covered calls provide yield at the cost of upside market appreciation.

Covered calls work similarly to earnest money received on a land contract. With a land contract, the potential buyer makes a contingent offer to the seller to purchase the property in the future at a price typically higher than the present value. In exchange for that agreement, the seller receives earnest money from the buyer. The seller keeps that earnest money whether the buyer purchases the property. The same concept holds with covered calls, except the property is not land but shares of stock, and the earnest money is referred to as premiums. Implementing covered calls into Target % models that fail to meet the targeted yield boosts the TGT % models' yield enough to meet their distribution objectives.

Target %'s Risk Overlay

Like our other Volume Factor Models, Target % also utilizes a Volume Factor risk overlay. In correspondence to its risk profile, I recommend tweaking the Target % risk overlay to be more defensive than the growth of income models but more aggressive than our growth strategies.

Another recommendation to differentiate between Target %'s risk overlay and the growth and growth of income models is the underlying risk-off investments. Employing income-producing alternative risk-off positions not highly correlated to either stocks or bonds may add to diversification. Suggestions of alternative income strategies include selling covered calls with commodities such as precious metals, selling deep-in-the-money calls on short-term treasury bonds, hedging out the equity in convertible bonds, and inversely correlated bonds such as agency MBS Interest Only (MBS IO) securities. (As interest rates go up in the MBS market either due to Treasury rates rising or mortgage yield spreads to Treasuries widening, prepayment rates decline, extending the interest-only cash flow stream and increasing the market value of MBS interest-only bonds).

Volume Factor's Harmonious Diversity

All Target %'s risk-off models should be positioned to generate the income needed to meet the targeted withdrawal while hedging against correlated assets. Note that each Volume Factor Model is designed to work with the whole Volume Factor ecosystem. For example, Bull Run Bear Hide might employ T-bills, Dividend Tree could use bonds, and Target %'s defensive position could be alternative income. In this way, when employed together, each model's risk-off positions add diversity to the whole. Additionally, although each model uses similar indicators and triggers, each employs the risk-overlay rules uniquely.

Additionally, each model can be in different risk-off positions depending upon the state of the indicators. There are situations when a dividend growth model is fully risk-on, whereas a growth model is fully risk-off, and a targeted yield model could be 50% risk-off. Such occurrences should be common in markets changing from bear to bull or vice versa.

Overall, the Target % models target a yield such as 5, 6 or 7% to meet the distribution needs of its investors. Secondarily, its objective is to grow both the model base and the distribution yield. Therefore, it is best suited for investors who require a higher level of withdrawal who may also wish to increase their income over time and pass on the portfolio corpus after their passing.

Conclusion:

In conclusion, this exploration underscores a fundamental paradigm shift needed in retirement planning – a shift from traditional total return strategies to a focused emphasis on generating income. The analysis of various model scenarios vividly illustrates the importance of prioritizing yield over cumulative return, particularly in the distribution phase of retirement.

The stark reality is that conventional safe havens like CDs and government bonds have struggled to keep pace with inflation, prompting a reevaluation of investment approaches. The Target % series emerges as a strategic response to this challenge, tailored to meet the specific needs of investors requiring higher withdrawals, income growth, and the preservation of wealth.

The presented study vividly demonstrates the superior performance of models with higher yields when accompanied by significantly larger distribution requirements. The study highlights the resilience and efficacy of income-focused strategies. The data advocates for a departure from the common misconceptions of growth and highest total return objectives, emphasizing the intricate balance required in retirement planning.

Ultimately, the Target % series, combines the Dividend Yield Factor with the Volume Factor for offense, a customizable Volume Factor Risk Overlay for defense, and of course the Volume Factor special team's unit for unique market transitions., In this way, the Volume Factor targeted yield models emerge as a dynamic and diversified solution. Our yield target approach echoes the broader philosophy that retirement is fundamentally about income replacement and reduced volatility rather than portfolio growth. As investors navigate the complexities of shifting market dynamics, this strategic approach aligns with the evolving landscape of retirement investing, offering a thoughtful and goal-oriented path towards financial well-being in one's golden years.

THE VOLUME FACTOR CONCLUSION

"Investing is solving a puzzle with missing pieces,
the Volume Factor was the last missing piece."

I hope you have enjoyed the book and now have hope that smooth and successful financial outcomes are possible through goals-based investment management. Infused by the Volume Factor, the Volume Factor suite of investment models are each tailored made to create a prolific offense through the Volume Factor Ranking System, a championship defense via the Volume Factor Risk Overlay, and a uniquely special, special-teams unit utilizing Volume Factor capitulation signals. Historically, our volume-infused, post-modern tactical models empircially work between 60 to 75% of the time. By work, I mean these models theortically beat their benchmarks with less risk assumed. However, what about the failing 25 to 40%?

Once, a retired doctor was distraught that his investments were not meeting his expectations. Part of his investments were under my asset management programs, and the remaining were shaped by his ideas and primarily consisted of aggressive stocks. With the foreknowledge that the investments I managed for him outperformed in the bull market two years prior, then lost significantly less in the down year that followed, I asked him about his expectations. To summarize, he believed he should beat the equity markets when they were up and meet or beat CD rates during down markets. I asked him if he had ever been able to accomplish this lofty goal. Never had he previously accomplished this expectation. Yet it was never considered a problem before. After drilling down further, I discovered it had never been an issue because when he was working, bear markets did not bother him. After reassessing his tolerance for risk and his appetite for returns, I found out that his risk temperament had not changed.

After further discussion and investigation into his frustrations, I told him I was very confident our models could accomplish his financial goals while meeting his risk and return appetite. However, I could not achieve his investment goals of beating the market when it is up while simultaneously beating bank rates when the market is down.

Similarly, a client called me once, very upset that his Growth of Dividends model of high-quality dividend stocks was underperforming his own personal portfolio of technology stocks. I asked how long this underperformance had lasted, knowing my strategy significantly outperformed the Nasdaq the prior two years. The client believed that underperformance relative to the Nasdaq lasted only a quarter, but it was actually two. I told this client I could not beat the Nasdaq every quarter, and if this was their expectation, they needed to look elsewhere. I simply cannot deliver on this expectation. However, I had full faith and confidence that our strategy would achieve the client's financial goals. I then reminded them how much the Nasdaq had previously declined, and how little their assets were down in comparison. Further, I reiterated that over the long term, we were beating those indexes handily, with significantly less risk.

The reality is that sectors, styles, and factors move in and out of favor. Although our volume-based model should identify shifts quicker than price trends while improving the accuracy of price momentum, it still takes some time for these shifts to emerge, and for volume to confirm them. Thus, during a shift from value to growth, it may take a quarter or two before our model verifies that these shifts are legitimate and not a rebound or recovery rally. Therefore, investors should be prepared for underperformance for a period of time. In the case of major shifts, a couple of quarters of underperformance could lead to an underperforming year. However, by applying these methods of "following the money," investments should not remain out of favor for years, unlike investments in styles, sectors, or other types of factor-based investing.

I share these stories because we have ambitious expectations. Yet, all strategies have strengths as well as weaknesses. There are times when the market is in transition. Our model is excellent at picking up most transitions from bear to bull. But not all. For instance, our model will most likely never get out at the top of a bull market. We will typically endure the first 7-12% of a bear market decline. If a 7-12% decline is too much to tolerate, I suggest pairing our model with a buffered ETF. A buffered ETF will avoid the first 10 to 20% of the loss. To avoid this loss, an investor must be able to give up something in return. In the case of buffered ETFs, that give up is a ceiling on how much the ETF can appreciate. The height of the ceiling is proportionate to the amount of the buffer. For example, a 10% buffer will commonly have a 17% ceiling. A 15% buffer may have a 14% ceiling. Our Volume-Factor Risk Overlay mixes well with buffered strategies, as the buffer will protect investors from the 7-12% sacrificed when employing the Volume Factor Risk Overlay. While in bull markets, the buffered strategies cap out, but our Bull Run keeps on running.

» Performance Summary (%)	3 Month	YTD	1 Year	3 Year	5 Year	10 Year	Since Fund Inception
Fund Performance*							
Net Asset Value (NAV)	5.73	5.73	-1.47	–	–	–	6.08
After Tax Held	5.73	5.73	-1.47	–	–	–	6.08
After Tax Sold	3.39	3.39	-0.87	–	–	–	4.69
Market Price	5.82	5.82	-1.39	–	–	–	6.13
Index Performance**							
S&P 500® Index - Price Return	7.03	7.03	-9.29	–	–	–	7.92

Performance data quoted represents past performance. Past performance is not a guarantee of future results and current performance may be higher or lower than performance quoted. Investment returns and principal value will fluctuate and shares when sold or redeemed, may be worth more or less than their original cost. You can obtain performance information which is current through the most recent month-end by visiting www.ftportfolios.com.

Source: ftportfolios.com

As illustrated in Figure 1, the 10% buffered model outperformed a non-buffered portfolio by preserving capital during period(?) that had a negative return, thus reducing the negative impacts of sequencing risk and withdrawals made during this particular market drawdown.

Everyone has a bias. My bias is to avoid risk and preserve capital. Earlier in my career, I employed tools to identify tops. Forgive me if I do not sound humble, but I believe I was pretty darn good at identifying peaks. In 2000, as portfolio manager of a family office, I called the top of the market. My problem as a Chartered Market Technician is that I was previously very successful, (timely and accurate), at identifying minor tops and turning points throughout the bull market. Yet, this was not a minor top call, but a major top call, and I was two weeks early. You might think two weeks is not a big deal. But due to our prior successes, my employer was not accustomed to missing much. We were already up over 50% for the year after more than doubling our gains the year prior. Moreover, the top in 2000 was no ordinary top, but a rare blowoff top. I looked quite stupid raising cash during those two weeks. With the market surging to a blowoff top, my top call caused a loss of confidence in me by my team and ownership. As a result, they went back in against my advice to stay in cash just as the market topped out. Those were difficult days that followed.

Over the course of my career, I have identified many "tops." Yet, I have discovered that most tops are not really tops at all, but merely pauses. Often, a pause appears to be a top. After reaching a peak supported by short-term leading indicators, the market will retreat to a level that appears to confirm the price breakdown. But then the market suddenly roars back, leaving weakhanded investors in the dust. Often, by the time the leading indicators confirm the breakout, the market is off, making new highs again. I've danced to this tune long enough to know that the cost of identifying a top is not worth the price of losing my position. Perhaps others can do it. Tom Demark and Larry Williams are legends at identifying turning points, as was my old friend Joe Granville. The Capital-Weighted Money Flow Indicator (CW-MFI) may be of unique value in finding toppy markets. Yet, I believe I can survive without exiting at the very top and still create value. Make no mistake, calling a top is heroic. But the risk of striking out is too costly. For this reason, I choose to follow the intermediate trends of our leading indicators to identify the shift from bull to bear, avoiding the temptation of utilizing momentum or short-term indicators to pick a top.

Additionally, it is not uncommon for market turns and shifts in market leadership to happen simultaneously. Even with all of our precautions in place, such major transitions can be painful. If investors cannot tolerate these short and shallow valleys, then the Volume Factor may not be an appropriate model for them. Investors applying the Volume Factor must have the resolve to stay with it when market transitions and style shifts occur. Those who consider employing these Volume Factor models to meet their financial goals should forget about trying to time their exits or entries. Such behavior will cause investors to miss the ride. Do not try to outthink the system; ride it out and stick with it, or don't employ it at all. Bypass your feelings and emotions. Instead, follow the data and trust the process. *"In every mystery, there's a missing puzzle piece waiting to be found."* In the end, outcomes are what matter. Wishing you and yours the very best.

Grace and peace. Buff.

ABOUT THE AUTHOR:

Hailing from Fort Wayne, Indiana, Buff Pelz Dormeier is not just a Technical Analyst and Portfolio Manager, but an esteemed award-winning figure whose expertise in volume analysis is unparalleled. He is the driving force behind VolumeAnalysis.com, VolumeFactor.com, DividendTree.com, and holds the position of Chief Technical Analyst at Kingsview Investment Management. With a career spanning over three decades, Buff Pelz Dormeier has navigated the intricate world of portfolio management for high-net-worth individuals, institutions, trusts, endowments, and financial advisors.

Distinguished as an industry trailblazer, Dormeier is the visionary mind behind a suite of groundbreaking concepts, including Volume Weighted Moving Averages (VWMAs), the VW-MACD, and the Volume Price Confirmation Indicator (VPCI). His ingenious contributions extend to VPCI Stochastics, Anti-Volume Stop Loss (AVSL), Trend Thrust Indicator (TTI), Volume Momentum Indicator (VMI), Capital Weighted Volume and Dollar Volume Indexes, as well as an array of breadth and capital-weighted volume-based indicators. Notably, his work is showcased in popular platforms such as Barron's, Stocks & Commodities, Bloomberg, C-NBC, The Financial Times, and Active Trader magazine. Additionally, his insights hold a firm place in the prestigious IFTA & CMT Journals.

Buff Pelz Dormeier's prominence transcends borders, as evidenced by his role as a featured portfolio manager in "Technical Analysis and Behavior Finance in Fund Management," a celebrated European book featuring interviews with 21 accomplished portfolio managers. As a Chartered Market Technician, he clinched the coveted 2007 Charles Dow Award, a distinction reserved for research papers that break new ground or ingeniously deploy established techniques in the realm of technical analysis. This accolade, a pinnacle in the field of technical analysis, underscores his visionary contributions.

Further embellishing his accolades, Buff Pelz Dormeier proudly holds the title of recipient of Technical Analyst's 2022 Best Product Research Award, a testament to his unwavering commitment to pushing boundaries. His influence extends to the global stage, where he has captivated audiences at both national and international conferences. His authorial prowess shines through in the critically acclaimed "*Investing With Volume Analysis*," a book that stands alone in securing both Trader Planet's STAR AWARD for top Book Resource (2012), as voted by end users, and the internationally prestigious Technical Analyst's Book of the Year Award (2013), peer-reviewed and endorsed by top industry luminaries.

In the world of investment, Buff Pelz Dormeier stands as a beacon of expertise, innovation, and accolades. His legacy is etched not only in his transformative concepts but also in the success stories of those embracing his theories. Buff's expertise can help you discover and embrace a new dimension of investment excellence redefining your journey toward financial prosperity with The Volume Factor.

ACKNOWLEDGMENTS

To my beautiful wife, Kathy, your love and encouragement have been as a guiding light throughout this process. Your willingness to shoulder additional responsibilities creating space to immerse myself into this writing has been nothing short of extraordinary. I am endlessly grateful for your presence in my life.

To Dessa and Kal, you have been my greatest source of inspiration. Your curiosity and boundless energy have infused every page of this book with a sense of wonder and joy. Thank you for understanding when I needed to retreat into my writing cave, and for your endless hugs and laughter that never fail to brighten my days.

To my partners and teammates at Kingsview, Don, Laura and Tia. Thank you for your unwavering belief in me. Your words of encouragement, thoughtful gestures, and understanding during moments of self-doubt have been invaluable. I am deeply appreciative of the sacrifices you have made to provide me with the time and space to pursue my passion. You deserve all the compliments and praise our clients frequently share with me on a daily basis. To our clients and friends thank you for your loyalty and the advocacy you champion. Your encouragement has been instrumental in shaping this book into what it is today.

I am profoundly grateful to the esteemed members of the Kingsview investment committee, Scott Martin, Sean McGillivray, Kevin Swanson, Neil Peplinski, Yash Patel, Jake Bauer, and Mitch Ehmka, thank you for your invaluable support, research expertise, and unwavering assistance throughout the journey of crafting this resource. Your collective wisdom, guidance, and dedication have been instrumental in shaping the ideas presented within these pages. I extend my deepest appreciation to each member for their insightful feedback, thoughtful discussions, and commitment to excellence, which have undoubtedly enriched the quality and depth of this work. This book stands as a testament to our collaborative efforts and shared passion for the world of investments. I am honored to have had the privilege of working alongside such a talented and dedicated group of professionals.

Furthermore, I would like to express my heartfelt gratitude to Neil Peplinski, whose exceptional contributions and tireless efforts have been pivotal in navigating the complexities of investment strategies and ensuring the accuracy and relevance of the content.

Additionally, a big gush of gratitude goes to the book's compliance review team of Kevin Swanson and Sean McGillivray. Kevin and Sean's expertise and professionalism have not only helped to streamline the compliance review but have also played a crucial role in maintaining the integrity and adherence to industry standards within the content of this book. I am sincerely thankful for Kevin and Sean's outstanding efforts and unwavering dedication, which have undoubtedly strengthened the credibility and reliability of this book.

I am profoundly grateful to Josh Lewis, whose unwavering support, boundless enthusiasm, and inspiring vision have been instrumental in bringing this book to fruition. From the initial spark of inspiration to every milestone achieved along the way, Josh has been the driving force behind this project.

His belief in the importance of this endeavor, coupled with his relentless encouragement and steadfast dedication, has been nothing short of extraordinary. Josh's unwavering optimism and infectious passion have not only fueled my own determination but have also served as a constant reminder of the significance of our shared journey.

I am deeply appreciative of Josh's unwavering commitment and enduring support, which is a source of strength and motivation throughout this creative process. His belief in the power of this book's content and his unwavering dedication to its success have been truly inspiring.

It is with heartfelt gratitude that I acknowledge Josh Lewis as not only the inspiration behind this book but also as its biggest cheerleader and supporter. His contributions have left an indelible mark on this project, and I am honored to have had the privilege of collaborating with such a remarkable leader.

I would like to express my sincere gratitude to Jerry Blythe for his invaluable editorial review of this book. Jerry's keen eye for detail, insightful feedback, and dedication to ensuring clarity and coherence have been instrumental in refining the content and enhancing its overall quality. Additionally, I extend a heartfelt thank you to Chris Wright and Lewis Charles Lewis for their diligent readership audience review.

Finally, I am sincerely grateful to Paul Arancio, Austin Pica, and Steven Lubrano, whose exceptional talents, dedication, and collaborative spirit have been instrumental in bringing this book to life. Their multifaceted contributions, from editing and proofreading to designing graphics and illustrations, have elevated the quality and visual appeal of this work.

Furthermore, their invaluable guidance, expertise, and unwavering support have played a pivotal role in shaping the direction of this project and ensuring its success. In addition to their creative endeavors, I am immensely appreciative of their efforts in establishing and maintaining the book's online presence through the creation of the book's website buffdormeier.com.

I extend my deepest gratitude to Paul, Austin, and Steven for their tireless commitment to excellence, their relentless pursuit of perfection, and their unwavering dedication to bringing our collective vision to fruition. Their contributions have been nothing short of extraordinary, and I am honored to have had the opportunity to collaborate with such a talented and dedicated team.

GLOSSARY

ABS Relative Strength: Absolute Relative Strength is the absolute value of relative strength where positive relative strength is unadjusted and negative relative strength is its inverse. For example, the absolute value of +5 is +5 whereas the absolute value of -5 is also +5. Absolute values have other practical uses like determining how far something traveled that went 5 ft one way and 5 ft back.

Advance-Decline Line: The running tally between the number of stocks closing up versus closing down.

Alpha: a measure of an investment's risk-adjusted return in relation to a benchmark. Alpha quantifies the excess return generated by an investment after accounting for its systematic risk (beta) against the benchmark. Positive alpha indicates that the investment has outperformed the benchmark after adjusting for risk, while negative alpha suggests underperformance.

Anti-Volume Stop-Loss (AVSL): A trailing stop-loss indicator developed by Buff Dormeier, CMT. AVSL provides an indication of where to exit a trade based upon trend support, volatility, and the price-volume relationship.

Average Directional Index (ADX): Trend strength indicator developed by Welles Wilder. ADX is designed to measure the strength of a trend. The higher the reading, the stronger the trend.

Average True Range (ATR): A range indicator developed by Welles Wilder. ATR is designed to measure the width of volatility within a trading range.

Beta: A measure of volatility comparing an investment to an index benchmark. A Beta of 1 means the investment has the same volatility as its benchmark. A Beta above 1 indicates higher volatility whereas Betas below 1 indicate lower relative volatility compared to the benchmark index.

Buffered ETFs: An ETF seeking to provide a defined level of protection or buffer in exchange for a cap or ceiling on upside return.

Bull-Run, Bear-Hide Risk Overlay: A risk overlay system developed by Buff Dormeier, CMT. The risk management system employees both Capital-Weighted Volume and Capital-Weighted Dollar Volume with the Advance-Decline Line acting as a doubler. The allocation can range from 100% equity to 100% T-Bills.

Bull-Run, Bear-Hide: A growth investment model developed by Buff Dormeier, CMT best paired with the endowment method of withdrawals when in the distribution phase. Bull Run Bear Hide is designed to run with the bulls when the trend of capital flows are positive, to hide from the bear when capital flow trends are negative, and utilize strategic reentries during possible bear-to-bull market transitions.

Capital-Weighted Dollar Volume: An index indicator developed by Buff Dormeier, CMT which measures how much capital is flowing into and out of an index.

Capital-Weighted Downside Volume: An index indicator developed by Buff Dormeier, CMT that measures how many shares are trading downward within an index on a capital weighted basis.

Capital-Weighted Money Flow Indicator (CW-MFI): A momentum indicator for index analysis similar to MFI (Money Flow Index) precisely employing Capital Weighted Upside and Downside Volume as opposed to presumptive volume assumptions based upon price direction.

Capital-Weighted Upside Volume – An index indicator developed by Buff Dormeier, CMT that measures how many shares are trading upward with an index on a capital weighted basis.

Capital Weighted Volume: An index indicator developed by Buff Dormeier, CMT that repairs volume tallies to their proportional index weights harmonizing price and volume index data.

Closed End Funds (CEFs): A mutual fund that trades like a stock that is closed to external capital inflow injections as well as outflow redemptions.

Direct Indexing: A tax management investment strategy intended to mimic an index that encourages the sale of losing positions to generate tax losses.

Directional Movement Index (DMI): A trend strength indicator developed by Welles Wilder used to compute the ADX (Average Directional Index)

Dividend Factor: A market factor suggesting that as a group, stocks that pay dividends tend to outperform the averages.

Dividend Tree (DT): A growth of income investment model developed by Buff Dormeier, CMT. The model invests in stocks that pay dividends, raise dividends, and are experiencing high Free Cash Flow. After screening for these variables, the remaining stocks are then selected and weighted according to their Volume Factor rankings. The Dividend Tree model further employs a risk mitigation overlay designed to mitigate risk during bear markets.

Dividend Tree Risk Overlay: A risk mitigation model developed by Buff Dormeier, CMT employed for the Dividend Tree model. The risk overlay analyzes the trends of Capital-Weighted Volume, Capital-Weighted Dollar Volume and the Advance-Decline Line. The allocation ranges from 100% equity to 50% Volume Factor Bonds.

Downside Capital-Weighted Volume: An index indicator developed by Buff Dormeier, CMT measuring how many shares are trading downward with an index on a capital weighted basis.

Exchange Traded Funds (ETFs): A fund or basket of pooled securities, usually tracking an index, traded on the exchanges that offer significant tax advantages over mutual funds.

Factor: An investment strategy targeting specific characteristics or traits that may be important drivers of investment returns.

Fama French Models: Asset pricing models developed by Eugene Fama and Kenneth French to explain equity returns based upon specific factors. The three factor model employs market risk, size, and value. The five factor model adds profitability and investment as quality metrics.

Free Cash Flow (FCF): The remaining cash after operating expenses and capital expenditures.

Endowment Method of Withdrawal: A withdrawal methodology based upon a fixed percentage of a portfolio's value. The percentage withdrawal may be based on multiple factors including expected rate of return and the investors financial needs. Its goal is to sustain the portfolio's purchasing power to perpetuity.

Enterprise Value (EV): A company's market capitalization plus debt minus cash.

Internal Relative Strength Volume Factor (IRSVF): A grouping of momentum indicators developed by Buff Dormeier, CMT noting volume's impact upon a securities momentum compared to its recent momentum.

Market Positioning System (MPS): An analysis technique plotting securities on a plane using X and Y axes.

Money Flow Index (MFI): A volume-adjusted price momentum indicator developed by Gene Quong and Avrum Soudack.

Moving Average Convergence Divergence (MACD): A trend divergence indicator developed by Gerald Appel.

Nasdaq-100 Index: An index of the 100 largest non-financial companies traded on the Nasdaq Stock Exchange weighted primarily by capitalization.

NYSE Index: An index of all the stocks traded on the New York Stock Exchange weighted by capitalization.

On-Balance Volume (OBV): An interday volume accumulation indicator popularized and likely invented by Joseph Granville.

Parabolic Stops: A trailing stop indicator developed by Welles Wilder utilizing trend and volatility.

P-Value: "Probability Value" quantifies the strength of evidence against the null hypothesis (the assumption that there is no significant relationship between variables). The smaller the p-value the stronger the null hypothesis. A value below 0.05 suggests strong evidence the results are not by chance.

Relative Strength (RS): measures the performance of an investment asset relative to a benchmark or another asset. RS helps identify which asset has outperformed or underperformed over a specific period. It is calculated by dividing the price performance of the asset by the price performance of the benchmark or another asset. RS helps identify if an asset has outperformed or underperformed over a given time period.

Relative Strength Index (RSI): a momentum oscillator developed by Welles Wilder measuring the speed and momentum of a security's price change relative to its recent past.

Russell 1000 Index: The top 1000 largest United States companies ranked and weighted by capitalization.

Russell 2000 Index: Is an index of the next largest 2000 United States domestics stocks after the largest 1000 (Russell 1000).

Russell 3000 Index: An index comprising of both the Russell 1000 and Russell 2000 components weighted by capitalization.

S&P 500 Equal Weight Index: The components of the S&P 500 index weighted equally, approximately 0.2% each stock.

S&P 500 Index: An index of large cap stocks weighted by capitalization.

S&P Small Cap Index: An index of approximately 600 small cap stocks weighted by capitalization.

SPY: The most popular S&P 500 exchange-traded fund (ETF).

Sharpe ratio: A risk/reward statistic developed by William Sharpe. The most common ratio used to measure risk-adjusted returns as determined by the excess return received relative to the volatility assumed.

Simple Moving Average (SMA): The average price over a specified time range.

Sortino ratio: A risk/reward statistic developed by Frank Sortino. The Sortino ratio is a modified version of the Sharpe ratio by removing upside standard deviation. This is my preferred risk-adjusted return metric as only downside standard deviation is relevant in protecting capital.

T-bill/s: U.S. Treasury bonds debt obligations with one year of duration or less.

Target % Risk Overlay: A risk mitigation model developed by Buff Dormeier, CMT employed in the Target % model. The risk overlay analyzes the trends of Capital-Weighted

Volume, Capital-Weighted Dollar Volume. The allocation can range from 100% equity to 50% Volume Factor Yield Alternatives.

Target % Series (TGT): An investment model developed by Buff Dormeier, CMT similar to Dividend Tree further weighted by dividend yield.

Trend Thrust Indicator (TTI): A trend indicator developed by Buff Dormeier, CMT. TTI is an adaption of the MACD indicator employing adaptive volume multipliers exaggerating the impact of volume upon price trend divergences.

Upside Capital-Weighted Volume: An index indicator developed by Buff Dormeier, CMT that measures how many shares are trading upward within an index on a capital weighted basis.

Volume Analysis: Employing volume data in market analysis.

Volume Factor: Volume analysis employed to create an investment factor.

Volume Factor Adjustment: Adjusting indicators and data with volume factors.

Volume Factor (Yield) Alternatives: An investment model developed by Buff Dormeier, CMT employing the Volume Factor ranking system on yield-bearing alternative ETFs.

Volume Factor Bonds: An investment model developed by Buff Dormeier, CMT employing the Volume Factor ranking system to a select group of diversified bond ETFs.

Volume Factor Risk Overlay: A risk overlay developed by Buff Dormeier utilizing the trends of Capital-Weighted Volume and Dollar Volume.

Volume Momentum Indicator (VMI): A volume momentum indicator developed by Buff Dormeier, CMT calculated through the difference of MFI and RSI.

Volume Price Confirmation (VPC): A trend confirmation indicator developed by Buff Dormeier, CMT calculated through the difference of a simple moving average and its corresponding volume-weighted moving average.

Volume Price Confirmation Indicator (VPCI): A trend confirmation indicator developed by Buff Dormeier, CMT unveiling the asymmetry between price trends and volume-price trends.

Volume Price Momentum Confirmation Indicator (VPMCI): A momentum confirmation indicator developed by Buff Dormeier, CMT unveiling the asymmetry between price momentum and volume-price momentum.

VPCI Most Bullish Volume Index: An index developed by Buff Dormeier, CMT consisting of the top 10% of securities in an index as ranked by VPCI.

VPCI V Bottom: A deep capitulation signal developed by Buff Dormeier, CMT employing the VPCI with Bollinger Bands.

VPCI W Bottom: A capitulation setup condition developed by Buff Dormeier, CMT employing the VPCI with Bollinger Bands.

Volume-Weighted MACD: An adaption of the MACD indicator using volume weighted moving averages developed by Buff Dormeier, CMT.

Volume-Weighted Moving Average/s (VWMA/s): A volume weighted adaption of moving averages developed by Buff Dormeier, CMT.

VOLUME FACTOR BIBLIOGRAPHY:

Equity Smart Beta and Factor Investing, Ghayur, Heaney, & Platt Wiley, 2019

Bollinger On Bollinger Bands, John Bollinger 2002 McGraw-Hill

Investing With Volume Analysis, Buff Dormeier, 2011 Pearson Publishing

Quantitative Strategies for Achieving Alpha, Richard Tortoriello, 2009 McGraw-Hill

"The Volume Factor", Buff Dormeier, December 2021 Journal of Technical Analysis

"Equity factor-based investing: A practitioner's guide", Grim,Pappas, Tolani, Kesidis Vanguard 2017

"Taming the Factor Zoo: A Test of New Factors" Feng, Giglio, Xiu Journal of Finance June 2020

"Factor investing considerations" FTSE Russell November 2019

"Low Volatility: A Practitioner's Guide" Edwards, Lazzara, Preston S&P Dow Jones Indices June 2018

"Factors – ways to pursue outperformance" Andrew Ang, Blackrock 2016

"Strategic beta's due diligence of dilemma" Trillo, Staines, Bovino, Stewart J.P. Morgan April 2017

"Factor exposures of smart beta indexes" FTSE Russell 2015

"Buff Up Your Moving Averages", Buff Dormeier Technical Analysis of Stocks & Commodities Feb 2001

"Between Price and Volume" Buff Dormeier Technical Analysis of Stocks & Commodities Jul 2007

"Trend Trust Indicator" Buff Dormeier Technical Analysis of Stocks & Commodities Aug 2011

"Fact Fiction and the Size Effect" Alquist, Israel, Moskowitz Journal of Portfolio Management Fall 2018

"A Case for Dividend Growth Strategies", Cheng, Wang, Srivastava S&P Dow Jones Indices June 2021

"Smarter Investing in Any Economy, The Definitive Guide to Relative Strength Investing", Michael Carr Banyan Hill Publishing 2018

"Decisions, Fast, and Slow" Ken Haman AllicanceBernstein May 2020

"An Introduction to Behavioral Finance" Ben McClure Investopedia January 2022

Bible, English Standard Version Crossway 2001

"An Overview of Factor Investing" Darby Nielson, Frank Nielson, Bobby Barnes Fidelity Investments 2016

"Ishares Factor ETFs Diversified Factor Exposure at the Core" Blackrock 01/31/2022

"Guide to the Markets" J.P. Morgan Asset Management 12/31/2022

"Factor Investing Ishares factor strategies for the core of your portpolio" Blackrock 2023

"The Relationship between return and market value of common stocks" Journal of Financial Economics March 1981

"Fact, Fiction, and the Size Effect" Ron Alquist, Ronen Israel, and Tobias Moskowitz *Journal of Portfolio Management* in 2018

"On the Evidence Supporting the Existence of Risk Premiums in the Capital Market" Robert Haugen and A.J. Heins December 1, 1972

"Value and Momentum Everywhere" Clifford Asness, Tobias Moskowitz, Lasse Pedersen *Journal of Finance* 2013

"Quality Minus Junk" Clifford Asness, Andrea Frazzini, Lasse Pedersen *Journal of Portfolio Management 2018*

"The Cross-Section of Expected Stock Returns" Eugene Fama and Kenneth French *Journal of Finance June 1992*

"Momentum Strategies in International Stock Markets" Kalok Chan, Allaudeen Hameed, Wilson Tong *Journal of Financial Economics 2000*

"Fact, Fiction and Momentum Investing" Asness, Frazzini, Israel *Journal of Portfolio Management 2014*

"Momentum Investing in Factor Portfolios" Huseyin Gulen, Yuhang Xing *Journal of Portfolio Management* 2018

"The High-Volume Return Premium," Simon Gervails, Ron Kaniel, and Dan Minglegrin The Wharton School, University of Pennsylvania January 1998

"The High-Volume Return Premium and the Investor Recognition Hypothesis: International Evidence and Determinants" Kaniel, Li, Starks University of Texas Austin March 2003

"Investing with Volume Analysis", Buff Dormeier FT Press 2013

"Profits in the Stock Market" H M Gartley 1935

"New Concepts in Technical Trading System" Welles Wilder Trend Research 1975

"Miss the Worst Days, Miss the Best Days" Michael Batnick The Irrelevant Investor February 2019

"Leverage For the Long Run" Charles Bilello & Michael Gayed Journal Of Technical Analysis Spring 2020

"Quality is Job One" BofA Global Research January 2023

" A Case for Dividend Growth Strategies" Cheng, Wang , Srivastava S&P Down Jones Indices June 2021

"Free Cash Flow and Dividends: How A Focus on Yield Can Help Investors Provide for Today and Prepare for Tomorrow" Manning & Napier April 2012

"The Power of Dividends: Past, Present and Future" Hartford Funds Insight 2023

"Strategy Slides" Chris Bush First Trust 2023

"Accumulated Capital Weighted Dollar Volume and the Volume Price Confirmation Indicator Factor Model" Matt Lutey, Indiana University NW Journal of accounting and business education 2022

"Fund Flow Trends and Investor Psychology" Rob Anderson Daniel Chin Ned Davis Research May 2011

"One to Rule Them All: FCF/EV"

"Quantamentals: The Quality Factor" GoldmanSachs March 16th, 2017

"Sequence of Return Risk: The Achilles Heel of Retirement Plans" CBOE January 2023

Printed in the USA
CPSIA information can be obtained
at www.ICGtesting.com
JSHW020728020624
63775JS00015B/21

9 781636 983226